BROKEN EARTH

BROKEN EARTH

The Rural Chinese

STEVEN W. MOSHER

THE FREE PRESS
A Division of Macmillan, Inc.
NEW YORK

Collier Macmillan Publishers
LONDON

The Free Press
A Division of Macmillan, Inc.
866 Third Avenue, New York, N.Y. 10022

Collier Macmillan Canada, Inc.

First Free Press Paperback Edition 1984

Printed in the United States of America

Paperback printing number
1 2 3 4 5 6 7 8 9 10

Hardcover printing number
2 3 4 5 6 7 8 9 10

Library of Congress Cataloging in Publication Data

Mosher, Steven W.
  Broken earth.

  Includes index.
  1. China—Rural conditions. I. Title.
HN733.5.M67   1983   306'.0951   83-47982
ISBN 0-02-921700-8
ISBN 0-02-921720-2 pbk.

For Huiya

Contents

Preface

As part of the extension of ties between the United States and the People's Republic of China heralded by the establishment of diplomatic relations on January 1, 1979, a cultural exchange program was initiated. It was as a research scholar under this program that I lived in a Chinese village during the last half of that year and the first half of the next. My goal was a community study of a production brigade, what in the years before collectivization would have been called a village, focusing on the usual array of anthropological exotica—kinship patterns, marriage customs, religious ceremonies, social structure, and the like. But upon returning to Taiwan (and another research project) at the end of my fieldwork and beginning to sift through and reorganize the copious notes I kept while in China, amounting to well over 100 notebooks in all, I discovered that they contained another story as well. Putting aside the esoteric and the academic, postponing the process of statistical analysis and sociological generalization, I found that there remained a tale of what it is like to live in today's China, told by the rural Chinese themselves.

In retelling their anecdotes and observations, I have sought to bring the rural Chinese within reach, to describe what it is like to live with them in their villages and celebrate the lunar New Year with *jian dui* pastries and lion dances, to mourn with them at funerals and rejoice with them at marriages and the birth of sons, to sit with them at collective meetings and listen to them discuss crops and policy, to take tea with them in their teahouses at dawn and to enjoy a game of basketball with them at dusk, coming over time to appreciate the bitterness of their past, the frustrations of their present, and their hopes for the future.

While this is a report of people encountered, events experienced, and anecdotes related to me during my year in China, it is also an attempt to compose from this collection of ethnographic miniatures a portrait of the rural Chinese. I do not pretend that my rendering encompasses all that it means to be a peasant in the People's Republic. Nearly all of my time in China was spent in the southern province of Guangdong (Kwangtung), and my configuration of what it is like to live in village China is grounded largely in the experiences of southern Chinese. But in understanding a people as different from ourselves—along whatever social, economic, cultural, or political dimension one cares to measure—as the Chinese, depth is often more important than breadth. All too often descriptions of the fabric of Chinese life have been cut from the whole cloth of stilted Marxist rhetoric as preserved in issues of the *Beijing Review* (*Peking Review*) or stitched together from the odd tatters of impression and sentiment collected during month-long tourist junkets. What I have attempted here is a more intimate, full-bodied description.

Though I was able to carry out my fieldwork without hindrance or even surveillance by the authorities, the People's Republic is nevertheless a police state, and those who were critical to me of the current order would face reprisals, up to and including lengthy imprisonment, if their identities should become known. This is especially so now that Beijing, furious over my unmasking of rural problems, has denounced me as a "foreign spy" and has demanded that I be punished. I have thus been led to take every possible precaution that this account does not cause unpleasant repercussions for those who have given me their confidence. While informants, usually higher-ranking cadres, who adhered closely to the official line have been correctly identified, those persons who ventured less orthodox opinions—and these are in the majority—have been carefully disguised by giving them fictional identities, that is, by altering their names and other unimportant aspects of their lives. These changes in no way affect the substance of their conversations with me, but should protect them from official retribution for their honesty. Considerations of confidentiality also dictated against writing the story of the village that I lived in—though I hope to do so in the future—and I have here drawn fairly heavily on visits I made to other communities in other communes during the course of my study, all of which are referred to by invented English names. The descriptions of these visits are otherwise accurate, just as the quotations, though not always attributable, are genuine. I recorded interviews as they were in progress and made notes on less staged encounters immediately after they occurred.

I have chosen to romanize Chinese words after the Pinyin system currently in use in the People's Republic and adopted by the Western press, rather than after the Wade-Giles system favored by scholars, though I have retained older conventional spellings of names of people and places when these are so well known that to do otherwise would risk confusion. Thus I have left Jiang Jieshi as Chiang Kai-shek, and Guomindang (Nationalist Party) as Kuomintang. For less well-known places and people I adhere strictly to Pinyin, though to assist the reader in making the necessary mental connection, the first appearance of a new Pinyin spelling is followed with its more familiar spelling in parenthesis. Chinese names are written in their proper order, with last names first and first names last.

A number of people have helped with the manuscript in various stages of preparation. Joyce Seltzer was everything an editor should be in giving constant encouragement and trenchant suggestions. Cynthia Parker and Cindy Nil typed many chapters of the manuscript as an act of friendship. My wife, Huiya, to whom this book is dedicated, was my most critical reader as she translated it into Chinese. Karen Strauss of The Free Press dealt expertly with the media when the storm of controversy over my research findings broke.

My primary debt, all the more deeply felt because it is impossible to repay, is to those Chinese, most of whom must remain anonymous, who led me to an understanding of their native land. Not least among those who can be mentioned is Joceline Lau, a Hong Kong Chinese who interrupted her education to serve as my research assistant largely out of a personal desire to come to a better understanding of conditions in her homeland. Her enthusiasm for the "New China" often spilled over into our daily discussions of the day's interviewing. "Much has changed for the better in the past thirty years," she stressed on more than one occasion. "You shouldn't be oversensitive to the venality of a few bad officials, the excesses of current campaigns to control births and modernize, or the superstitions of a handful of old women." Valuing her admonitions as a corrective to any possible ethnocentrism on my part, I tried to focus on the positive, especially near the end of my stay when the burden of confessions, confidences, and complaints that officials, workers, and peasants alike had disclosed to me had grown achingly heavy, but in the end I could only report what I had seen and heard. I alone bear responsibility for the account of life in contemporary rural China that follows.

Toucheng
August 19, 1982

BROKEN EARTH

1

Introduction: Beyond the Chinese Shadow Play

. . . *under the conditions in which foreign residents and visitors now live in the People's Republic of China, it is impossible to write anything but frivolities, and those who think they can do something serious when reporting their Chinese experiences, or who pretend they describe Chinese realities when they are in fact describing the Chinese shadow play produced by Maoist authorities, either deceive their readers or, worse, delude themselves.*

Simon Leys*

Late in March 1979 I first arrived, elated yet diffident, in the South China commune that I hoped to study. As an anthropologist whose goal it was to penetrate the private world of the villager, I saw getting through to the Chinese as people as the main challenge of the coming year. I was an outsider, neither Chinese nor Communist, and I wondered how long it would take to make contacts with local peasants and cadres, and worried that it might not be possible at all.

Friends who had been to the People's Republic had not been optimistic about my chances. One acquaintance, just back from a year of intensive study of Chinese at the Beijing Language Institute, told me how he had been put up by the PRC government in a dormitory restricted to foreign students where he had met

* *Chinese Shadows* (New York: Viking Press, 1977), p. xiv.

1

and made friends with Australians, Germans, Africans—students
of various nationalities—but no Chinese. His instructors at the
institute had been the only Chinese he had come into regular
contact with. While they had been cordial enough in class, they
had discouraged socializing after hours. His trips about the city
of Beijing, to such places as Tiananmen Square, Beihai Park, and
the Forbidden City, had engulfed him in vast, swirling crowds
of people but had not helped him to break through the social
barriers that separated him from these Chinese millions. Outside
of the institute he had been treated as a walking spectacle, interesting to observe but dangerous to approach too closely. People
stared at him, pointed him out to their companions, but generally
avoided talking to him, unless it was about some simple matter
such as directions to a nearby restaurant or bus stop. Exchanging
names or dinner invitations was out of the question. He had not
set foot in a single Chinese home during his year in Beijing, and
despaired that he could have made more Chinese friends by staying in California. "You will get to know Chinese in their official
roles as cadres, teachers, and Communist Party members," he
warned bleakly, "but you will not get to know them as people."

At first this pessimistic appraisal seemed to be coming true,
at least in my relations with cadres (the Chinese term for officials
of all stripes), who were invariably polite, correct, and standoffish.
It was as if each cadre carefully wrapped himself in a private
Bamboo Curtain of political orthodoxy that made the easy friendships and open give-and-take that Westerners are accustomed
to impossible. But I soon had an experience which taught me
that under the right circumstances this barrier of reserve could
come down.

One morning I paid a visit, arranged in advance through
the local "foreign affairs" cadre, to Equality Commune's industry
and transportation department, which was responsible for the administration of the commune's twenty-odd factories. I was taken
to the office of Jian Liguo, who was introduced to me as one of
the leading cadres of the *zhanxian*, or department (literally, battle
line). Jian offered me a seat at one end of the green felt-covered
table which took up nearly half of his small office, while he and
two other ranking officials took seats at the opposite end. For
the next two hours we discussed the work of the "battle line"
that they were in charge of, covering a wide range of topics from

the organization of local industry to the day-to-day work of the department staff. My questions about current problems in production or with personnel, however, met with only the briefest comment.

Still, despite their stonewalling where difficulties were concerned, I learned a great deal about the work of the department during the course of the morning, and I offered my genuine thanks to the cadres for their cooperation as the interview ended. After the Chinese fashion, all three courteously ferried me down the stairs to the building's entrance to see me on my way, and Jian Liguo even walked with me the final few paces to where I had parked my bike. As we bade farewell, out of earshot of the other two cadres, who had already turned to go back inside, he casually invited me over to his house. "If you have time one of these evenings, why don't you come over and sit for a while," he said. Though his invitation was tendered with the usual Chinese diffidence (no Chinese would ever say, "We must get together again"—it would sound too much like an imperial summons), I was struck by an underlying earnestness, and immediately asked him when would be most convenient. Before we parted, we had agreed that I would call at his home the following evening.

The next night I waited until 8 P.M. before setting out by bicycle for the village where Jian Liguo lived. By that hour, to avoid the damp chill of March evenings, most peasants had retreated to the relative warmth of their homes, and I found the road deserted. I rode slowly along, picking out a path by means of the flashlight I held in one hand, trying to avoid the worst of the potholes that pitted the dirt surface of the road. Reaching Jian's village, I dismounted and entered the narrow, stone-paved alley leading to the village center that he had described. The high walls of the houses loomed over the alley, leaving it in a pitch darkness unbroken by street lights, and I flicked on my flashlight at intervals to pick out my way. I came to Jian's doorstep pleased that I had not encountered a single person.

The double wooden doors of Jian's outer gate stood ajar, and, like a villager, I stepped into his courtyard without knocking and called out his nickname, Old Jian. A moment later he stuck his head out of the door of the house proper and, seeing who it was, stepped out and greeted me with obvious pleasure. He came out, took me by the arm, and led me inside. I stepped over the threshold of his house and received my first surprise of the night. His living room was packed with twenty or more peasants, seated on wooden stools or simply squatting on the floor. Sensing my pang of uncertainty, Jian gestured at the roomful of watchers and told me that they came to his house to watch television for an hour or two after dinner on the nights when there was electricity. "Tonight there is a Hong Kong kungfu program on," he went on, "so the crowd is especially large." As he was speaking, I noted that they were indeed all intently watching the TV set in the far corner of the room. My entrance had caused scarcely a ripple.

Jian invited me to sit down in a chair away from the TV and went to make a pot of tea. His living room, with its set of lacquered if plain wooden furniture and its tiled floor, seemed to me to be a class above those of the other village homes I had been in, which usually had only a motley collection of battered and pock-marked furniture placed haphazardly about a packed earth floor. As a commune cadre, Jian obviously had good local connections, and benefited as well from occasional remittances from Hong Kong relatives, to judge from the TV set. Jian returned with the tea, which we sipped as we waited for the program to end, talking pleasantries. He pointed out with pride that he had fashioned the TV antenna himself, confiding that it was one of only two in the village, out of a total of twelve sets, that could consistently receive broadcasts from Hong Kong 45 miles down the Pearl River. The reception did not seem good to me that evening. The kungfu fighters leaped and feinted through a miniature blizzard of snow and challenged one another through the crackle of static, but this did not seem to distract the villagers, who were totally absorbed in the action.

The program over, Jian flicked off his TV set. The peasants stood slowly up, shouldered their stools, and unhurriedly began to file out of the room. Only then did they take me in, young and old alike staring at me with the unblinking yet benign stares of so many roughhewn children. Some of the men glanced at Jian, as if to ask what could have brought this foreigner to his house so late at night. At least that's the way I uneasily read their expressions, and I wondered again if I had made a mistake in coming here. Jian seemed to sense my thoughts, smiled again— he was certainly much more expansive at home than when engaged at the "battle line"—and told me, even while the last of the peasants were still shuffling out of his house, that they were only peasant neighbors of his and that it made little difference what they thought about my presence. (He later told me outright that it was his commune comrades that he had to be careful of. No one really listened very much to the peasants, he maintained, but it would go badly for him politically if he allowed the people he worked with to get anything on him.)

Then his mood became serious, and, without prompting, he opened up to me. I said very little about anything during the next several hours, concentrating rather on listening and taking notes. He poured out no-holds-barred assessments of his own "battle line" ("Only a handful of our commune enterprises make a profit, though the accounts are jimmied to show that they all do"), the local medical care system ("poorly administered and of low quality"), the political system ("The problem is the system itself, which needs a thorough overhaul"), and the several decades of Communist rule ("It was the Hundred Flowers campaign of 1957 that made everyone first question where the Communist Party was taking us"). So it continued until after 1 A.M., when, my notetaking falling ever further behind his narrative, I suggested that we stop for now and meet again a few nights hence, after I had had a chance to absorb and think about what he had told me. We settled on the following week, and I took my leave, though not before he cautioned me to keep quiet about this late-night visit.

I rode slowly home, amazed at how much I had learned in a single evening about how the commune world looked from the inside, and even more astounded over Jian's transformation from a loyal, by-the-book cadre to a sharp-tongued social and political critic. He had clearly exulted in the opportunity to speak his mind freely, something that he told me he was able to do only in the company of trusted friends, and then only in small groups of two or three. Why he had decided he could trust me as well, after we had only met once for a rather formal interview, was initially a mystery to me, but as a result of this decision he had relaxed his carefully conditioned political reflexes and had become honest and outspoken.

What was remarkable about this transformation, apart from the fact that it occurred at all, was that it was total. Rather than the gradual, stepwise progression to mutual trust and intimacy that marks Western confidences, it was a sudden plunge into personal confession that left no subject, even politics, taboo. I was so taken aback at first by Jian's unexpected revelations concerning politics that I briefly suspected entrapment, worrying that his remarks might be a ruse to trick me into making comments unfavorable to the Beijing regime, at which point I imagined a trio of public security agents would appear in the room and my stay in the PRC would be over. I even asked him to show me around his house, under this pretext satisfying myself that, except for the members of his immediate family, who had just gone to bed, the two of us were alone. Later, after I came to better understand Jian, I had to laugh at my momentary fear that he was an actor in a scheme to entrap me.

Yet Jian was an actor of sorts. Like everyone in China with the exception of the peasants, Jian wore a mask of political orthodoxy in public, carefully projecting the image sanctioned by the state. ("People here are very, very careful about what they say and how they behave in public," a rural physician confirmed to me.) At home, in the company of someone he trusted, Jian's mask came off and he could be himself—a warm, spontaneous, and remarkably free-thinking human being. By unmasking himself, Jian had given me my first glimpse of the human face of China, and it was considerably different than I had been led to expect.

As my stay in China lengthened and numerous other Chinese took me into their confidence as Jian Liguo had, the sterility of conventional images of the People's Republic became increasingly apparent. Everywhere I looked, the richly complex reality of Chinese life, with its fascinating irregularities of opinion and behavior, seemed to deflate, if not demolish, exaggerated or romantic clichés about socialist China. Though I had long since set aside the myth of monolithic Chinese communism, I was still unprepared to hear a young Communist Party member mock Mao's famous bluster that the United States is only a paper tiger. "*We* are the paper tiger," he told me. Despite being suspicious of Beijing's claim that the PRC has left feudalism behind in its march toward the socialist millennium, I was still taken aback to hear the Party secretary of a production brigade complain to me that the nationwide birth control campaign was making it difficult for his clan to attain its rightful, pre-World War II size.

Few socialist clichés survived careful and lengthy scrutiny. I found that instead of being unflagging builders of socialism, peasants work a lethargic six hours a day for the collective and spend their remaining time tirelessly cultivating their private plots, feeding their domestic animals, and selling their produce on the free market; that in a country that espouses state and collective ownership of property, most people still own the homes they live in, and build new homes themselves when their families grow large and divide; that many Chinese—peasants, workers, and cadres alike—are alienated from politics by the endless cycle of political movements that the quixotic Mao sent hurtling down on their heads; that in a state where equality of the sexes is not only a law but a point of official pride, women do almost no administrative work, nearly all domestic work, and a good half of collective work; that despite efforts by the Communist Party to instill in its cadres a new morality of selfless devotion to the common good ("Serve the people"), the Chinese I spoke with insisted that most cadres look out for their own interests first, last, and always; that despite decades of political conditioning by the world's best-coordinated propaganda machine, most Chinese retain their traditional values and beliefs.

I knew beforehand that the state's efforts to create "new socialist men" out of China's peasant masses had not been entirely successful, but I was still surprised at the traditional ways villagers ordered their lives. Village temples had been mostly destroyed or converted to collective headquarters during the "Great Leap Forward" (GLF), but I discovered that most villagers still worshipped the gods regularly on the first and fifteenth of the lunar month in the privacy of their home. Ancestral tablets had been marked for burning during the "Great Proletarian Cultural Revolution" (GPCR), but peasants told me how they had hidden the inscribed tablet itself, casting only its wooden frame on the bonfire, and continued to memorialize their forebears on the prescribed days behind closed doors. As the months passed, I saw that peasants still feast on festival days, marry on "lucky" days, pay bride prices for new daughters-in-law, celebrate births with full-month ceremonies, prefer sons to daughters, invite Taoist priests to chant following a death in the family, bury their dead on "lucky" days, and then rebury them seven years later in "golden pagodas" set above ground in a "lucky" spot.

I also had to learn that despite the state's vow to reduce material inequality, cadres and the well connected led much more comfortable lives than their less influential neighbors. The findings of Western scholarship, that rich peasants in rural collectives earn only twice as much as poor peasants, held true for the villages I visited as well, but turned out to matter far less than I had originally imagined. Money alone counts for little, I was told repeatedly by Chinese friends, who never tired of complaining that they had "money but nothing to buy." They explained that not only is the production of consumer goods insufficient to meet demand, but the bicycles, tape recorders, and television sets that are produced go to those who have *guanxi* (connections) or *ganqing* (influence or sentiment) with key cadres that can be manipulated so one can *zou-houmen* (go in the back door). The annual quota of bicycles allotted to every village, for example, is spoken for well beforehand by peasants who are either related to or on good terms with, or in desperation have bribed, the cadre in charge of distributing what the peasants revealingly term "treasures."

It was this ineradicable selfishness in a system predicated on selflessness that dispelled for me the propaganda vision of socialism in the making. I was not overly surprised to find that individuals and families were still motivated primarily by personal or familial gain, for I had surmised in advance that they had not been radically transformed, but I had not been expecting collectives—production brigades and their constituent production teams—originally created by the state to have been captured by the peasants, who use them to advance their own interests. I did not fully come to see how particularistic and partisan the rural Chinese remained, however, and how openly they violated socialist mores both individually and in groups, until I was told by a young teacher about the misadventures of an attempt by the Guangzhou (Canton) municipality to build a middle school in Longwei County, a poor county located in the mountainous periphery of the municipal area and well in need of better educational facilities. School district officials located a building site for the proposed school on uncultivated land near the road which linked the county seat to Guangzhou. They then approached the local production team— the lowest level of collective agriculture, under the production brigade and commune—whose hamlet lay nearest the projected site to discuss terms. The team head asked only a modest annual rent of 100 *renminbi,* or *rmb,** for the approximately 5 acres of land, or roughly the value of the wild herbs and firewood formerly gathered off that plot each year, and readily agreed to provide laborers to help with the construction of the school. He would cooperate fully with the state's effort to help his culturally backward district, he assured the visiting cadres. They then returned to Guangzhou, pleased that the negotiations had gone so smoothly, and a dozen teachers were sent to supervise the construction of the school and start classes.

Then the demands began. The team head first requested an indefinite loan of 2,000 *rmb* ($1,333) from the school, and the newly appointed school principal had no choice but to comply. Then the head insisted that the laborers he was sending over be paid 1 *rmb* ($0.67) a day, or three times what they normally earned in collective work. Next came a demand that the school "lend" the production team enough bricks and cement from the stockpiled building materials to allow the construction of a sizable grain storage silo. Worst of all, nearly all of the twenty-odd families in the team had taken advantage of the convenient store of nearby materials to begin replacing their original huts of thatch and mud brick with new homes of fired brick with tile roofs.

With supplies disappearing almost as fast as they were shipped in, the beleaguered teachers decided in desperation to take up residence at the building site itself and moved into the four classrooms that had been completed by that point. Their presence proved to have little effect, however. The peasants kept pushing their wheelbarrows over to the building site, loading up a 50-kilogram bag of cement or a barrow of bricks, and shoving off for home to continue work on their half-completed houses. If their piracy chanced to be discovered by a teacher, they would sing out cheerfully, without a trace of embarrassment, "Just borrowing a bag of concrete" or "load of bricks, teacher," and trundle off with their prize. The teachers were furious, but there was little they could do. "We couldn't complete the school without their assistance, and they knew it," the teacher I talked with said

---

* At the 1981 official exchange rate $1 was worth 1.5 *renminbi* (literally, people's currency). This would make 100 *renminbi,* or *rmb,* worth approximately $67, but I calculated that its real buying power in the countryside was only about two-thirds of this amount. Whenever dollar figures are given they are based on the official conversion rate.

helplessly. "And if we had really tried to stop their thefts, they probably would have broken all of the windows in the schoolhouse or worse." Senior cadres from the brigade and commune to which the production team belonged simply shrugged their shoulders when approached by the teachers for aid, my informant said. "This is a very poor area, they would say, as if that explained everything."

———————

The unruly richness and anarchic complexity of Chinese life has remained largely hidden from the view of Western observers, in part obscured by the flat projections of official propagandists and Maoist apologists, in part because opportunities for Chinese and foreigners to associate in the PRC openly and easily are few. There are a formidable series of hurdles, mechanical, political, and cultural, standing in the way of foreigners hopeful of making contact with ordinary Chinese in everyday settings. Those in China for brief stays are shepherded about in tour groups and official delegations by interpreters and guides from the China Travel Service, or by cadres from the Ministry of Foreign Affairs, who never leave the visitors' sides as they make their predictable rounds of model schools, model nurseries, model factories, model communes, and other tourist haunts.

Foreigners who actually reside in the People's Republic live lives of privileged isolation, either in the suburban ghetto near Beijing that passes for a diplomatic quarter or in one of the hotels for foreign guests that are found in each of China's major cities. In these all-purpose institutions, such as the Beijing Hotel in the capital or the Dongfang Hotel where I stayed on my trips to Guangzhou, foreign residents play out a dreary suitcase existence, eating, sleeping, and working in the same building. The only Chinese they see are the members of the hotel staff and the cadres with whom they deal professionally. For ordinary Chinese these hotels are off-limits.

Stretching around each of these alien outposts is a high wall—the one at the Dongfang Hotel in Guangzhou, for example, is 9 feet high and topped with metal spikes and glass shards—broken only by one or two entrances manned twenty-four hours a day by guards who sit in a sentry box checking all who enter and leave. While those who arrive in chauffeur-driven automobiles are not challenged, because only cadres of some rank have cars at their disposal, any Chinese who tries to enter on foot is stopped and questioned. Unless they are overseas Chinese (ethnic Chinese resident abroad) or can prove that they are on official business, they are turned back. More serious consequences may follow as well. During one of the times I stayed at the Dongfang Hotel, a handful of local youth successfully crashed the gate twice by disguising themselves as tourists from Hong Kong. On their next try, however, their real identity was discovered by the guards at the gate, who handed them over to the city's public security department for questioning. Since a record is kept of interrogations, this is a serious matter, the equivalent of being booked and more, and these youth did not put in any further appearances at the Dongfang while I was there.

Near the beginning of my stay in the PRC, when I was still unmindful of this *cordon sanitaire,* I casually invited several village friends to have lunch with me at the Dongfang, telling them to meet me in the lobby at noon. I waited in the lobby until nearly 1 P.M. before it occurred to me that they might have been held up at the gate. I walked out to the main gate to look for them, finally coming upon them sitting forlornly on the curb some distance from the entranceway. They had indeed been turned back by the guards, who evidently had taken one look at their plastic sandals, baggy trousers, and generally scruffy appearance, marked them for peasants, and denied them entrance. They had waited immediately outside the gate for a while, but a guard had shortly come out again and waved them along, warning them against loitering.

Still thinking that this misunderstanding would be cleared up as soon as the guards saw that I knew them, I attempted to lead them back through the gate. To my astonishment, a guard came charging out of the sentry box to order my friends back out of the compound. I attempted to explain that these three villagers were my guests, that we were merely going to have lunch together, but my entreaties fell on deaf ears. The guard didn't even look my way when I spoke to him, so engaged was he in demanding of my companions, in a loud and imperious tone of voice, what they thought they were doing by trying to enter the hotel again. After a minute of this I finally caught the guard's attention by stepping between him and my friends, and quickly explained that I was a guest in the Dongfang Hotel, that these comrades were *my* guests, and that I was inviting them to lunch. "We will register inside," I told him. The guard regarded me briefly, took in the crowd that had started to gather, and grudgingly let us pass rather than risk an incident over such a trivial matter. But from that time on, when I wanted to invite friends for lunch or dinner, I brought them in in my van, which the guards would simply wave through as they did all vehicles. My politically unsophisticated village friends and the recklessly imposturing youth were unusual, though. Most Chinese made a wide berth around the isolation ward for foreigners.

The foreigners themselves are allowed to venture out into the cities that surround their living quarters, but those who would range farther afield quickly come up against another barricade: travel outside of the city limits is forbidden to foreigners without a difficult-to-obtain travel permit from the public security organization. What excursions to the countryside do occur are carefully stage-managed so that no possibility for improvisation exists. Foreigners are not permitted to roam freely about the countryside, where plain-spoken peasants would quickly disabuse them of any romantic notions they might have about idyllic commune life in the rustic Chinese countryside. They are instead led on short tours of one of a dozen or so model communes, the Red Star Commune outside of Beijing being the most famous example. There visitors tramp dutifully through the same commune industry and health clinic, eat lunch at the same reception center, and walk about the same production brigade viewed by countless other "foreign guests" before them. These rustic *tableaux vivants*, to borrow a phrase from Simon Leys, are interesting in the limited way of agricultural pavilions at an international fair, but they are hardly rural China.*

The cadres who man these Potemkin pavilions feel a strong sense of pride that their unit has been chosen as a model, a sentiment that is indubitably reinforced by the government slush funds that are funneled in to buy extra tractors, purchase chemical fertilizers, complete a small reservoir with electric generator, generally spruce up, and most important, build a spacious reception center. The rewards of being singled out as a model are so great that local cadres spare no effort to put their best collective foot for-

---

* Simon Leys, *Chinese Shadows* (New York: Viking Press, 1977), p. 3.

ward, even if that means deliberately constructing series of production data showing stepwise yearly increases in grain yields and family incomes. The *People's Daily* revealed in 1980 that the most famous model of them all, Dazhai Brigade in Shanxi Province, had been doing this for the better part of the previous decade. But foreigners in the countryside for short visits are hardly in a position to question the testimony of these practiced and seemingly straight-arrow witnesses, and come away with impressions that are more art than life.

Between the city "wall" closed to foreigners and the hotel wall closed to Chinese lies the vastness of urban China where the two, it might seem, could freely mingle. Unfortunately there are bars to contact here as well, less tangible than the all too obvious mechanical segregation of Chinese from the hotels and foreigners from the countryside, yet equally impenetrable. One of the world's most difficult languages, unfamiliarity with the public transportation system, the discomfort of overcrowded buses, shops, and streets—all this and more serves to quickly dampen the exploratory enthusiasm of all but the most hardy and curious foreigners.

One obstacle to communication with the Chinese man in the street in that setting is that at most hours of the day the streets, parks, and other public places of urban China are awash in what the Chinese call "seas and mountains of people." In such circumstances ordinary conversation is not only impossible, it is foolhardy. The foreigner *en voce* immediately attracts an audience of the curious, and the hapless Chinese with whom he attempted a dialogue finds himself the center of an unwanted attention. He begins to sidle nervously away, his responses growing terser and less distinct, until he has merged safely into the roiling crowd. This body, which by now has coalesced into what Erving Goffman calls a "focused gathering," is collectively engrossed in observing, with the patient intensity of a group of birdwatchers viewing a strange specimen, the now isolated and discomfited foreigner, who wonders what could have possibly prompted him to speak in the first place.* I was caught in such a human vortex of my own making several times and always found it to be a profoundly depersonalizing experience.

* Erving Goffman, *Encounters: Two Studies in the Sociology of Interaction* (Indianapolis: Bobbs Merrill, 1961), pp. 9–10.

Meeting Chinese at home is equally fraught with difficulties. In the cities, apartment buildings are the rule, and even former single-family dwellings have customarily been divided up among several families. There are no *dezhurnaya*, the old women and men who watch the entrances of buildings in the USSR, but the crowded conditions of Chinese cities, the presence of street committees, the monitoring of each other's behavior habituated during past political movements, and the fact that many apartment buildings belong to a particular unit, such as a factory or department, making all the residents co-workers as well, leave the Chinese with precious little privacy.

But it is not only the lack of privacy for casual conversation that hinders the foreigner in his efforts to break through to the Chinese; it is also a reluctance, born of fear and conditioning, on the part of the Chinese themselves. This self-enforced segregation by Chinese, who are by nature warm and gregarious, springs from the Cultural Revolution, when even to own a classical recording or Western novel, much less to be seen in the company of a foreigner, was evidence of bourgeois reactionary tendencies and an almost criminal act of disloyalty to the revolution.

A former Beijing resident revealed to me that this fear of foreign contact is constantly reinforced by the Ministry of Public Security (MPS), whose overzealous operatives often act as though every chance encounter between a foreigner and a Chinese is contrived. To illustrate her point, she told me of seeing two Westerners, obviously lost, approach a group of people waiting at a bus stop and ask for directions. A young college student, in halting English, told them how to get back to their hotel. This exchange was observed by a plainclothesman, who came hurrying over as soon as the foreigners had left to barrage the student with questions—"Have you seen them before? Where are they going? What did they want?" The boy stammered out, red-faced, that they were just asking directions and that he didn't know them. This did not satisfy his interrogator, who made as if to take him to Public Security for further questioning. But the others present, who up to that point had been silent, raised a chorus of protest at this, saying that the student was telling the truth. The MPS man, "half-believing half-suspicious," as my friend put it, finally let the boy go, but not before sternly warning him not to have anything further to do with foreigners. My friend assured me with a bitter smile that he would probably hide if he ever saw foreigners on the street again.

If a foreigner should visit a Chinese at home, even under the most innocent of circumstances, the result is often an MPS investigation. A friend in Hong Kong told me of how his aunt, a 72-year-old Catholic, had collapsed while attending Mass with her husband in Beijing's recently reopened Catholic church. An American couple who happened to be present volunteered their car as an ambulance, and the distraught husband agreed. On the way to the hospital the woman regained consciousness, was wide-eyed to find herself in the midst of foreigners, and insisted on going home instead. There was no need to go to the hospital, she anxiously told the American couple, adding that she and her husband would walk home. But the foreigners insisted on taking them home anyway, and once there the old couple, being Chinese, had to thank them by inviting them in for a cup of tea and a few minutes of polite conversation. On leaving, the American husband wrote down his address and telephone number for the old couple. If they ever had need, he told them, "just call us at this number. And we'll stop by on the way to Mass next Sunday to give you a lift. It will be no trouble at all."

No sooner had the American couple left than an MPS cadre arrived, demanding to know why the old Chinese couple had invited foreigners to their home. The MPS had been notified by the local street committee, which was charged with keeping an eye on resident antisocialist characters, a category which includes not only local thieves, reactionaries, and other bad elements but also Christians. The couple explained the events of the morning, but their visitor did not seem fully satisfied. Pocketing the address and phone number that the Americans had left, he told the couple it would be best if they had no further contact with them. The following Sunday, when the Americans knocked on their door, the old couple pretended not to be home. From that day onward, they stopped attending Mass.

Though it is impossible to know how frequently Chinese citizens are intimidated after innocent encounters with Westerners, with depressing frequency urban Chinese I spoke with could relate at least a cautionary tale or two similar to the one above. This general awareness that unsanctioned, spontaneous contact with Westerners might lead to trouble with the public security hierarchy serves as a powerful deterrent to approaching foreigners. Chinese are not impetuous—the Chinese equivalent of the American "Think twice" is a prudent "Think thrice" and few have the temerity to risk the displeasure of the authorities.

Those few urban Chinese who seek out such contact, or who accept glancing, one-time encounters if they are somehow private or can be explained away, are all in some way unusual—former Red Guards, intellectuals, young people, emigrating Chinese, or those with relatives in Hong Kong or overseas. Former Red Guards are often cynical closet dissidents, outspoken in private, whose views, particularly on politics, are invariably revealing. Intellectuals, especially establishment types who have some sanction to mix with foreigners, are interested in maintaining contacts in the U.S. and other countries to facilitate trips overseas and to increase their prestige and usefulness to the Party at home. Young people, out of a touching mixture of naiveté and curiosity, and emigrating Chinese, who become bolder as their time to leave the PRC approaches, are both eager to learn about the outside world, and often speak with considerable candor about their own society. Those with overseas relatives often want no more than help in writing, or sometimes simply addressing, a letter to relatives they may have had no contact with for decades, or help in interpreting or filling out the emigration forms that their American cousin has finally sent them. Many of those whom I helped over this linguistic hurdle stayed to share their thoughts and experiences about China.

Yet at least some of those who are willing or somehow specially motivated to associate with foreigners come under increasing pressure from the MPS in proportion to their boldness, as I found out from a young Briton named Brian. His Chinese girlfriend, whom he had met while working in Beijing for a foreign trading company, had literally been hounded by the MPS after they discovered that she was seeing a foreigner on a regular basis. They warned her personally to stop her "indecent" behavior, visited her family to hint of serious consequences, and even contacted her superior at the primary school where she taught to bring additional pressure on her. She was incredibly gutsy, for not only did she refuse to break off the relationship, she went to the MPS, protested that she had done nothing wrong, and demanded that they stop harassing her. This only served to make matters worse, however, for it led the authorities to intimate that if she continued not to cooperate, they would see to it that she was transferred from Beijing to another part of the country. Brian and his girl-friend had already given up seeing each other openly by the time he spoke to me. Instead, dressed in the blue jacket and baggy pants worn by Chinese workers and with a workman's cap pulled down low over his forehead, he would ride a bicycle over to her neighborhood for an occasional late-night tryst.

All in all, though, the Chinese MPS is probably less aggressive in harassing Chinese who have contacts with foreigners than the Soviet KGB (the Soviet secret police), and is generally very polite to foreigners. Whereas in Russia foreign journalists and others have occasionally been roughed up by police goons, the most that has happened in the PRC is some police heckling in 1979 of those covering the Xidan Democracy Wall* in Beijing. The very visibility of foreigners in China makes it unnecessary to put a continuous tail on them. The exception is East Asians, who are said to be the MPS's biggest headache in the foreign commu-nity, because of their ability to blend in with their social surround-ings and, in the case of the Japanese, to read Chinese. Wherever other foreigners go, they leave a large wake of witnesses behind them, and any Chinese they encounter is immediately stricken with the sure knowledge that there is little possibility the meeting will go unnoticed.

But at least as important as segregation and fear in preventing communication between Chinese and resident foreigners, though not as immediately evident, is the deep cultural divide separating China and the West. This is, paradoxically, both the cause and the consequence of the long-standing but superficial fascination of the West for China, which dates from the time Marco Polo came back to Italy after many years abroad bearing tales of a fabulous oriental civilization. Italians of the fourteenth century may have laughingly dubbed Marco Polo *Il Milioni* for his Munch-hausen-like tales of huge, populous, and ancient Cathay, but they nevertheless listened in slack-jawed wonderment. From that time onward the West has always had an insatiable appetite for Chinese cultural exotica, which over time has given rise to some strange

* The Xidan Democracy Wall became the focal point of the brief Democracy movement, its 100-yard length festooned with posters large and small demanding governmental reform and human rights. It was closed in late 1979.

accretions of images—"the good earth" and communes have fused
together into a mindscape over which roam mythical dragons and
surly Red Guards, long-gowned Confucius and peasant-garbed
Mao, needle-wielding acupuncturists and barefoot peasant doctors. Westerners never tire of hearing how odd the Chinese are.

China continues to be seen as a source of entertainment rather
than enlightenment, a kind of never-never land where the normal
laws of social gravity don't hold. This has perhaps never been
truer than during the past decade, when dozens of tourist journalists padded out their impressionistic, sketchy accounts from the
only truly abundant source material available: the propaganda
printed by Beijing's Foreign Languages Press, whose guiding bea-
con is the principle of socialist realism, that is, how China is supposed to be, not how it really is. It is revealing of how little
Westerners know about the basics of life in China that a tourist
who doesn't read, write, or speak Chinese, who understands nothing of Chinese culture, literature, or the arts, whose knowledge
of the vast panorama of Chinese history would barely suffice to
fill a comic book, can consider himself qualified to write an entire
book. Yet the interest in China has been sufficient to absorb the
last ten years' enormous outpouring of travelogues and journals
out of all proportion to the degree they contribute to an understanding of Chinese life. American travelers, with their tourist-
eye view of culture and history, seemed all too ready to believe
that they had had an encounter with the real China, and they
had little trouble enchanting a sizable readership.

For all this playful fascination of Westerners for China, there
is a dismal lack of even basic knowledge of China's history, language, and culture in the minds of most Westerners, even those
resident in China. In fairness, it must be said that there are few
countries where it is harder to find your feet than present-day
China. In China are combined a culture the oriental equal of
Japan and a political economy the totalitarian rival of the Soviet
Union. But Japan's cultural alienness is tempered by the machinery
of democracy and the market economy, while under the smooth
totalitarian facade of the USSR are indissoluble links to Greece,
Rome, Christendom, and other elements of Western civilization.
The PRC's socialist economy and totalitarian polity, unfamiliar
as these are to Westerners, are more easily comprehended than

what lies underneath: a Chinese civilization which from its inception has developed entirely independently of the West. The Westerner in China comes face to face with an alternate civilization whose distinctiveness is little moderated by assimilation to the West, a singsong language with a difficult-to-master ideographic script, a land where nods don't necessarily mean yes and smiles may indicate embarrassment rather than pleasure. Rather than Christianity, Greek civilization, and the Roman Empire, the Chinese past is written in terms of Confucianism, the Warring States Period, and the Han Dynasty, names whose very unfamiliarity betrays our ignorance. The development of a true world humanism through integration of the Chinese experience and the Western experience is only in its beginning stages, regardless of whether the problem is viewed from Paris or Beijing (where it is not viewed as a problem at all).

All of these barriers combine to place the foreigner in China in a sort of quarantine, one that wears particularly hard on those accustomed to a more open society (which is not to say that it doesn't wear hard on the Chinese themselves). The impossibility of foreigners' having any sort of a normal social life while living in China was brought home to me by a phone conversation I happened to overhear in the lobby of the Dongfang Hotel between a young American exchange student at Zhongshan University in Guangzhou and his father in New York. "My Chinese is coming along good," he began, "a little slower than I had hoped but still OK. I have a good academic program here, but everything else is going crazy." His voice started quavering, and he started pleading with his father to let him come home over the summer. "My mental attitude is not very good right now," he explained to his obviously worried parent. "I've just got to get away from this isolation." And if students able to speak Chinese and living on university campuses with thousands of Chinese of similar age can be, at best, marginal participants in Chinese life, they are nevertheless better off in this regard than members of the resident diplomatic and business communities, who are altogether outcasts. Not only are they, like the students, treated as nonpersons by most Chinese they happen across in unofficial contexts, their opportunities for such unstructured contacts are restricted as well. The upshot of all these barriers is to produce the desired result:

most resident foreigners do not long persist in their urban wanderings, but retreat into the cloistered comfortable life-style devised for them by the Maoist authorities.

A number of fortuitous circumstances surrounding my stay in China combined to loosen somewhat the normal restrictions on foreigners. I was in China in 1979–80, when the lingering euphoria over "the Four Modernizations"* and the Xidan Democracy Wall made it relatively easy to make unsupervised contact with Chinese.** "Vice Premier Deng Xiaoping himself has said that we can talk with foreigners," I was told repeatedly in the months after my arrival by Chinese, who often used this assertion of their newly granted freedom as a conversation opener.

The arrest and trial of the dissident Wei Jingsheng in late 1979 and the abolition of the Democracy Wall in December of that year did put a chill into my relations with certain cadres, who correctly saw which way the wind was blowing, but by that time I had formed friendships with enough Chinese that this didn't matter much. (It wasn't until after I had left the mainland that the Chinese authorities attempted to fully reimpose their peculiar institution of apartheid. In early 1981 a party directive warned Chinese against mixing with foreigners, and shortly thereafter foreign reporters in Beijing, a group that Beijing in any case regards as being no better than spies, were reined in. All interviews and visits must have official authorization, they were told.)

Being an American in China only a few months after the establishment of diplomatic relations between the U.S. and the PRC was an advantage as well, for that announcement generated a groundswell of good will and friendship that allowed me to

---

* The Four Modernizations, designed to lift China out of the ranks of underdeveloped nations by the year 2000, involves industry, science and technology, agriculture, and military.

** For several months in late 1978 and early 1979 journalists and other foreigners resident in Beijing were able to mingle freely with Chinese at the Xidan Democracy Wall and even visit them at home. This relaxation evidently came about because the MPS was uncertain to what degree the Democracy movement was supported by the top leadership, in particular Deng Xiaoping, and so delayed cracking down. An interesting account of the short-lived Democracy movement by a correspondent in Beijing at the time is John Fraser's *The Chinese: Portrait of a People* (New York: Summit Books, 1980).

move more easily in cadre and peasant circles alike. My status as an exchange scholar, whose stay in the countryside was arranged by Beijing ministries and whose officially sanctioned purpose was to investigate rural conditions, gave me entrée to commune and county cadres who would normally have been inaccessible to foreigners.

The longer I stayed in China, the more I came to realize how anomalously advantageous my situation was. While most foreigners resided in Beijing, the taut political nerve center of China, I spent my time in the relatively relaxed countryside of Guangdong Province, half a continent away from the capital. While most foreigners are sequestered in hotels and deal only with officials who professionally manage foreigners, I lived in a village farmhouse and spent my time with peasants and rural cadres. While foreigners are normally restricted to the cities, visiting the countryside only for short periods under the escort of officials and guides, I was allowed in the countryside for nearly a year, and lived and worked unaccompanied and unobserved. While most foreigners rely on interpreters, especially when visiting areas like Guangdong where Mandarin is not in widespread use, I was able to speak conversational Cantonese before my arrival, and found the villagers so pleased that I could manage their local dialect, and so patient when my speech came out off-pitch* or garbled, that I dispensed with an interpreter from the beginning.

Despite these advantages, I experienced my share of frustration from uncommunicative dialogues with supercautious higher-level cadres who would not let down their guard even briefly and with factory heads who insisted that they had no problems with production (or personnel or management) even though, from well-placed friends, I knew better and politely told them so. And away from the several villages where I did most of my interviewing, I sometimes found the villagers more curious than cooperative and the local cadres more guardedly polite, not to say deceitful, than open and informative in their remarks. The difference was that such occasions were neither common nor insurmountable, because when they did occur, a personal introduction from an acquaintance with ties of friendship or kinship in the village or

* Cantonese, like all Chinese dialects, is a tonal language in which different inflections affect not just emphasis, as in Western speech, but the very meaning of the word itself.

enterprise where my inquiries had been initially rebuffed was often sufficient to generate a warm welcome the second time around.

I soon discovered that peasants were often far more reliable and revealing informants than many of those they were led by. Though nearly all officials I encountered seemed to suffer more or less from an inability to speak candidly about problems, at least in the presence of others, most peasants spoke honestly and artlessly about topics ranging from suicides during the Cultural Revolution to failed harvests. The sturdy sense of loyalty that peasants feel toward their families and communities stops a long way short of the state. In this they are unlike commune-level and higher cadres, who are revealingly described by the peasants as "eating the nation's rice and speaking the nation's words." Moreover, again unlike cadres, peasants have little to lose by their indiscretions, having precious little to begin with.

My acceptance into the plain-spoken world of the peasant began two days after I had moved into Sandhead village when I was feasted by my neighbors. It was a very Chinese initiation. The eight men present, ranging in age from a 23-year-old production team head to the poor 63-year-old peasant named Ah Shi who was our host, all sat around a large circular banquet table, the women having repaired to the kitchen. Ah Shi opened a fifth of the local brand of cheap rice liquor as soon as we had taken our seats, pouring the liquor directly from bottle to rice bowl. We would not eat rice until we had finished this bowl and more.

Ah Shi began the toasts by "respectfully offering a glass to our foreign friend," and we both raised our bowls high as a sign of mutual respect before downing part of the fiery contents neat. While Ah Shi finished the equivalent of several shots, I took only a small sip, all that the ritual minimally requires, for I had been the guest of honor at a number of feasts in Hong Kong and Taiwan and knew what was coming. Each of my other companions followed Ah Shi's lead and raised his bowl to me in turn, and I received seven more toasts in quick and pungent succession. Then it was my turn to salute them, and so it went.

As we continued, the women began serving the food, a small plate of fried freshwater fish from local ponds, a bowl of boiled greens, a sizable dish of fried pork fat, and a small helping of salted turnips. Occupying the center of the table was a broiled goose, steaming in its succulent juices. All of the food had been cut into chopstick-sized pieces, with the strongly flavored salted turnips chopped up more finely still to make their sharp, briny flavor palatable. While the guests drank their liquor with abandon, they were much more frugal with the food. Only occasionally would someone reach out with his chopsticks and deftly snare a small piece of salted vegetable or fried fish. While Ah Shi kept urging pieces of goose meat on me and I accepted them, the rest of the guests left the goose practically untouched. It was, I found out later, an unheard-of extravagance, killed for the occasion, and none of the other guests could bring themselves to eat it, contenting themselves with bites of commoner fare.

We chatted in a combination of Cantonese and the local dialect. My Cantonese, learned in Hong Kong, proved passable, but my efforts to imitate the local dialect produced gales of laughter. My companions were fascinated by the fact that they were speaking with a foreigner, but showed almost no curiosity about America or anywhere else outside of their part of China except Hong Kong, Macao, and Singapore, where some had relatives. Though I had carefully laid plans to talk to them about life in America and the West, thinking it best not to appear too curious too soon about local affairs, the liquor and their friendliness soon weakened my resolve. They were talking about local events to each other, and so I joined in. Many of their comments were too compressed for me, as a newcomer, to follow, but this was far less important to me than the folksy sociability of these peasants and their matter-of-fact openness about village life.

My meeting the next day with one of the leading cadres of Equality Commune, to which Sandhead Production Brigade belonged, was the other half of the equation. Upon arriving at the commune headquarters, I was ushered into the foreign affairs office (every unit in China, regardless of its size, has a foreign affairs office for dealing with foreigners, overseas Chinese, and Hong Kong and Macao compatriots). The cadre in charge, a spare man in his mid-fifties, stood up from his desk as I entered and greeted me politely, introducing himself as Wu Tian and offering me his smooth and uncalloused hand. The handshake, the introduction, and his politesse were all stylized conventions alien to the peasantry. His clothes, carefully tailored and pressed, offered another contrast with my new village friends, who dressed in rough peasant garb. Speaking impeccable Cantonese in the accent of the provincial capital, he welcomed me to the commune, wished me a pleasant stay, asked if there was anything that he could do to make that stay more pleasant, and so on. My first impression, which the passage of time confirmed, was of a careful and calculated reserve, only partly camouflaged by a kind of officious politeness.

Neither at that meeting nor on any of the other occasions when we met did I ever hear Wu Tian freely offer his opinion on any issue. He was invariably polite, and there were no strained silences in the conversations that I had with him, but he proved formidable in deflecting a query with an irrelevant aside or parrying it with a question of his own. There was an air of solicitousness about him, as if he would go to any lengths to resolve a problem for you, whereas in fact I found him to be one of the least helpful individuals around as I began my village research.

Wu Tian proved typical of middle-level cadres—commune heads and county leaders—who with few exceptions were almost as reticent in private conversations as they were in public ones. These cadres have a built-in conditioning that both inhibits them from unauthorized contacts and protects them from political errors. Perhaps the system rewarded them so handsomely with political authority and material luxuries that the rigid ideological conformity demanded by the state in return was not very burdensome. Or perhaps they were adept game-players who were all too aware of what they stood to lose by ignoring their political conditioning. In any event, with a very few exceptions, I was unable to tap the reservoirs of their dissatisfaction, if in fact they existed. Questioning them most often elicited only a bland recital of current policy, remembered newspaper articles, and recalled directives with the life squeezed out of them.

But while all cadres to some extent share an ability to adopt a protective coloration blending in with the current political line, many cadres, especially those lower in the rural hierarchy, have not internalized the Party line to the point where they are incapable of having their own, sometimes quite heterodox opinions. Knowing enough to consider carefully the consequences of any deviation from the political straight and narrow, under the right circumstances they would still pour out their frustrations at the system that gave them so little freedom of thought and action, as Jian Liguo had done. Cadres whose answers read like *People's*

Daily editorials in discussions in front of others often proved to be vigorously independent individuals with their own viewpoints when I met with them in private at their house or mine. They possessed a chameleon-like ability to adjust their political coloration to their environment, and had become excellent judges of the extent to which they could trust those around them. More sophisticated and articulate than most peasants and less inhibited than their superiors, commune and production brigade cadres became my best guides to the Chinese way of life.

I learned also from Chinese who sought me out with more specific motives. My ready access to the Friendship Stores, a chain of department stores which sell hard-to-come-by manufactured goods like radios, electric fans, and watches to non-Chinese, led a number of people to ask me to make purchases for them. One assistant team head, who had apparently gone to some lengths to persuade his fearful uncle, a former landlord, to agree to an interview with me, visited me shortly after that event with 30 *rmb* and a request that I buy a watch for him at the Guangzhou Friendship Store. (I always refused such requests, preferring to pay back debts by invitations to dinner.) Some wished to use me as a conduit of information and cash to and from family in Hong Kong, especially so-called bad elements—landlords and ex-Kuomintang (KMT) officials—who were afraid to contact their relatives by ordinary mail. Others came to complain about this policy or that restriction, apparently preferring to share their grievances with someone from outside the system who could be more objective and, perhaps more important, would not betray them during the next political movement. What these wanted was not a conduit to the outside world, but an opportunity to bear witness to the shortcomings of their own.

For a time I received frequent calls from a young cadre who worked at the commune-run limestone factory. Perhaps once a week on his own initiative he would ride over on his bicycle, a trip that took forty-five minutes even at his brisk pedaling speed, and we would visit for an hour or so. Without prompting, he told me much about the foibles of factory management and about the corruption, cheating, and bribery that marked commercial transactions between his factory and other units. I finally asked him, after a particularly revealing session, why he was telling me all this. He knew that I was doing research, he replied without hesitation, and wanted to make sure that my information was complete.

Even away from the Pearl River Delta, where I enjoyed unusual entrée, it was sometimes possible to break through the barriers erected by the authorities and make rewarding, if fleeting, friendships with Chinese in certain urban settings, such as parks and restaurants, or while traveling. On a train trip from Guizhou (Kweichow) to Hunan I recall going to the dining car for breakfast and finding it arbitrarily divided into two sections. The six small tables at the far end were crowded with Chinese talking and eating, while the six tables nearest the single soft-sleeping car, where I had been put in a private compartment, were vacant. The waiter quickly laid out a tablecloth, place setting, and even a vase of grimy plastic flowers on a table in this section and gestured for me to take a seat there. Irritated that none of the other tables had such tourist trappings and longing for some company after half a day alone in a private compartment, I asked the waiter if it would be all right if I sat with the others. He stared at me as if the wall had just spoken. Whether surprised that I spoke Chinese, aghast at my suggestion, or both, he made no reply, and I walked over and took a vacant seat. He brought my order of fried rice and stir-fried vegetables to me without reproach, though I noted with a spasm of embarrassment that this was far better fare than my tablemates were eating, which was a kind of coarse noodle stew served in metal tins.

Pleased with myself at having escaped from solitary confinement, I settled down to enjoy my meal and strike up a conversation with my new companions, a woman and a young man. This didn't go as well as I'd hoped, sputtering along with awkward pauses, although the woman proved more communicative than the young man, who confined himself to nervously remarking how good my Chinese was. I did find out that she was 30 and from Shanghai, that he was 22 and from Fujian (Fukien) Province, and that they worked together in the same unit in Chongqing (Chungking, the old wartime Nationalist capital). Fortunately the fourth seat at the table was quickly taken by a friendly Cantonese fellow, outgoing like most of his fellow provincials, and we were soon off into the topic of education. Trying to draw the other two into the conversation, I asked them at one point how far they had gone in school. They replied with their customary curtness. The woman said "upper middle school," while the young man to my surprise grunted "college." When I asked him what college, he looked nervously at his companion and then down at his bowl of noodles before finally replying in a barely audible tone of voice, "PLA University." As it was dawning on me why he and the woman had been so reluctant to speak with me, these two People's Liberation Army officers traveling in mufti chugged down the remainder of their noodles and literally bolted from the table. I couldn't help chuckling at their panicky exit and looked up to find my Cantonese friend amused as well. In sudden rapport, we switched to his dialect, ordered another bottle of Qingdao beer, and for the next two hours talked about our lives and countries as the train rolled through the Hunan countryside.

2

Village Life: The Chinese Peasant at Home

[The supermarket had] aisle after aisle stacked with 10,000 kinds of food. It was unbelievable. So much food in one place.

Equality Commune cadre, 1980

It was mid-morning when the 30-foot cargo launch I was riding in chugged slowly up to the Sandhead lock. I stood on the bow, impatient to breach the high dikes that had mostly frustrated my efforts to observe the Pearl River Delta during the three-hour trip upriver from near the Portuguese colony of Macao. A hail brought a young man in a blue Mao jacket up to the concrete overspan and the heavy concrete doors of the outer gate swung slowly open, then closed again behind us. The launch began to settle lower in the lock as the water was pumped down to the level of the canal that led to Sandhead. Finally the inner gate opened to reveal the delta locale that was to be my home for most of the next fifteen months.

I found myself viewing a world half land, half water. Huge, man-made ponds were scattered across the landscape as thickly as puddles after a summer rainstorm. The embankments between were crowded with miniature forests of tiny mulberry trees, whose leaves went to feed voracious crops of silkworms. Higher ground was given over to tall stands of sugarcane interspersed with banana

28

trees. The only breaks in this tropical panorama were made by occasional low hills. These had been coastal islands until accumulating river silt had gradually lifted them out of their watery isolation and joined them together. Chinese peasants from the north had completed the transformation from islet to hill ten centuries before when they had settled on the safety of their lower slopes and built dikes encircling the adjacent mudflats. Five of these hills and 1,300 acres of surrounding cultivable land comprised the holdings of the 8,000-member Sandhead Production Brigade, my destination.

Crouched against the nearest hill lay Sandhead Village, headquarters of the brigade and its largest settlement. From a distance it appeared a solid mass of gray brick walls and even grayer tile roofs, penetrated only by a few narrow alleyways. The village, I knew, was home to some 1,000 families, but the whole occupied scarcely more than a city block. The launch reached the landing and I bounded up the stone steps and into the nearest alley after my escort. The homes were built so closely together that their high walls almost touched, and each brick front was broken only by a high, recessed entryway and a single small, barred window. I felt as though I were being ushered through some ancient catacomb, an effect enhanced by the stone slabs underfoot, the low-lying clouds above, and the total absence of greenery. The alley twisted and branched haphazardly as it went, and after a turn or two I was utterly lost. It would be many days before I could find my way through the maze of alleyways without assistance.

Stepping through the flanking wooden double doors of my destination, I found myself in a small, stone-paved courtyard. The far end was occupied by a low shed-like kitchen, its interior blackened with creosote from the box-like brick stove. A basket of dried Chinese cabbage sat on a stone bench beside the entrance to the house proper. A covey of chicks scattered before me as I advanced to the threshold of the house, blinking for a minute at the unaccustomed darkness, adjusting to a way of life that spoke of familism and continuity, of clearly defined roles for all ages and both sexes, of a private community of fellowship, of a refuge from the omnipresent state.

I was standing in what I would in days to come recognize as an ordinary peasant home. The corners of the central room were deep in shadow, as they remained even on sunny days, for the one or two glass tiles placed in the otherwise opaque roof let in only enough light to dispel the worst of the gloom. When the electricity is turned on at dusk, the single 25-watt light bulb that is all each family is allowed is even less effective against the encroaching darkness. Brigade and commune cadres may have floors paved with tile, but more common in the countryside are homes like this one with floors of hard-packed earth. Furniture is sparse and starkly utilitarian, hewn out of wood in simple patterns by the village carpenter. At a minimum each family has a dinner table, a few straight-backed chairs reserved for the household head and favored guests, and a scattering of stools and short benches for the women and children. Besides the indispensable dinner table, the only substantial piece of furniture likely to be in evidence is a glass-faced cabinet, centered against the wall opposite the entranceway and used as the repository for the family head's bottle or two of rice liquor and a motley assortment of family bric-a-brac. In some homes walls are covered with a layer of unpainted plaster, while in others the brick is left barefaced, but in nearly all I saw, an effort had been made to add a touch of color by pasting up bright posters along the walls at eye level and more somber-hued printed portraits of Mao Zedong (Mao Tse-tung) and Hua Guofeng over the mantelpiece-like family altar. The bedrooms off to the side of the central room are narrowly functional, filled up by the family's beds, which occasionally spill out into a corner of the central room for want of space. Not only is the bedroom not divided into separate sleeping quarters for adults and children, but the generations sleep together in the same beds. While it is considered unseemly for couples to share a bed after their children are grown, sex being a matter of procreation, grandparents enjoy the comfort of a grandchild nestled in warmly beside them at night, and siblings unselfconsciously curl up together on the same single bed. Closets are nonexistent, their place being taken by a wooden chest or two, providing all the storage space necessary for the family's few personal belongings. Though few Chinese women are meticulous housekeepers, to Western eyes accustomed to wall-to-wall furnishings their homes leave an impression of spare tidiness.

But I found the material austerity of Chinese dwellings to be more than compensated for by the human richness of their domestic life-style. With the small, only partly enclosed kitchen reserved for cooking and the bedroom set aside for slumber, the central room provides the setting for most other activities of family members, serving as combination dining room, family room, utility room, and parlor. Nothing better illustrates the natural togetherness of the Chinese family than the scene in the central room following the evening meal. Around the table the father relaxes after a day in the fields, perhaps sharing a pot of tea with a visitor, while opposite him the older children sit doing their homework. The mother sits on a bench to one side doing her mending and sewing, while the grandmother gazes contentedly at her youngest grandchildren playing on the floor. Chinese relish the gregarious intimacy and physical proximity of such a setting in a way that it is difficult for Americans, with their penchant for privacy, to understand. It is no accident that the Chinese language is without a word for privacy.

As family members do not carefully divide the domestic hearth into personal domains, so village families do not erect gratuitous barriers among themselves. The casual visitor to a Chinese home is greeted not by a frantic effort to spruce up place or person, but with the simple, unvarnished hospitality of a seat at the family table and a cup of tea (or sometimes just hot water). Indeed, there is little time to put one's home in order on the arrival of a guest, because it is not the custom for visitors to wait to be invited in. Rather they straightaway advance through the outer gate without knocking and go directly to the living quarters. All the while they call out the name of the person they are seeking in a bellow that would be the envy of a court herald, until they either find the object of their quest or determine that he is not at home. The evenings especially are filled with such comings and goings, as neighbors call on each other to discuss village affairs or just to exchange the latest gossip.

For me, coming from a culture that draws the distinction between public and private much more sharply, this sort of communal familiarity was initially difficult to adjust to. Particularly during my first few weeks in the village, I lived a fishbowl existence as a steady stream of unannounced visitors flowed through my two-story house in casual reconnaissance. After checking out my living room and downstairs bedroom, they would saunter up the stairs to my study. There they would take a slow turn about the room, eye the make and estimate the value of my electric fan, marvel over my portable typewriter, riffle through my notes and books, and scrutinize whatever my assistant was writing, all the while kibbitzing with anyone I happened to be interviewing. My initial reaction to these unrelenting intrusions was to consider latching the main gate when I was otherwise engaged within. This urge was promptly vetoed by friends, who told me that people never locked their gates during the day. "People will talk," my cook said worriedly. "They will think you lock the gates because something suspicious is going on."

Fortunately, I soon came to feel less oppressed by my visitors, even to see their casual calls as a token of acceptance. The turning point came when I was called over to a neighbor's house to help decipher the English instruction booklet for the new portable black-and-white TV that a relative had brought back from Hong Kong. During the course of the fifteen minutes or so it took me to show him how to work the set, at least a dozen people, alerted by the grapevine, trooped into his living room to have a look at his new acquisition. Most, I observed, entered and left without exchanging more than a nod or grunt of mutual recognition with the head of the household. After this experience I made an even more determined effort to overcome my Western craving for privacy and extend my unbidden guests a genuine welcome, recognizing that by allowing my living quarters and activities to become community property, I was coming, in a small way, to belong.

Behaving as a member of a Chinese community is not the same as being of that community, though. However much the newcomer follows local customs, he can never come to share its deep taproots in time. The social bonding that knits together the people of a Chinese village begins in a sense even before their birth, for even today most peasants worship annually at their grandfather's tomb not far from the village and can trace their family trees back to a first ancestor who came to the village many generations earlier. In the cities the unit—a factory, office, or service enterprise—forms an encapsulated urban community whose members work and live in as close proximity as the inhabitants of any American company town. But the population of even the most staid of American towns appears in hyperkinetic flux by comparison with that of Chinese villages, whose inhabitants, like all Chinese, are forbidden under the 1958 population control law to change their place of residence without permission. With the cities and towns closed to him by a government intent on curbing unplanned urban growth and unemployment, and with all of China's arable land already divided up among 5 million production teams who are understandably unwilling to share limited collective resources with outsiders—except those women brought in by male members in marriage—the peasant is left with no place but his home village. Where he happens to be born, there will he grow up, marry, raise children, grow old, die, and be buried. It is a long course for such a narrow compass.

Another result of life-long encounters on village paths is an effortlessly acquired and altogether exhaustive fund of knowledge of each fellow denizen's finances and possessions, history and hopes, strengths and weaknesses, allies and enemies. One sign of this intimate communal familiarity lies in the revealing nicknames which Chinese everywhere assign one another, and which I found to be uncannily accurate appraisals of a person's appearance and character. The best are truly inspired sobriquets. One brigade Party secretary surnamed Wang is known to everyone in his village as Toad Wang, which is precisely the image evoked by his squat body and flat, powerful head, as well as by a certain distasteful deviousness he is known for. Then there is Cherrystone Shen, a tightfisted peddler whom, as many of his neighbors have discovered, it is next to impossible to get the best of in a deal. Some handles are obvious choices, like Big Head Yan for a man whose head is unusually large and dome-like, or Wine Rice Su for a villager who is well known for his habit of scooping only a finger of steamed rice into his bowl and then filling it up to the brim with rice liquor. Others ring unpleasantly, even cruelly, to Western ears, for instance the nickname of one Sandhead brigade official who has a severe speech impediment. He is called Cripple Mouth Lin. But wl.en I asked Comrade Lin, as I carefully addressed him, if his seemingly disparaging appellation had ever made him angry or uncomfortable, he was perplexed. "Why should it have?" he answered mildly. "After all, my mouth *is* crippled." As he well knew, his nickname carried no hint of taunt or blame, but was simply the public recognition of the obvious fact of an infirmity. More generally, these names stem from the down-to-earth unpretentiousness of Chinese life, where people are seen—and identified—as what they are. Unlike Americans, Chinese do not hold the individual strictly accountable for everything that he is. If someone has a bad temper and is constantly getting into arguments with his neighbors, people merely shrug and say, *"Ta shi zheyang de ren"* ("That's the way he is"). In the villages, where sustained deception is impossible, a person can be ugly, argumentative, and crippled and still be recognized and accepted as a member of the community.

Except for the late summer, when the dead heat of particularly stifling evenings drives the men out of their homes to sit on their haunches alongside the canal or on the granite steps of one of the old ancestral halls, the dinner table is the focal point of social life, a center for conversation and companionship. After the supper hour neighbors wander in and out throughout the early evening, with each new arrival greeted by a chorus of calls to come take a seat around the table. There the men—for these gatherings are exclusively male—sit for hours at a stretch talking, smoking, and drinking tea. The tea is weak, for Chinese are as frugal with tea leaves as they are in the rest of their life, but is taken piping hot, regardless of the season. My Chinese friends were amused to hear that Americans put ice in their tea during the summer, a practice I related to them with more than a twinge of nostalgia during the humid summer months when out of politeness I was forced to down cup after cup of scalding tea. As comings and goings swell and diminish the crowd around the table, the conversation ranges from lively to listless, but somehow meanders affably along through the long evening hours. Disagreements are rare and quickly patched over. Always there is the wonderful sense of humor of the Chinese gently poking fun at friends without the hard edge of sarcasm that so often marks American humor, self-deprecatingly pointing out their own foibles and joining unselfconsciously in the general laughter, ever amused by the small absurdities of their impoverished existence. I recall one evening telling the crowd around my dinner table that some people in the States deliberately affected grubby, torn, or faded clothes, and that for this reason some articles of clothing, such as jeans, were actually bleached and patched before being marketed. This broke them up into incredulous laughter, for although rural Chinese dress as well as they can given their circumstances and frayed and torn clothing is quickly patched and mended, it must still be worn until it is literally in tatters. One quick-witted youth suggested that the village organize an export company to ship old Sandhead clothes to the U.S. in exchange for new. As everyone roared with laughter, he tugged at his own ragged and weather-beaten cotton jacket and chortled, "We'll never run short of goods."

The friendships that are slowly nurtured over the dinner table require an intensity of commitment seldom found between friends in the West. This stems in part from the character of rural life. Compressed within the confines of the village, relationships easily attain an unusual depth of feeling—friendships tribal in their strength, enmities atavistic in their intensity. But there is something essentially Chinese at work here too. A young Chinese engineer in Hong Kong, who had studied in both England and the United States, put the difference this way. "Imagine that you find yourself walking down a street exactly one block long with three strangers—an American, an Englishman, and a Chinese. The American will probably strike up a conversation with you before you have taken two steps and will immediately profess a great regard for you, but by the time you get to the end of the block he will have forgotten that you exist. It will take the Englishman half a block to overcome his reserve and engage you in conversation, but he will also have forgotten you before you reach the end. The Chinese, on the other hand, will have been friendly from the beginning, but in a less self-interested way than the American, who is interested in being popular, and in a less self-conscious way than the Englishman, who has difficulty overcoming his reserve. And by the end of the block, if you are of like temperament, you may have found a life-long friend."

This spontaneous warmth and generous friendliness of the Chinese is one of their most attractive characteristics, and one that I found to be especially strong within the circle of the village. When the work crew of seven bricklayers that I had hired set about in July laying the foundations for my house, the work progressed slowly even though difficult-to-obtain building materials were already on hand, having been expedited by Beijing officials. It soon became apparent to my new neighbors that there was little chance of the structure's being completed by the first of September when I would return to the village to officially begin my fieldwork. What happened over the next five weeks was like an old-fashioned house-raising. Over thirty friends and neighbors lent a hand mixing cement for the bricklayers, carting heavy hods of bricks, hoisting the roofbeams into place, and hauling loads of tile up the stairs to the roof. Some pitched in for only a day or two, but others, mostly youth who had no fixed collective duties, came to work every day for a month. This tremendous volunteer effort enabled the house to be finished on schedule, and I consulted a close friend concerning how much I should pay them. "No need," he cried emphatically, slightly shocked by my Western tendency to hang a price tag on everything. "They helped out because they are neighbors. It would not be appropriate to give money. But you should invite them to your 'bringing in the fire' feast" (housewarming). This I did, but because I was not going to be around to help in years to come when they raised homes of their own, I also bought two dozen brightly colored ski jackets as gifts for the young workers whose natural industry and warm neighborliness saved me so much inconvenience.

    As this joint effort suggests, if ever there was a people to make collective agriculture into a going concern, it was the Chinese. They simply excel in cooperative ventures that, by dint of hard work, mutual trust, and faith in the future, almost invariably succeed. The Chinese who came to America overcame prejudice and endured years or decades of separation from their families to add Chinese-American to the long list of successful immigrant groups. The Chinese of Southeast Asia parlayed their ability to act in concert into fortunes and became that region's trading class. The Chinese of Taiwan, Hong Kong, and Singapore worked the most impressive economic miracle of all in transforming their resource-poor islands into enclaves of wealth and prosperity. Nor were the Chinese who remained home any different. The nose-to-the-grindstone perseverance of the peasants so awed one nineteenth-century missionary that he wrote, ". . . when the far-distant West comes into close and practical competition with the patient Chinese for the right to exist, one or the other will be behindhand in the race and it is safe to venture the prediction that it will *not* be the Chinese."* I was thus totally unprepared

* Arthur H. Smith, *Village Life in China* (New York: Revell, 1899), p. 53.

for the foot-dragging sloth and lack of collective spirit that I found when I spent a day working with the members of Sandhead's Production Team No. 12, a group of forty-nine families farming some 40 acres of fish ponds and fields.

I arose at dawn, gulped down a steaming bowl of rice congee to ward off the January cold, and set out briskly for the team headquarters in the center of the village. I need not have hurried. The team hall, a large building in the traditional style that had been erected seventy years ago to honor the village ancestors, was silent, its 11-foot-high wooden doors chained shut. For half an hour I waited on the stone steps, passing the time admiring the vividly detailed bas-reliefs of dragons, tigers, and skull-capped Chinese I discovered under the eaves, wryly amused that a collective farm should be quartered amidst such incongruous ornamentation. Finally at nearly 7 A.M. the team head appeared, Lai by name, a stocky man of medium height and easygoing manner. He was always the first one to arrive mornings and afternoons both, Lai told me good-naturedly as he unlocked the padlock. He had to come early to plan the day's work.

The massive doors swung open to reveal a gloomy, cluttered interior. The team's only building, the hall served at once as repair shop, storeroom, meeting room, and office, a snarl of competing functions that left it in a perpetual state of disorder. In the center of the hall, where the ancestral altar and tablets had once stood, was an untidy woodworking area. A punt, the main means of transport on the canals, was up on sawhorses awaiting the new bottom that was being fashioned out of the wood stock strewn on the floor beside it. A long, ramshackle storage shed, looking as out of place in the high-ceilinged hall as a chicken coop in a church, crouched against one wall. Locked inside were the team's small, easily pilfered agricultural implements—hoes, baskets, buckets, carrying poles, and the like. Near the door stood two 20-bushel tubs of dried corn, tarps thrown over their tops to foil rodents; behind them a dozen punts were stacked in groups of four. For the rest, the hall could have been an abandoned warehouse. Here a heap of bamboo poles of different lengths and a mound of fishnets and floats. There a cobwebbed stack of crates and boxes.

The only area relatively free of clutter was the team "office." This was not a room at all, but merely a corner near the door where the team officers—the head and assistant head, the accountant, the cashier—had their desks, and where notices and production charts were posted. Its most eye-catching element was a large blackboard covered with rows of hooks and small wooden tags. Here Lai stood, moving tags from hook to hook and row to row as if playing some kind of solitaire.

"There are 110 tags in all," Lai began to explain, seeing that I was interested. "Each represents a worker. Has his name on it. See this large group of tags on the bottom two rows here? These are people who have been spending their time planting beans and peanuts on land that has been let out to their families. I don't have to worry about them. They are themselves responsible for meeting state production quotas. For the rest, everyday I have to decide what work needs to be done and who to send to do it. One thing the collective has to do today is seed a number of ponds with fingerlings. That's what this group will be doing," he said, pointing to a cluster of five tags underneath which had been written in chalk "Move fingerlings." "These other larger groups will be hoeing fields for planting sugarcane," he continued. "Since you want to participate in collective labor, why don't you go with one of them?" I nodded agreement.

By now other team members had begun straggling into the hall. All the new arrivals sauntered over to the tag board to check out their work assignments for the day, often exchanging a few words with the team head, and then wandered off in search of a corner to lounge or squat in. Their numbers grew only slowly. By 7:45 A.M. there were still many more tags on the board's upper rows than there were people. Impatient to be off, I asked Lai when we would leave. "We are supposed to assemble here at 7:30 in the winter," he answered, "but—." The sentence trailed off into an embarrassed smile as yet another team member appeared in the entranceway. "Now everyone is waiting for the last stragglers to arrive," he went on. "And no one wants to be the first to leave for the fields. They're all afraid that the others will sneak a few minutes more of leisure [*tou lan*]." Shortly thereafter I heard Lai going around and quietly urging everyone to begin work. A line began to form in front of the storage room as people went to check out hoes. Even so, ten more minutes passed before those present began to drift, like a leaderless gaggle of geese, toward the door. As I left with them for the fields, I saw the team's carpenter walk over to the punt he was repairing and begin to lay out his tools. He had arrived fifteen minutes before but had spent that quarter hour dawdling about in the hall. Like the other team members, he did not want to work while others were resting.

The peasants reached the edge of the village and split into half a dozen separate streams. The eight men I was with headed in ragged file for a field near the Sandhead lock. Walking briskly, one could reach the lock from the village in ten minutes, but my companions shuffled along so slowly that it took us twice as long. "No one wants to be an activist," one villager shrugged when I asked about the tortoise-like pace. It was 8:15 before we arrived at our assigned plot. This was one-third of an acre of land sloping down from the inside of the dike to the canal. We formed a line at its lower end and set to work turning over the sodden soil with our long-bladed, heavy hoes. For all their lack of concert in assembly and march, by some unspoken agreement the group now fell into rhythm. But what a rhythm. Their hoes rose and fell together with the cadence of a dirge. I would have preferred to work faster to warm myself in the frigid air, but my own hoe was soon striking the earth with this same measured and compelling beat.

So we continued for about an hour, creeping up the slope toward the dike. Then, as if at some signal, the men threw down their hoes and squatted in little clusters to talk and smoke. I was already getting chilled fifteen minutes later when they went back to work. At 10:30, when we were still less than halfway up the slope, the men suddenly stopped for good, shouldered their hoes, and started back to the team headquarters, where they quickly checked in their tools and left. The hall was deserted by 11. The afternoon turned out to be a repetition of the morning as we went out to the fields at 2:10 and returned at 5:10. In all, we were in the fields for less than six hours that day and actually at work only about five.

Early that evening I went to see Team Head Lai at home, telling him of my surprise at how little in the way of work my group had accomplished that day. "There's nothing to be done," he replied, smiling his resignation. "It is useless to have them work longer hours. They just rest more in the fields. People aren't lazy all the time, just when they do collective labor. When they work on their private plots, they work hard. There is a saying, 'Energetic as dragons on the private plot, slugglish as worms on the public fields.' "

"Have things always been like this? I queried.

Lai did not answer immediately. The unsteady flame of the kerosene lamp that was his central room's only illumination that night—Sandhead was supplied with electricity only every other night—cast flickering shadows across his face, making him look older than his 51 years. "Before collectivization people worked hard," he said finally, breaking his silence. "Take that piece of land you worked on today. At the time of the land reform one person could have hoed it in six days or so. Now it takes eight people two full days to do it. Everyone works at the same slow pace. People have learned from collectivization to do just enough to get by."

———◆———

Collectivization had not been intended to work out that way, of course. Mao's purpose in organizing the countryside into agricultural collectives during the mid-1950s was to move the countryside from capitalism to socialism in one fell swoop. As a Marxist he took as an article of faith that the economic development of village China would accelerate once the land—the all-important means of production—was in communal hands. He believed also that this shift would recast peasant nature, undermining old allegiances to self, family, and friends as it fostered new loyalties to collective, Party, and state. This creation of socialist man out of the stuff of propaganda and production was the core of Mao's Faustian quest for a China truly Communist. But he reckoned without the tenacity of economic man.

As I pieced together from discussions with Lai and others, it had not been long before the peasants, ever alert to their own interests, had caught on that it did not pay to work hard in the new collectives. Diligence, they saw, went unrequited, all receiving nearly the same in work points—the currency of the collective— regardless of how much they actually accomplished in the fields. But the fatal defect of the new system was that by eliminating individual accountability, it actually encouraged sloth. The fruits of any extra effort were diluted among twenty to fifty families, so that any work done beyond the average was nearly a dead loss. Labor that could be shirked, on the other hand, was nearly cost-free because any losses that resulted were borne equally by all. In the egalitarian collective, the villagers discovered, indolence is its own reward.

Neither could the peasants be brought round to work by propaganda alone. A Stakhanovite frenzy was exhibited by the Chinese during the first few months of the Great Leap Forward (1958–60), a frenzy that probably had more to do with the free-rice policy of that time than with incessant appeals of the Party to "love the commune as you love your own home." But whether it was because they were ultimately unconvinced by such utopian precepts or because the rice ran out, peasants thereafter ignored the exhortations that blasted out of village loudspeakers, the directives that were read at mass meetings, and the stilted slogans that marched in huge characters over any convenient wall. The Party had hoped by such saturation propaganda to permanently indoctrinate the people in a secular version of the Protestant ethic: analogous to the worker collaborating with God in a cosmic design whose completion ushers in the millennium, the peasant was to make a pact with the Party to work for the Marxist scheme whose fulfillment in history would bring the dawn of the Communist utopia. But most peasants were not equipped to understand what it meant to be building something called socialism, to connect their little corner of the countryside with the needs of the nation as a whole, or to grasp such niceties as the inherent virtue of hard work. And insofar as they understood these ideas, they seemed inherently implausible, especially the Communist exaltation of labor (*laodong*) and the laboring class (*laodong jieji*).

The Chinese never cherished any illusions about work. They regarded it not as the divinely ordained purpose of life—there was no Confucian, Taoist, or Buddhist work ethic—but merely as its grinding, inevitable, and endless business. The goal of Chinese peasants was to escape toil by accumulating a little land, hiring tenants to till it, and living off the sweat of others. This dream of leisure lent their labors a hopeful energy, even a certain dignity. But Mao foreclosed on these peasant aspirations by taking the land out of private hands and substituting a collective alternative that proved inviable.

Western economists have been puzzled by the poor performance of Chinese agriculture, which, despite improved irrigation, increased use of chemical fertilizers, and the adoption of high-yielding varieties of rice, has barely kept pace with population growth since 1949.* But this paradox dissolves when the human quotient, the Chinese peasant psyche, is considered. Forced to share more or less equally what they earned, peasants slacked off, working just hard enough to feed themselves. Hence every potential gain in agricultural production was offset in the making by increasingly shiftless peasants, whose declining labor productivity held them to the subsistence level. Collectivism, which had been held out as the deliverance of the peasantry, had become its curse.

To all appearances, Mao Zedong went to his grave unshaken in the belief that rural collectivism was the highroad to communism. If the production teams failed to produce the hoped-for agricultural surpluses, their leadership should be strengthened. If "eating out of one big pot" seemed to cut against the grain of Chinese peasant nature, efforts to alter that nature should be stepped up. Deng Xiaoping, Mao's more pragmatic successor, seems, on the other hand, to have long recognized the obvious: China's twenty-five-year experiment with collective agriculture was, by any reasonable criteria, a failure.

In the end, the peasants outlasted both Mao and the egalitarian collective. In its place is a rural economic policy, gradually introduced from 1979 onward, that not only allows but encourages a return to family farming. The heart of the new policy is the "responsibility system," under which the land is no longer worked in common, but is cultivated by individual households. Each year the team parcels out its land to member families and, following state guidelines, sets production quotas for each tract. But it is the family, not the team, that is responsible for turning over this amount of its produce to state purchasing stations. More importantly, it is the family, not any larger group, that owns all production in excess of this quota, free to consume, sell, or store these fruits of its labor as it sees fit. County officials, mimicking their Beijing superiors, rather disingenuously denied to me that all

* From 1952 to 1978 agricultural production rose at a rate of 3.1 percent a year, only slightly higher than the 2.4 percent annual growth registered by population. See Nicholas R. Lardy, "Food Consumption in the People's Republic of China," in *The Chinese Agricultural Economy*, edited by Randolph Barker and Radha Sinha with Beth Rose (Boulder, Co.: Westview Press, 1983), pp. 147–162.

this means the abandonment of collectivism, pointing out that the land is still owned by the state rather than the households that till it. In fact, the responsibility system is neither collective agriculture nor rural private enterprise, but a return to a form of tenant farming. Thirty years after dispossessing China's landlords, the state has itself become an absentee superlandlord, with the emasculated collective serving as its local representative, each year contracting out its land to hundreds of millions of tenant farmers in return for a share of their crops.

However it is characterized, there can be no doubt that the responsibility system, which came to Sandhead the year I was there, delighted most peasants, who early realized what their leaders long denied, that the rural economy develops faster when the land is farmed by family units. The only peasants I talked to who were ambivalent about the new program were those whose households had many dependents and few laborers. The primary beneficiaries of past welfare policies under which a portion of team income was distributed according to family size rather than work points, they now stood to lose this income supplement. A few commune and brigade cadres also expressed reservations about how well quotas would be met, although one lower-ranking official privately dismissed their concern as merely disguised self-interest, noting that the responsibility system will reduce the power of the organizations that they control. In any case, such doubters were a distinct minority. Upwards of 75 percent of the villagers I discussed the new system with fully approved of it, and were more than willing to trade off the security of the herd for the prospects and hazards of tenant farming. Not only had twenty-five years in the collective failed to make good collectivists out of the peasants, it had convinced them that they had been sold a social security policy by the Communist Party that they neither wanted nor needed nor over the long run could afford.

Equally surprising, years of ruthless condemnation of "the capitalist road" of material incentives and private profits—at one time rural households were even forbidden to raise pigs or more than a handful of chickens—failed to quench the entrepreneurial spirit of the Chinese, which flared anew once opportunity presented itself. "The first thing I'll do when I get my own mulberry patch," one excited Sandhead woman gushed to me when she first heard about the new program, "is plant beans between the

rows of trees. You can't do that now because people are careless
when they work. They would step on them when they are spreading mud [as fertilizer] or picking mulberry leaves. But I'll be careful because they'll be mine." She went on to detail for me how
she and her family would more efficiently manage the 2-acre mini-
farm of fish pond, mulberry patch, and sugarcane field that would
be theirs to till if the team let out its land. The topic of farm
management quickly eclipsed all others around the dinner table
as peasants throughout the village discussed similar plans.

She and the other villagers did not get to put all of their
plans into practice that first year, though, for the conservative
county bureaucracy timidly allowed only more distant fish ponds
and the winter vegetable crop to be leased out to the peasants.
Still, even on this limited basis the responsibility system with its
built-in profit motive was a resounding success. Peasants who
were working their own tracts of vegetables that winter could
be seen at all hours of the day hoeing, weeding, fertilizing, and
otherwise working harder and longer hours than their fellow team
members who remained on collective land. This extra expenditure
of effort and care paid off in yields that were higher by half than
those in the past, enabling peasants to easily meet quotas and
keep a sizable surplus besides. As a result household incomes
in Sandhead rose by 15 percent in 1980, about what other parts
of the country are reporting under the new system, and the following year most of the land was parceled out to families.

Even so, the program did not go far enough to please the
peasants, most of whom would prefer to permanently disband
the collective and return the land to private ownership. What I
initially dismissed as the muttering of unreconstructed old men
took on somewhat larger significance when I began asking about
the distribution of land before and after the 1952 land reform.
I found that despite orders to burn their old land deeds from
this period, most families had instead carefully secreted them away
in their homes, in the hope that they would one day prove useful
in reclaiming the land that had once been theirs. Though economics figured largely in this preference for the private family farm,
another reason often cited was the ease of cooperation within
the intimate household unit as compared with the larger, often
conflict-ridden collective. "People get along better when families
farm alone," was how one cadre, whose team headquarters had

been the scene of angry brawls in the past, put it to me. Chinese villagers remain staunch familists who, given a choice in the matter, center their economic and social life around the domestic hearth.

The home is also a place where Chinese seek relief from the unremitting toil of their workaday existence. Village men have an apparently limitless capacity to sit or squat in nearly motionless languor and, like the serfs in Tolstoy's novels, an ability to curl up like cats any time of the day and go to sleep. And when they have slept enough, men prefer the easy, indolent human communion of the dinner table, where they can relax in the company of friends. The main leisure-time activity in rural China is nothing other than leisure itself.

Officially organized sports competitions on public holidays draw few participants because these activities require an amount of physical exertion that even the youth are loath to make on their few days of rest. Basketball courts, a fixture of rural communities, are used mostly for outdoor meetings and movies. Except for occasional sports broadcasts and a rare Cantonese opera, local television programming has little entertainment value, and TVs are rare in the villages anyway. Newspapers and magazines are difficult to subscribe to—it took me one month and intervention by the county foreign affairs office to succeed in placing a subscription to the *People's Daily*—repetitive in content, and of no use whatsoever to the large numbers of older peasants who are illiterate. The Great Leap Forward–vintage loudspeaker systems that unceasingly broadcast a steady diet of official speeches, news bulletins, semioperatic ballads, and People's Liberation Army marches are appreciated even less, and I was amused to discover that peasants had early ended this unwelcome intrusion of officialdom into their quiet menages by the simple expedient of installing a switch on their home's loudspeaker and keeping it in the "off" position.

Traditional games of chance have not fully recovered from the attacks on "bourgeois amusements" made during the Cultural Revolution, and are still not given free rein by the authorities. The itinerant Chinese chess shark has reappeared in the market towns, the pieces on his several boards set up in end-game configurations that the passerby is invited, for a few *fen* (cents), to play out against the master. The outcome is only rarely in doubt. The occasional clicking of Mahjong tiles can be heard again in towns and villages, but the game is still officially frowned on as a waste of time and an incitement to gambling. During my year in Sandhead, several groups of men, including a number of cadres, got into the habit of a noon poker game at the brigade headquarters, often with a little surreptitious betting on the side. So popular did this activity quickly become that for a time men were getting to work late in the afternoon as they played out a few more hands, and before long a notice appeared on the brigade propaganda board stating that men under 60 were not permitted to play cards during the noon hour. This did not spell the end of noon poker in Sandhead, though, for the retired continued to congregate at their old haunt, while the younger card players moved their action to a less conspicuous location.

The only manufactured entertainment enjoyed by any sizable number of Chinese in country or town is the movies. In the countryside this is usually an outdoor activity, for during good weather a member of the commune's movie projection team visits each village once or twice a week, setting up his projector at one end of the basketball court and his screen at the other. While some young people bike in to catch an occasional movie at the commune theater, people of all ages regularly attend the open-air village cinema; it is like a drive-in movie without the cars. The show begins at dusk. As the hour approaches, the alleyways fill up with villagers filing slowly out to the basketball field, each shouldering a chair, bench, or stool for seating. In Sandhead and other villages the motion pictures draw enormous crowds of thousands of people, more even than mandatory political meetings. Often three-quarters of the local population will be mustered on the basketball court by the time the projector is turned on.

These enthusiastic multitudes were initially difficult for me to reconcile with the sorry quality of the movies themselves. "Red Day," a black-and-white movie filmed in the early fifties about the last phase of the Chinese civil war, is typical. The copy of the film that circulates through the commune is so grainy, scratched, and spliced from its hundreds (thousands?) of screenings that the characters hop about like figures in an old silent film. Added to this is the poor quality of the loudspeakers, which produce a cacaphony of barks, growls, and squeals that only faintly resemble human speech. But even if the speakers were top-flight, the movie would still be unintelligible to villagers on another count: the entire sound track is in Mandarin, the national language, which few understand. The projectionist is thus forced to double as a narrator, stopping the film every fifteen minutes or so to tell the crowd in Cantonese what is about to happen. Despite these several handicaps, most villagers have the plot of "Red Day" and other movies down pat, and spend as much time chatting with their neighbors as they do watching the movie. The 22-year-old who sat by me during my maiden viewing of "Red Day" explaining the significance of each troop charge and howitzer bombardment casually mentioned to me at the end that despite having missed some showings, he had seen this movie at least fifteen times over the past few years.

This solved the riddle of how the villagers came to be so familiar with the dozen or so films in the local repertory, but created another: why did villagers outdistance even the most ardent of "Star Wars" groupies by sitting ten or more times through movies that seemed to me unworthy of even a second viewing? In part I saw that it was the mundaneness of village life that led them out to the basketball court each time a movie was announced, and on sultry summer evenings I noticed that the crowd of moviegoers swelled even larger than usual as people came to enjoy the coolness of that alfresco setting. But I came to realize that the root appeal of these movie evenings to the Chinese, a consummately social people, is that they provide another opportunity to relax among friends and intimates and rehash the events of the day, never mind that the movie is one they have seen countless times before. Like the dinner table, the outdoor movies are a place to lounge and a meeting ground.

The Chinese leisure-time activity par excellence, the ultimate recreational and social event, is the feast. Here are combined all of the indispensable elements of a good time Chinese-style— the friendly cakes-and-ale camaraderie of the dinner table, the sensual contentment that comes from "drinking until full and eating until drunk," and the high-spirited boisterousness of people in groups that the Chinese call *renau.* Each ritual meeting of the brigade, commune, or county Party organization, each ceremonial event such as a birth, death, or marriage, each one of the elaborate yearly round of traditional festivals, provides the Chinese with an opportunity to do what they enjoy most—eat. So closely are feast and festivities identified with each other that to "eat good things" is another way of referring to a wedding, festival, or other occasion on which "good things" will be served. At these times eating is elevated from an essential activity to a passionate pastime, peaking with the Chinese New Year, when the obsession with good food verges on a national mania. For Chinese, the good things in life are mostly edible.

The Chinese love a feast, approaching it not with the wary ambivalence of chronically overfed and weight-watching Westerners, but with a gusto that bespeaks the skimpiness of their diet at other times. The Pearl River Delta where I lived is one of the richest agricultural areas in all of China, yet ordinary meals of most of the people I knew were meager to the point of subsistence. They often sat down to dinners that consisted of nothing more than steamed rice and a single plate of diced salted turnips. Some evenings an extra side dish of turnip greens, string beans, or spinach from the private plot would be stir-fried, and once or twice a week a small fish or a few slices of pork fat would appear on the table.

It was not just from observation that I came to know this diet: after my arrival in Sandhead I initially took my meals with a peasant family. But a month of recurrent minor illnesses and steady weight loss convinced me to make other arrangements. Nor was my experience unique, for in the course of my stay in China I encountered a number of commune and county cadres who complained of chronic stomach trouble that they traced to extended stays in villages during the land reform, when the "Four Togethers" policy required them to live, study, work, and eat with the peasantry.

In the midst of this Sahara of ordinary fare, feasts beckon like salvatory oases. On these occasions the usually barren dinner table blossoms with seven or eight dishes, customarily including lean pork, fried fish, steamed prawns, broiled chicken, scrambled eggs with diced green onions, mixed vegetables with pork cubes and peanuts added, and one or two dishes of leafy green vegetables, most prepared with a reckless profligacy of peanut oil or pork drippings. Such rich spreads offer a temporary respite from the monotonous starch diet of other times, a rare opportunity to gorge on fatty meats. Most Chinese are still less gourmets than gourmands, less interested in *haute cuisine à la Chinois* than in a decidedly full belly. The highest compliment that a guest can pay his host is not that his food is good, but that it is plentiful.

That food has often not been plentiful is a point instinctively understood by every Chinese, not least because it is deeply imbedded in his language and culture. An ancient Chinese adage, as true today as it was 2,000 years ago, states that "to the people food is paramount." The Chinese greets others not by inquiring vaguely, "How are you?" but by striking right to the heart of his neighbor's well-being with a pointed "Have you eaten yet?" A person in China with job security is said to have an "iron rice bowl," while one who has been fired has had his "rice bowl broken." The Chinese lays carefully prepared dishes before his family's ancestor tablets in worship, only to consume them himself after a brief ritual. His most biting criticism of cadres concerns their incessant feasting, and he envies his Hong Kong, Taiwan, and American cousins above all for the good things that grace their tables. A commune cadre whose boyish face and slender build made him look far younger than his 45 years told me the reaction he and his friends had to an hour-long TV program on life in the U.S. that had been broadcast a short time before. "What most impressed us," he said, "was not the cars and the freeways, nor the homes with their appliances, though we were all struck by how rich America is. What left the deepest impression was a shot of the inside of a supermarket. It was only about ten seconds long, but you could see aisle after aisle stacked with 10,000 kinds of food. It was unbelievable. So much food in one place. We still talk about it."

The agricultural cornucopia that is the United States provides a sustenance so substantial that most Americans have trouble understanding the razor-thin margins that separate rural Chinese from hunger and famine, and the seriousness of the charge of gorging on food that I often heard leveled at cadres. As it has been for centuries, the diet of the Chinese peasantry is systematically and necessarily abstemious. It is nearly impossible for an individual to gain weight on the rice and other rationed foodstuffs he receives, which add up to just under the caloric intake required to maintain a stable body weight. In America members of lower income groups, socially less motivated toward slenderness and with a diet in which carbohydrates bulk large, are more often overweight than those who earn more. In mainland China it is the opposite. Peasants and workers are generally slender, at best achieving a lean fitness from field and factory work, whereas officials, whose feasting provides them with extra calories, are generally pictures of florid, fleshy health. In the old China only merchants, mandarins, and large landowners had a chance at corpulence. In the People's Republic, the only overweight individuals I saw over the course of a year were county-level and higher cadres.

What ultimately motivates the frenetic Chinese celebration of eating is the haunting memory of starving. Seen in this light, the enormous and inventive cuisine of the Chinese is the product of a millennium-long effort to extract from nature every possible bite of provender. During my time in China I tasted—gingerly and often in no more than polite helpings—mole, snake, dog, silkworm pupae, fish eyes, fish liver, bamboo shoots, and one particularly tasty dish made from Chinese grapefruit peels. What is a delicacy in a year of bounteous harvests may provide the thin margin of subsistence that means survival during the next, which may very well bring one of the periodic famines that have punctuated China's long history down to the present day. During the "three difficult years" immediately following the disastrous Great Leap Forward, 20 to 30 million Chinese may have died in famine-related deaths. Sandhead residents recalled to me that in 1960 their rice rations were cut and then cut again, until finally rice disappeared altogether from their diet and they had to live on sweet potatoes. But soon these were gone as well, after which they had only what they could scavenge from the countryside, and they were eating field mice and wild grasses. The people were consumed by their own hunger and before the spring of 1961 not a few families had buried an elder in a simple grave or an infant in an unmarked one.

No one was dying of starvation in the Pearl River Delta when I was there, but villagers in places like Equality Commune where the land was planted in commercial crops did complain to me that the grain ration they received from the state fell short of their needs. The basic allotment was 35.2 pounds (16 kilograms) of rice per month per head, but this was parceled out to individual households by each production team following a complex scale of age and sex. As there was not enough rice to go around, neither adult laborers nor rapidly growing teenagers were ever quite able to eat their fill. Likewise, residents of villages in grain-growing areas grumbled that state purchase quotas were set too high, leaving them with too little grain for their own larders. Pleas to increase rations or reduce quotas had not been heeded by the provincial government, which needed every catty of grain it could collect to supply the cities.*

Even those Chinese fortunate enough to reside in the capital, which is far better supplied with food than other parts of China, were grimly reminded of how close to starvation many of their countrymen live by the famine that smoldered through much of the North China plain during 1980–81. By March 1981, when the authorities belatedly admitted to the existence of widespread famine and asked for international aid, Beijing residents had already known of the tragedy for almost a year. With the failure of the 1980 spring wheat crop the peasants of Hebei (Hopeh) Province, who as in the past still live largely from crop to crop, had descended like a plague of locusts on the cities, rummaging through garbage cans, scavenging the produce markets, and begging openly in the streets for food, money, and ration coupons. A young worker in a government ministry told me how they would also congregate in the larger restaurants. As a diner took his seat, he would hear a plaintive begging begin from behind his chair: "Comrade, could you spare a little food for me? Please leave a little food in the bowl for me. My family and I are starving." "It simply takes away your appetite when they beg like that," this man recalled, sighing deeply. "But the last time I went to a restaurant it was even worse. A teenaged girl stood behind my chair crying, not saying a word. I got a lump in my throat and couldn't eat more than a few bites. I let her have most of the meal. After that experience I decided not to eat out again until after the famine was over and the poor peasants had gone back to their villages."

Even if famine and grain shortfalls had not repeatedly falsified the claim, accepted even by many who are otherwise highly critical of the current regime, that the Communist Party brought full

---

* One catty equals 1⅓ pounds or 600 grams.

rice bowls to the improvident Chinese people, it would still be basically wrongheaded. It is the peasantry, after all, not the Party, that grows the grain. This much should have been obvious all along. And the evidence is now accumulating that the Party's major rural innovation, yoking up the peasants into collectives, was counterproductive. Far from easing the peasants' monumental task of feeding China, the Party actually seems to have exacerbated it. This is the reality that forced Deng to take the very unsocialist step of returning many collective farm responsibilities to the peasant family. In spite of its all too evident agricultural failings, though, the three-tiered system of communes, brigades, and teams will almost certainly be continued in one form or another. It would be naive to think that a Party and state bureaucracy so obsessed with keeping its vast population under close control would ever voluntarily give up an organization so admirably suited to that purpose.

3

The System: The Iron Cage of Bureaucracy

Here even routine matters are often impossible to take care of unless you know someone on the inside.

Heaven's Gate Brigade cadre, 1979

My first quandary after the official beginning of my fieldwork was how to get myself and my equipment from the Dongfang Hotel in Guangzhou to the rural commune 45 miles to the southeast that was my destination. I had been warmly received at the Guangzhou train station by members of the Guangdong Provincial Institute of Social Science and Philosophy, my official liaison unit in China, and at first thought to hire their passenger van to make the short journey.

"It's inconvenient," the short female cadre who had only the day before warmly insisted I call her "older sister" nervously told me after I broached my request. "Our unit was only issued this van a few months ago, but it's ten years old. The last time we drove it out into the countryside it broke down, and it took our driver several weeks to get the parts to repair it. Besides, it's against regulations for nonunit people to use the van. You had better take up the matter with the provincial department of foreign affairs."

I took a taxi to this department's office, where Wen Minglu, a sleekly handsome official who looked 30 but was actually ten years older, told me after a short deliberation with colleagues that I could rent a vehicle from the Dongfang Hotel's motor pool, which regularly hired out cars and drivers to Hong Kong Chinese returning to their ancestral villages. But back at the Dongfang, things did not go smoothly.

"You want to rent a van to go to the countryside," the head of the hotel's motor pool said warily, repeating my request. "But foreigners are only permitted to travel by taxi, and only within the city limits." When I remonstrated that it was not my idea, but that of the department of foreign affairs, he asked for documentation—the standard ploy of the Chinese petty official. Heart sinking, I showed him the visa in my passport indicating my rural destination.

"Not enough," he said, shaking his head. "You will need a written authorization from foreign affairs and a travel permit from public security." As it turned out, a letter from Wen Minglu was sufficient to resolve this impasse; still, two days had gone by before the necessary arrangements were completed, a delay that seemed interminable to me in my eagerness to begin research. Nevertheless, I put the whole episode down as one of the petty bureaucratic snafus that impede foreign travelers in many countries.

I was finally able to leave Guangzhou on the fourth morning after my arrival in a rented van. But my pleasure at arriving in the village diminished somewhat when I was presented with a bill of 170 *rmb* ($113) for the two-hour trip. "One hundred *renminbi* to rent the van for a day," the driver explained, "and mileage at half a *renminbi* a kilometer for 140 kilometers." When I pointed out that we had only come half that distance, he replied imperturbably that the regulations require the passenger to pay milage for the return trip as well, whether he was aboard or not.

Nor were the Dongfang motor pool fares unusually expensive. I soon discovered that even rural communes charged upwards of 100 *rmb* a day for a car and driver. These rates may have been reasonable elsewhere, but in the People's Republic, where drivers earned less than 2 *rmb* a day, they were positively predatory. The state and its constituent units take full advantage of the monopoly they hold on transportation to exploit the tourist trade.

After doing a few depressing calculations on the cost of future rides and reflecting on the inconvenience of arranging for a van and driver each time I went any distance from the village, I decided to seek permission to import a van for research use. This request had to run the gamut of a host of Chinese bureaucracies—including the Guangdong provincial department of foreign affairs, the Ministry of Public Security, and the Chinese Academy of Social Sciences—and it took nearly two months for it to be approved, but in my satisfaction at finally hearing from Wen Minglu that my request had been granted, I didn't give these bureaucratic complications much thought.

But I began to appreciate the dimensions of China's bureaucratic phenomenon after the van actually arrived and I attempted to register it and apply for the driver's license I had been promised. Wen Minglu assured me that he had made all necessary arrangements, including contacting the county transportation office about the matter, and so it was that I set out for the county seat 35 kilometers away early one morning, hopeful of taking care of the matter in a day. My mood began to sour when my arrival at the county transportation office created consternation among the functionaries, who announced after a brief huddle that they had had no advance notice of my coming and that I should go on to the prefectural transportation office in Foshan (Buddhist Mountain) City. I would be helped there, they assured me.

But the Foshan transportation office cadres proved as nonplussed by my sudden appearance as the county branch office personnel had been, and after a short, whispered conclave, they steered me politely but firmly to the prefectural office of foreign affairs. There the now familiar scenario was repeated—the initial perplexity, the private hand-wringing session, and the automatic effort to shift responsibility upward. After an unsuccessful attempt to call Guangzhou for instructions (the phones are unreliable and time-consuming in the PRC), prefectural foreign affairs cadres courteously advised me that it would be best if I went on to their main provincial office in Guangzhou. By this time, I was rather exercised at the official runaround that I was being given, but my driver, Ah Bing, remained in good spirits, jesting on the way to Guangzhou that he would not be surprised if they told us there to drive on to Beijing to register the van.

This did not happen, but we encountered a bureaucratic obstacle of a different kind after arriving at the foreign affairs department. Wen Minglu was out of the office for the day. The cadre on duty, whom I had met on my previous visit, listened expressionlessly as I recounted the day's difficulties. "You are Comrade Wen's charge, and only he can help you," he responded with the primness of the petty official, obviously worried about overstepping his authority. "I'm sorry, but I can do nothing."

After this episode, I resolved to stay home and let my driver register the van, postponing until later the question of my driver's license. Ah Bing left again for Guangzhou the following day and was gone for three days. He returned to the village with even his considerable Chinese patience exhausted, ranting against "bureaucratism" as he told me how he had been batted back and forth like a ping-pong ball among half a dozen government bureaus, none of which wanted to take the responsibility for registering my van. "And after all that, they finally issue only a temporary license plate and a certificate waiving the yearly road tax. I still must go back and apply for permanent registration," he fumed.

Nor did my transportation difficulties end with the van registration. Even such an outwardly simple matter as buying gasoline turned out to be unexpectedly trying, though not for me personally. Ah Bing would first go to the brigade headquarters, where the cadre in charge of administrative work would write out a request to purchase gas. His next stop was the commune headquarters. There, after obtaining the endorsement of the foreign affairs cadre, he would present the completed request to the cadre in overall charge of commune commerce, who would write out an authorization for the sale of 100 liters of gas, the maximum amount that could be purchased at any one time. Ah Bing would then proceed to the state-run public sales store itself, where he would hand over his purchase order along with 35 *rmb* for the 100 liters of gas and receive in turn a receipt for payment and a stock order for the gas. His final stop was the commune storage depot, where he would present the stock order and wait while the employees brought the gas out in 20-liter containers for him to fill up the van's gas tank. The extra would go into an oil drum that he would bring along. This administrative obstacle course could be completed in a morning if Ah Bing was lucky enough to find all of the essential cadres in their offices, but it could easily stretch out to engulf an entire day if, as often happened, he had to hunt down the cadres one by one for their signatures.

I heard from other drivers that I could have bypassed the trying state supply system entirely by purchasing black market gas from drivers who worked at large county- and commune-level truck depots for the slightly higher price of half a *renminbi* per liter, but I vetoed the idea.

More frustrating for me personally was my drawn-out and ultimately fruitless effort to obtain the Chinese driver's license that I had been promised and end my total dependence upon my driver. On several occasions when I asked Wen Minglu when the license would be issued, he was blandly evasive, saying only that the matter was "being researched." After I came to understand this phrase as officialese for killing a request by putting it off indefinitely, I pressed Wen for an explanation. It turned out that besides the consular staffs, whom the Chinese were bound by diplomatic convention to issue licenses to, only one foreigner in the entire province of Guangdong was holding a Chinese driver's license and operating his own private car at the time I applied. This privileged fellow was a North Korean engineer working on a joint North Korean–Chinese industrial venture. He was also accident-prone, for within six months of arriving in the PRC he had been involved in no fewer that four separate accidents, probably because he had never driven before coming to China. (Few are the private cars that ply the streets of Pyongyang.) This unhappy precedent was enough to unnerve faint-hearted department of transportation functionaries, who invoked the bureaucratic pocket veto of procrastination to stall my request, although I did receive permission to drive locally later in my stay.

Nor was the transportation office unique in its timidity, for I found this to be characteristic of all the Chinese bureaucracies I had contact with. Not long after I arrived in China, I received an invitation from a cadre in the education field to hold a day-long seminar on how to teach English. This man, a graduate of a three-year teacher's training school, was concerned over the considerable difficulties that local English teachers were having mastering the new, considerably more advanced, Four Modernizations textbooks that had just appeared, and had conceived the idea of a seminar to help them over this hurdle. I agreed immediately, happy to think that I could be of assistance, and the cadre promised to get back to me after the necessary arrangements had been made. But months went by and nothing happened. One day I encountered the cadre and asked him if a date had been set yet. He looked embarrassed as he told me that the planned seminar had been canceled because it was "inconvenient." My disappointment must have been evident, for the cadre paused, looked around to make sure we were not being overheard, and then asked quietly if I wanted to know what had *really* happened. No longer bothering to hide his exasperation, he told me that the head of the county office of education—"who has no back-ground in education at all"—had become worried about the pro-priety of the proposed seminar and so had contacted the head of the county office of foreign affairs to clear the plans with her. This beadle had been equally unwilling to take the responsibility, though, and had relayed the request up to the prefectural level, which had in turn passed it up to the provincial level, where it had ultimately been denied. "The reason they gave was that the seminar raised a problem of *fanwei* [proper jurisdication]," he snorted. "They said that for you, research was permitted, but not teaching English."

Administrative timorousness, sluggishness, and inefficiency arise from the very nature of the Chinese Communist system—the huge size and complexity of the bureaucracy, the extraordinary importance of human relations, and the dominance of leadership positions by technically incompetent apparatchiks and superannu-ated guerrilla leaders. The problems go far beyond the red tape that Westerners sometimes experience in their occasional dealings with their own state organizations, because in China nearly all aspects of life are under the surveillance and control of some many-storied pagoda of officialdom that peaks in Beijing.

Bureaucracy is of course not new to China. Indeed, it took root there earlier than anywhere else. Two thousand years ago during the Han Dynasty (202 B.C.–A.D. 220) China already had a civil service divided into twelve grades, each of which received a set annual stipend, from the 100 measures of grain of the lowliest clerk to the 2,000 measures of grain of the highest minister of state. So inbred in the Chinese consciousness is the concept of official that another name for God is "celestial bureaucrat."

Its early appearance notwithstanding, the absolute size of the civil service remained small as dynasties came and went. As late as a century ago, during the last decades of the Qing (Ching) dynasty, the total number of officials did not exceed 40,000, although nonstatutory employees of the officials themselves—personal secretaries, clerks, and police personnel—probably numbered several million. The number of government employees expanded rapidly after the founding of the Republic of China as billets for these personnel were incorporated into the lower ranks of an expanded civil service, but it was only after the People's Republic came into being that the bureaucracy exploded in size. Showing no sign of the withering away predicted by Marx, the new socialist state grew luxuriantly, extending powerful roots downward to enfold rural hamlets and villages, and branching outward to encompass agriculture, industry, commerce, and intellectual and social life. To man this vastly expanded state apparatus and discharge its labyrinthine administrative tasks, millions of new government cadres and employees were recruited.

The backbone of the system is a bureaucratic superstructure with a total of twenty-four grades. Implemented in the early fifties to regiment the world's largest army of state employees, it incorporates everyone from powerful government ministers to lowly commune cadres into the same hierarchy, assigning them a grade from 1 to 24. In contrast to Western convention, in China the smaller the number, the higher the grade.

The major divisions in this stratified pagoda of power fall at grades 7, 13, and 17. Grades 18 and below include the vast lower echelons of state employees, considered to be ordinary national cadres and accorded no special privileges. Grades 17 and up are held by *lingdao ganbu* (leading cadres), who occupy positions of command. Those in grades 14 to 17 are considered to be middle-ranking cadres and are assigned to positions of leadership at the commune and county levels, while those in grades 13 and up are *gaogan*, or high-ranking cadres, holding power in the prefectures, provinces, and Beijing. So well known is this latter breaking point that another term used by the Chinese interchangeably with the term *tequan jieji* (privileged class) is "grade 13 and higher cadres." Grades 7 and higher are the supercadres, the elite of the bureaucratic elite.

Occupying the pinnacle of this pagoda are the Chairman of the Communist Party, the Chief of State, the Chairman of the National People's Congress, and the Premier of the State Council, positions formerly held by Mao Zedong, Liu Shaoqi, Zhu De, and Zhou Enlai, all of whom held the first administrative rank, grade 1. These positions are filled from the powerful Standing Committee of the Chinese Communist Party (CCP) Politburo. Although in theory the Politburo is elected by the Central Committee and then elects a Chairman and the other members of the Standing Committee, in reality this democratic system of indirect election exists only on paper. What actually happens is the reverse: instead of being filled from the bottom up, posts are assigned from the top down. The top leaders personally approve selections for the next several administrative grades including Vice Premiers of the State Council, Vice Chairmen of the National People's Congress, Vice Chairmen of the People's Political Consultative Committee, the members of the Military Commission of the Central Committee of the CCP, and the members of the Politburo. The members of the Politburo in turn appoint cadres of grade 7, who include government ministers, provincial first Party secretaries, the commanders of military districts, and the 200 regular members of the Party Central Committee. The Central Committee then selects assistant ministers and provincial Party committee members. From province to prefecture, prefecture to county, county to commune, and commune to brigade the process continues, each level of Party government filling offices at the next lower level with its protégés. The only concession to democratic sentiments in all of this is that brigade Party secretaries are almost always selected from among the Party members of the village that they are to rule.

The result is a vast patronage system in which those at each level in the Party-run government and military owe their position and perquisites to those at the next higher level in the hierarchy and remain dependent upon them for continued sponsorship, protection, and promotion. Tammany Hall pales before the scale and perfection of PRC patronage, and Boss Tweed would have especially admired the way it operates out of the public eye. The system as a whole resembles a closed corporation, whose board of directors—the Politburo and especially its Standing Committee—serves as an all-powerful interlocking directorate of the Party, military, and government bureaucracies.

Although pay increases substantially with grade, the main rewards of those who faithfully serve the organization are privileges that money cannot buy in the form of chauffeured limousines, personal staffs, state residences, and access to special stores. These favors are carefully doled out by rank. Following the regulations of the State Council governing transportation, for instance, *gaogan* of grade 7 and above are allotted a limousine for their exclusive use. Cadres of grade 13 and above are allowed the use of a limousine to commute to their ministries, while cadres of grades 14 to 17 may travel by car when necessary for the conduct of state business. All persons in grades 18 and below, whether they are state employees, PLA personnel, members of rural collectives, or Communist Party members, belong to the rank and file and receive no transportation privileges.

Although China has characteristically not released figures on the combined size of its Party and government bureaucracy, most estimates place the total at around a staggering 20 million. Around 100,000 of these are based in the capital itself, cycling to work at one of the ninety-eight ministries, commissions, and independent bureaus that comprise the State Council, or at one of the ten units directly attached to the Communist Party's Central Committee. The bulk of public employees are located in lower administrative centers—those of provinces, municipalities, prefectures, counties, and communes—where they serve in the regional and local branches of Beijing ministries. Even county governments in China have many thousands of government employees and Party functionaries attending to their duties in a jungle-like proliferation of over sixty committees, offices, and departments.

Many of these myriad units tend to be top-heavy with overage officials, a consequence of the lack of a mandatory age for retirement coupled with the absence of strict limitations on the number of bureaucratic billets. With length of service the primary determinant of almost pushbutton promotions, the number of nominal leaders an office has can easily swell to a dozen or more. The most extreme examples of echelon creep are to be found at the very top: the Communist Party, with its five Vice Chairmen, the State Council, with its thirteen Vice Premiers,* and the National People's Congress, with its twenty Vice Chairmen. But the problem exists also at the most mundane levels of government. In the Pearl River Delta, I toured an electric motor factory which

---

* Reduced to two in late 1982.

had four assistant managers and visited a county education office which had no fewer than five vice heads, and these were not unusual cases.

The oriental scale and bewildering complexity of this state establishment led me to anticipate that it would be inundated in great seas of paperwork and vast sloughs of minutely detailed rules and regulations. Paperwork there is, and it constitutes considerably more of a burden in China, where reports must be written, copied, and duplicated by hand, than in the West, where the flow of information is speeded by modern technology. But I found the Chinese bureaucracy to be less governed by regulations than comparable Western organizations, because the natural tendency of the hidebound and conservative Chinese functionary to go by the book is overshadowed by another bureaucratic characteristic—timidity. The political line has changed too often for even high-ranking administrators and managers to commit themselves readily in writing. The directive signed today may be the death warrant of tomorrow. Neither can petty officials blindly follow rules handed down from the past; they must act with one eye to a future shift of ideology. One measure of the degree to which officialdom has been unnerved by past political movements is that the directives and statutes that are promulgated are commonly marked "provisional" or "temporary," are couched in fairly general or even ambiguous terms, and close by emphasizing that modifications of the letter of the law to suit local conditions are permissible as long as the spirit (*jingshen*) of their contents is followed.

These are all artifices designed, it would seem, to allow the official sponsors of a directive an escape hatch should their handiwork be declared rightist reactionary or leftist deviationist, but they have another consequence as well. This waffling language has the effect of giving local officials extraordinary discretionary powers. These powers are further enhanced because even the most ordinary regulations are usually stamped "for internal use only" and are thus accessible only to officials, who freely interpret them depending on circumstances. One time I took a package of paperback books, all of which were innocuous stuff that I had purchased over the counter at a state-run New China Bookstore, to the main post office in Guangzhou to mail down to Hong Kong. Before even looking over the material, the fiftyish postal inspector asked me what my status in the People's Republic was. Startled by his unexpected and seemingly irrelevant query, I automatically asked what difference it made. Clearly not used to being questioned, he was startled in turn, but after a slight hesitation he evidently decided to humor me. "Mailing privileges vary depending on *who* is doing the mailing," he explained in a schoolmasterly tone of voice. "Local Chinese are not permitted to mail any printed matter out, and neither are Hong Kong Chinese except in special cases. Foreign tourists may mail back materials with certain restrictions, while visitors invited by the Chinese government are granted even more in the way of mailing privileges. And of course," he finished in an upbeat fashion, "if you are a member of a consulate staff, you are allowed to mail materials without inspection." Bowing to the inevitable, I told him that I was in China under an official exchange program. "In that case," he responded, flipping quickly through the books I had brought, "there is no problem at all."

Chinese officials at all levels seek safety less in scrupulous adherence to regulations than in a cat's cradle of mutual involvement with others of their class. The essence of the Chinese bureaucratic style is to rely on informal consensus rather than, as in the West, on formal authority. This means that byzantine backroom negotiations form an intricate and essential prelude to decision-making, as a young cadre in the Guangdong provincial department of foreign affairs revealed. "We say that decisions are made in four stages—consideration, research, discussion, and decision," he told me. "The first stage, consideration, is the most important. Here we consider the issue from a personal angle. We weigh how it will affect us, how it will affect those with whom we have a personal relationship [*ganqing*]. In this way we arrive at a personal position on the issue. This comes ahead of everything else." He fixed me with a glance to underline this point before going on. "The second stage is research. Here we study any rules and regulations that relate to the issue. The third stage is discussion. We discuss the content of the regulations in relation to the issue and various proposals. We also contact all other units concerned and ask for their opinions at this point in an informal way. Of course, we don't voice our personal position to anyone except maybe privately to those we are very close to. The final step is a formal meeting. The decision has already been reached by this point, so this meeting is really just a formality. The highest-ranking cadre puts forward the proposal already agreed upon and the others present approve it unanimously."

Basing decisions primarily on personal considerations is merely one of the ways in which cadre behavior contradicts the strictures of scientific management. The average Chinese cadre is nothing less than the living antithesis of the ideal bureaucrat described by the German sociologist Max Weber. Instead of being impersonal, rational, and reliable servants of the state, Chinese government employees are partisan, self-interested, and inconstant; instead of being committed to an impersonal order, they are loyal first and foremost to friends, allies, and superiors. What from the outside, especially to closely monitored and narrowly restricted foreigners, appears to be a cold and impersonal bureaucratic machine looks from the inside more like an unregulated maze of tribal friendships and feudal ties. A brigade cadre well versed in the ways of officialdom told me that he had not been sanguine about my success when I set out to register the van. "I didn't think you'd be able to get a license in one day," he said with a wry smile a few days after I had returned from my futile foray. "You didn't have any *guanxi* [connections] with the transportation office, you see. Here even routine matters are often impossible to take care of unless you know someone on the inside." This was it in a nutshell. As in dynastic times, it is *ganqing* and *guanxi* that are the essential lubricants of an inert, inept, and timid bureaucracy.

They also, of course, come high on the list of reasons why the bureaucratic works came to be so gummed up in the first place. Although no bureaucracies are truly rational and depersonalized, Chinese organizations are extraordinary in the degree to which they are given coherence by the pattern of personal commitments linking individual members. While the continuation of what the official press blasts as feudal tendencies owes something to residual Confucian ideals of administration by influence, persuasion, and personal example, the current government has unwittingly fostered just these tendencies by its personnel policies. Undereducated but ideologically reliable "Red" cadres have often been favored over professionally trained "experts" with less pure political pedigrees in assignments and promotions. I ran into these "Red" cadres everywhere—a head of a county education office who had only an elementary school education, a director of a commune clinic who was out of his depth as soon as we got beyond barefoot doctors and basic hygiene, a head of a county construction unit who was formerly a bricklayer. But the most unforgettable member of this class of petty "Red" bureaucrats that I encountered in China was the head of a county transportation office. This character, I was told by his disgruntled subordinates, was a former lieutenant in the PLA infantry with no prior experience in transportation, whose assignment to head the transportation office had come through because that was a position befitting his impeccable army and Party credentials. He clearly appreciated the source of his karma, for even in retirement he continued to sport his military uniform complete to the visored cap with its prominent red star. The arrival of this impressively accoutered ex-officer several years prior had scarcely made a ripple in office routine, though, since he limited himself to morning appearances three times a week and to attending occasional meetings with other county-level Party functionaries. The real work of registering and inspecting vehicles, communicating with the transportation hierarchy concerning technical matters, and directing the commune transportation substations was carried on by the three assistant office heads as before.

But for me, the conclusive evidence of the paternalistic character of the Chinese bureaucracy came from a young commune cadre who told me that it was often easier to be promoted for ineptitude than for doing one's job well. "When brigade Party secretaries don't do a good job managing production, they are never demoted," he revealed to me. "They are promoted." What he went on to lay out for me was a Communist Chinese version of the Peter Principle, where managers rise not just to their level of incompetence, a: in the West, but one step beyond. "It's all a matter of face and *guanxi*. The brigade Party secretaries operate very close to the commune leaders. The two groups develop close personal ties with each other. Should a brigade leader fail to do his job well, he will not be demoted. How could he go back to working as a peasant or even as an ordinary brigade cadre after having been in charge of everything? He would have no face left. And how could the commune leaders do this to him? It would be like "dismantling the bridge after you have crossed it." The commune leaders feel an obligation to him and will protect his face. So they will promote him to be the assistant head of a commune factory or something. In our commune administration, maybe 100 of the 400 cadres are former brigade Party secretaries or assistant Party secretaries who were promoted in this fashion."

To Americans used to the complex and contentious overlap of municipal, county, state, and federal governments, the command structure of the Chinese Party and government possesses an awesome simplicity. The bureaucratic edifice grounded in commune and township rises up so monolithically through county, prefecture, and province to the capital that it seems a foregone conclusion that Beijing has an absolute monopoly on power. But hidden underneath the flat surface of the formal order are interlocking networks of relationships that cut across and emasculate loyalties to Party and state. While this occurs to some extent in bureaucracies everywhere, the innate ability of the Chinese to form widely ramified and resilient coalitions based on personal allegiances poses serious problems of control for those in command. Not only is the center far from having absolute control over the provinces or even its own ministries, but these administrative levels and units often take on a life of their own.

The first indication I had that there was more to the Chinese bureaucratic structure than met the eye came from a young Eastwind Brigade cadre who caught a ride with me into Guangzhou one day in order, he told me, to deliver a large bamboo basket of fresh fish to the brigade's "liaison office" there. It intrigued me that the brigade should maintain an office in the provincial capital, but he said matter-of-factly that all of the communes and most of the larger brigades in the counties immediately around Guangzhou also had representatives stationed there. We arrived in Guangzhou, and he directed me to an old prerevolutionary office building along Xinde Road. Eastwind Brigade's office turned out to be two smallish rooms rented on the quiet from the municipal department that was the officially designated occupant of the premises for 20 *rmb* a month. The back room, furnished in wall-to-wall plank beds, was a kind of brigade hostel where cadres in the city on business could spend the night, avoiding the expense and bother of registering at a state-run hotel; the front room with its motley collection of desks and chairs served as the "liaison office" proper. But the real work of the liaison office was not carried out in the office at all, according to the resident brigade representative, who candidly explained that his primary task was to develop useful personal contacts with provincial personnel. Rather than commit brigade requests to regular administrative channels, where they often sank into the bureaucratic sands without a trace, the representative would entrust them to these contacts to walk through. The fish that we had brought from the village was destined, he said, for a department of agricultural machinery cadre as thanks for his assistance in a machinery purchase.

My experience was corroborated by a Beijing friend, who said that each of the provinces maintained an unofficial liaison office in the capital. He had visited the Tibet Autonomous Region office and described to me how it occupied the spacious grounds of a once beautiful temple complex. The original four temple structures, one for each of the four points of the compass, still survived, but the interiors had been gutted and converted into offices, while a number of dormitories and living quarters had been built in the temple gardens. The permanent staff of this regional legation numbered over 200, he said, not counting the special delegations on more temporary sojourns in the capital. The staff's task was to represent the various interests of the regional government and Party bureaucracies in their dealings with the central ministries and Party organization.

That lower-level units find it not only expedient but essential to supplement the formal organizational chain of communication and command by stationing semiofficial representatives at higher levels is nothing short of bizarre, rather as if the Sixth Fleet was forced to set up offices a few blocks from the Pentagon to ensure that vital supplies arrived on time and in sufficient quantity for the fleet by wining and dining Pentagon employees. On one level, these informal liaison offices are symptomatic of the many crippling institutional illnesses that afflict the Chinese bureaucracy— the primitive and awkward communications, the all-consuming importance of personal ties and allegiances, the unregulated arbitrariness of petty officials, and the inertia and inefficiency of the whole massive system. But the informal liaison offices suggest more than this. They indicate that what exists in China is not, properly speaking, a pure bureaucratic system at all, but an admixture of bureaucratism, patrimonialism, and feudalism. They imply that these lower administrative levels are far more than mere extensions of the center and, in fact, constitute discrete entities or, as the Chinese say more imaginatively, "independent kingdoms."

It is not only from irreverence that ordinary cadres call provincial and prefectural Party leaders "feudal lords," nor is it a Bunyanesque exaggeration when peasants refer to long-time commune, brigade, and team heads as *tu huangdi,* or "local emperors." For the rock-bottom rule of Chinese political reality is that bosses of all stripes use the brick and mortar of *ganqing* and *guanxi* to build up personal organizations which allow them to rule their domains like independent kingdoms. In the same fashion, they cement relations with Party superiors who, as long as they meet basic production goals, will offer them protection against outside pressures and interference. The better connected—both inside and outside of his unit—a leading cadre is, the more easily he is able to exempt himself from the generally accepted rules or professional standards of job performance, set himself apart from the jurisdiction of the law (what little exists), and even insulate himself from the redoubtable authority of the public security apparatus. He becomes subject only to the control of his immediate Party superiors and, except in the unlikely event that these collude against him, is almost impossible to dislodge from the niche he has carved for himself.

So thick are officials that they instinctively close ranks like musk-oxen to repel an attack on one of their number. Campaigns to curb the corruption that is endemic to the Chinese bureaucracy (see Chapter 4) have stumbled on the block resistance of the bureaucrats. The classic case involved the *Liberation Daily,* the official organ of the Shanghai municipal Party committee. In early October 1980, this newspaper began an attack on bureaucratism with an editorial inviting readers who knew of cases in which cadres had abused their power to write in, promising to investigate each case individually, press for redress where misconduct could be shown to have occurred, and report the results in a continuing series of articles. Although such ombudsman-like services are common enough in the U.S. media, for the controlled Chinese press the offer was unprecedented. So, it turned out, was the public response. Within the month the newspaper had received over

13,000 letters, and an additional 1,200 plaintiffs had visited the editorial offices *in person* to register a grievance. On November 18, 1980, the *Liberation Daily* published a special report in which the dazed editors candidly admitted that they had encountered "three difficulties": it was "difficult to conduct the interview, difficult to review the report, and difficult to resolve the problem." Reporters sent to conduct interviews with the cadres concerned to check on the accuracy of the charges against them were either "treated coldly and their questions evaded, or they were met with anger and, in some cases, cursed." The few reports that were completed were sent back to the heads of the departments concerned for review. These leading cadres, to protect their subordinates and their own reputations, attacked the reports and slandered the reporters who had prepared them. Stunned by the fury of the bureaucratic counterattack, reporters began to say that "sending a report was like commiting suicide." Reaching a satisfactory resolution of the abuse that had led to the original complaint proved to be an even more intractable problem. The *Liberation Daily* complained that "while a few units unenthusiastically corrected the problem, others made no effort to do so and refused to answer the paper's queries on this point. Some tried to find out who had written the original letters and take revenge. Some even stormed to the newspaper offices and created a disturbance."

An even more blatant case of a local bureaucracy, in this instance the Party itself, brazenly sheltering its own came to light shortly after I arrived in China. The security defense committee of a neighboring brigade had taken a teenaged boy into custody on suspicion of poaching collectively owned fish. He had been spotted by a patrolman near midnight standing on the bank of a fish pond some distance from the village. Back at committee headquarters, he proved unable to explain satisfactorily what he was doing in such a deserted location at that late hour. Though the patrolman had found no evidence of a net or stolen fish, he recalled that he had heard a splash as he approached and ventured the opinion that when the lad noticed his coming, he had thrown his net and fish into the pond in order to escape detection. This became the premise on which the police chief, who had been awakened when the prisoner was brought in, based his interrogation. The boy steadfastly refused to admit that he had been stealing fish, however, and the questioning continued throughout the night. Near morning, the brigade Party secretary, known as a strict disciplinarian, came in and took charge. In no-nonsense fashion, he demanded that the boy confess his crime and began to threaten him when he proved still obstinate. Some villagers also maintain that he beat the boy, though the Party secretary and the police chief have repeatedly denied this. Be that as it may, there is no disagreement about what happened next. At 7 A.M., the boy suddenly collapsed, and efforts by brigade cadres to revive him proved unsuccessful. He was then rushed to the commune clinic, but died without regaining consciousness later that morning.

The grief-stunned parents appealed to the public security department for justice, but the brigade Party secretary, twenty years in office, proved to have powerful patrons. A proposed county public security department investigation was blocked by the county Party committee, which voted to consider the incident an internal Party matter. The secret Party investigation had already ground slowly along for the better part of a year with no end in sight when I left China, but it was rumored that the brigade leader would receive only a written reprimand—a slap on the wrist under the circumstances—and would keep his post.

If cover-ups rarely reach such criminal dimensions, they are common enough, especially among cadres seeking to hide the inept performance of the farm or factory under their supervision. At one point in my research, I was given a unique set of economic data for Dragonshead Commune containing all major accounting indices for each of its eighteen commune-run enterprises for the previous ten years. I was initially elated, but when I happily showed my find to a local factory manager I knew, he smiled at my innocence and quickly set me straight. "Many of the figures are absolutely worthless," he cautioned. "According to these figures, all eighteen factories have showed a profit every year for the past ten years, right? In fact, the only real money earner is the bicycle parts factory. This is because its raw materials are supplied by the province, which also purchases its entire output. The others earn little or nothing. The agricultural machinery factory and several other factories have lost money for years, but the figures are adjusted to disguise this fact." According to this factory manager, the commune authorities send false reports up to county superiors in order to avoid criticism for the faltering economic performance of many of the factories under their direction. He went on to say that although those who run the county government are not taken in by the fudged figures, they have taken no action, preferring to pass the figures off as accurate to their superiors in the prefectural government to put themselves in a better light.

This was only one of a number of stories I heard about "cooking the books" and falsifying official reports—from counties over-reporting grain production to impress superiors, to communes exaggerating crop losses after a typhoon to get government purchase quotas reduced, to brigades underreporting earnings from local enterprises to avoid heavy state taxes, to a commune education office proudly announcing that the latest literacy campaign had succeeded in entirely eradicating local illiteracy, a piece of academic legerdemain finagled by hiring (at 1 *rmb* apiece) hundreds of literate peasants to take the end-of-campaign literacy exam in place of "character-blind" neighbors. So widespread is such deception that the State Statistical Bureau's figures on nearly everything can be at best no more than approximations. I left the People's Republic convinced that top leaders, because of their lack of accurate information, have only a general idea of conditions in the provinces.

Max Weber argued that bureaucracies are difficult for the central authorities to control because bureaucracies' monopoly on specialized knowledge makes it possible for them to oppose policies on technical grounds.* That direct, sometimes confrontational approach is not the Tao of the Chinese bureaucracy. Rather, when local Party organizations receive directives from the Central Committee, or local government offices receive instructions from their ministries, they ritually kowtow in the direction of Beijing, send off reports that gush of "great victories on all fronts," and then quietly proceed to carry out the new policy in accordance with their own best interests, if at all. Bureaucratic independence and obstructionism are the main reasons why a system designed to concentrate all power at the top falls short of absolute totalitarianism.

Repeatedly foiling the plans, frustrating the ambitions, and cramping the authority of PRC leaders, Chinese officialdom has

* Max Weber, *The Theory of Social and Economic Organization* (Glencoe, Ill.: The Free Press, 1947), p. 338.

hardly endeared itself to them. Both Mao and Deng, despite their in many respects antithetical approaches to governing, have worried about the loyalty and efficiency of the bureaucracies under their nominal command. Mao was the more overtly hostile, accusing bureaucrats of being alienated from the masses and, worse yet, of identifying with their own unit rather than with the Party and the state (that is, with Party Chairman Mao himself). This indictment led to action during the Great Leap Forward, when he launched his first major onslaught against the state administrative system. Professionals who occupied the middle reaches of industrial management and government administration were attacked, and many were dismissed. Whole administrative and managerial structures were dismembered, and supernumerary officials were ordered out to the front lines of production.* Party cadres, whom Mao believed at the time would more reliably carry out the Party's will, replaced the fallen bureaucrats.

But it was during the Cultural Revolution that Mao, like the Taiping rebels of the nineteenth century, set out in earnest to "smash the officials" (da guan). The Red Guards held mock trials for officials of all stripes—this time not even Party apparatchiks were spared—who were paraded down the streets in dunce caps, abusively criticized, brutally assaulted, and not infrequently killed. Power passed from prostrate Party committees to newly constituted "Revolutionary committees." Much of government, paralyzed by the political struggle, simply ceased to function, and the military had to be called in to maintain essential services. Armed troop contingents appeared at airports and railway stations, broadcasting and telegraph stations, grain storage depots and banks and other key points. Cadres were sent down to state farms in large numbers to sweat off their bourgeous beliefs during extended periods of manual labor.

If Mao the Ideologue saw the bureaucracy as an evil to be expunged, then Deng the Pragmatist sees it as a tool to be used in the country's development, but only after being properly shaped, honed, and balanced for this task. Soon after returning to power in 1977, Deng declared that there were "too many gods in the temple" (miao xiao pusa duo), and a flurry of directives followed encouraging committees at all levels to undertake a reduc-

* Franz Schurmann, *Ideology and Organization in Communist China,* 2nd ed. (Berkeley: University of California Press, 1968), p. 71.

tion in their membership. Even lowly rural brigades and teams were to cut their numbers of cadres to the bare minimum. Two years later a freeze was put on government hiring, and office heads and factory managers were warned that those who violated this order would be administratively punished. Press articles about the necessity to reform the Party and government bureaucracy began to appear with increasing frequency, and by 1981 the coming reorganization was being touted as "revolutionary" in scope. In an essay in the *People's Daily*, Deng rebuked the Party for the "bad practices" of "bureaucratism, power concentration, commandism, lifetime job tenure, and the pursuit of special privileges," and declared that "corrupt and impotent" cadres must go. Shortly thereafter, at the December National People's Congress, Premier Zhao Ziyang identified bureaucratic "timidity, inertia, and obstructionism" as the most serious obstacles to China's long-term development. Not only was the government bureaucracy to be reduced in size, it was also, as Zhao was quoted saying several months later, to be made more "revolutionary, youthful, knowledgeable, and specialized."

An outline of the first phase of China's bureaucratic revolution, a reorganization of the central government, was unveiled by Zhao Ziyang in March 1982. The plans called for the number of Vice Premiers to be slashed from thirteen to two, for the ninety-eight committees, ministries, and bureaus to be reduced to fifty-two by amalgamation, and for the total number of employees to be cut back from 49,000 to 32,000. Superannuated officials were to be pensioned off, and a mandatory retirement age of 60 was to be set for all except ministers of state, who would be allowed to keep their posts until 65. It was estimated that the shake-up at the national level would take at least a year. From the center, the reorganization would spread downward in ever-widening circles, reaching the provinces in 1983 and the prefectures, counties, and finally communes in 1984 and beyond, taking a minimum of several years to complete.

The Deng leadership is genuinely dismayed at the "timidity, inertia, and obstructionism" Zhao saw in the bureaucracy and is set upon removing this impediment to the country's development by carrying out a thoroughgoing reform. But while it seems reasonably certain that officialdom can be crudely cut down to size and excess bureaucratic appendages lopped off, the prognosis for the delicate surgical operation necessary to produce a bureaucracy more "revolutionary, youthful, knowledgeable, and specialized" must be more guarded.

In Chinese political doublespeak, making the bureaucracy more "revolutionary" seems paradoxically to mean making it less radical by removing from office those who rode radicalism to power during the Cultural Revolution. But hundreds of thousands of the 12 million people who joined the Party during this period now hold positions in the government and the Party, and most of these officeholders are in their thirties and forties, relatively young by the standards of mainland officialdom. To purge all or most of these would make it difficult to achieve the second goal of rejuvenating the bureaucracy by promoting the young. Another difficulty is that the planned rejuvenation requires the mass departure of elderly officials. But Deng has already stated that "valuable" cadres will be permitted to retain their posts even if they are over the age of mandatory retirement, opening the loophole which will allow him to stay on in office but through which many thousands, perhaps tens of thousands, of politically agile sexagenarian and septuagenarians will also scramble.

But the most serious dilemma that the reformers face follows from the fact that it is not feasible to build a completely new bureaucracy from the ground up. Rather, the reorganization must work from the top down, using the existing structure as the framework around which to reconstitute an improved bureaucracy. Superiors at each level will be called upon to recommend which of their subordinates will go and which will stay, opening the way for the perpetuation of present problems. The regime may specify that the youthful, knowledgeable, and specialized are to be preferentially retained, but it seems likely that many leading cadres will pick and choose among subordinates more on the basis of personal considerations such as loyalty or *ganqing* than on the basis of their ability or knowledge, specialized or not. Some may even seize the opportunity presented by the shake-up to settle old scores. It is possible that the reorganization may thus prove, in part, counterproductive, strengthening the personal allegiances of cadres to their department heads or office chiefs, whose favor allowed them to escape reassignment to the provinces or worse.

Ironically, whatever degree of success the bureaucratic shuffle currently in progress enjoys, the PRC's administrative crisis seems fated to continue. Pruning back a bit of the bureaucratic under-growth by retiring or reassigning a few hundred thousand—or even a few million—overaged and underqualified functionaries will leave untouched the root of the problem: bureaucratic prolif-eration is the unavoidable consequence of a political system that not only sanctions but mandates official intrusions into every nook and cranny of everyday life. In *The Revolution Betrayed*, Trotsky argues that "when there are few goods, the purchasers are com-pelled to stand in line. When the lines are long, it is necessary to appoint a policeman to keep order. Such is the starting point of the power of Soviet bureaucracy." But in fact the Soviet bureau-cracy, like the Communist Chinese, has innumerable starting points, each of which leads to a small but significant loss of individ-ual and family autonomy. Freedom of choice is narrowly circum-scribed in the PRC, where the authority to decide where to live, where to work, what to eat and wear, and even how many children to have has been largely taken out of the hands of individuals and given over to government officials. The economic improbabil-ity that is bureaucratic totalitarianism drains the national treasury by forcing the population at large to support an ever-growing army of nonproductive bureaucrats, who justify their existence by busily controlling more and more of the business of everyday life. This cancerous growth represents a danger to the long-term health and stability of the socialist machine that currently rules China, and is a disease that can only be temporarily held in abey-ance by Deng's projected reforms.

4

Corruption: The Art of Going in the Back Door

There is no scale of fixed fees in China regulating the charges for official work performed by mandarins or by their underlings, as in Western lands. Here the official demands as much as he imagines he can get, considering the circumstances of the case.

J. Doolittle

Not long after I arrived in Sandhead, a mandatory mass political meeting was called one evening after dinner. As the last of the stragglers crowded into the open space centering on the village basketball court used for such occasions, the wiry police chief, head of the local security defense committee (*zhibao hui*) and second-ranking Party member in the brigade, stood up and began to address the nearly 2,000 assembled adults, reading from a directive he held in his hand.

"Comrades," he commenced, "under the direction of the Guangdong provincial Communist Party committee—." Realizing that his voice was all but drowned out by the buzz of the crowd, he paused and fastened the peasants with an impatient gaze.

After they had become quiet a minute later, he began again. "Comrades. Under the direction of the Guangdong provincial

---

* *Social Life of the Chinese* (1865), vol. I, p. 304 (reissued 1966 by Ch'eng Wen Taiwan).

Communist Party committee, the local prefectural Party committee has determined that we will hold a movement, the 'Criticize One, Hit Two, Rectify Three' [*yi pi, liang da, san zhengdun*], this spring throughout the towns and villages of our district. We must thoroughly criticize the Gang of Four's antirevolutionary revisionist line. We must strike a blow against class enemies and their destructive activities and strike down embezzlers, thieves, speculators, and all illegal capitalist elements. And finally we must rectify the free peasant markets, rectify commune and brigade cooperative enterprises, and rectify enterprise management practices. The Eleventh Party Congress has set out this line, and we must ensure that the will of dictatorship of the proletariat is carried out at the basic levels of government. Every Communist Party member, revolutionary cadre, proletarian worker, poor and lower middle peasant, and revolutionary intellectual must wholeheartedly participate in this people's war to criticize, strike down, and rectify."

The directive was written in *putonghua,* or Mandarin, the national language, but was being read in the local dialect of Cantonese, producing a stilted effect that was exacerbated by the police chief's monotone delivery. I noticed that not a few peasants, after a day's work in the fields, were nodding off as he continued. "At the present time the corrupting influence of capitalism and its subversive activities in our towns and villages are rampant. The special characteristics of this lawless capitalism are that it involves thefts committed by crime syndicates which include residents of cities, villages, and even overseas Chinese as conspirators. They carry out large-scale thefts and injurious speculation which throw national plans into disarray, negatively affecting not only production but also transportation, storage, distribution, and sales activities. They try by every means possible ('1,000 stratagems and 100 plans') to corrupt and collude with national cadres, in this way planting operatives within the revolutionary ranks who can aid them and serve as their 'protective umbrellas.' The number of crimes committed by these criminal elements, the malevolence of their schemes, and the size of the destruction they cause have reached astonishing and frightening levels."

Reaching the final lines of the passage, the police chief raised his voice to a higher pitch. "We offer a grave warning to all criminal elements: You must immediately come to your senses and repent of your ways. The only way to save yourselves is to completely confess your crimes and make a clean breast of things. If you continue to resist, the state will mercilessly bring you under control."

"Mercilessly bring you under control" was, I knew, a code phrase for execution, but the police chief's threatening words rang out over the impassive heads of the assembled peasantry without any palpable effect. He stepped back toward the sidelines without further ado, and a younger man, whom the peasant sitting next to me identified as the assistant police chief, came forward. A short, sturdy fellow with a voice like a bullhorn, he picked up where his chief had left off, reading individual cases and their disposition.

He boomed out the title of the first case—"If You Refuse to Reform, It Is Difficult to Escape the Dragnet of the Law"— and the crowd fell silent as the story began. The reader gave the particulars of the criminal: "Liang Jianxian, male, 53 years old, resident of Siquao Brigade, Xiaogang Commune, Xinhui County." Absorbing the fact that the man was from a neighboring commune, the audience grew yet stiller. "Before the liberation Liang Jianxian was employed as a clerk, and learned a whole book of black capitalist business methods. When businesses were co-operativized following the liberation, he went to the county department of commerce, where he served for a decade as a salaried employee. In 1962 he applied to resign his position and return to his native place.

"Following his discharge he did not return to Xiaogang Commune, however, but improperly transferred his household registration to Shuangshui Commune, where he began doing private construction work on the sly. At the same time, using vouchers from Daling Brigade's agricultural machinery station and other units, he went to a total of twenty-two factories and enterprises located in twenty cities and counties and purchased large quantities of public property, including 10.15 tons of steel, 4 tons of charcoal, over 300 tons of coal, as well as aluminum, copper, concrete, lumber, engines, electric wire, truck and automobile parts, and other important goods. Daling Brigade, with the whole-hearted collaboration of Criminal Liang, ignored the Party line for the sake of profit and operated a total of four underground factories employing more than 100 local workers. When local labor ran short, the brigade even dared to exploit outside labor by hiring fifty-six workers from neighboring brigades. With five junks obtained from the nearby city of Huaicheng, the brigade also ran an illegal shipping company engaging in illicit trade up and down the Pearl River. Criminal Liang's share of the profits from these antisocialist activities was 1,419 *rmb* [$946].

"In 1972 Liang became involved with the manager of the purchase and sales department of the Jiangmen Woodworking Company, a certain Lu by name, and went into speculation in a big way. He used the names of the Daling Brigade primary school, Tianma Brigade, and other units to arrange purchases of charcoal, steel, oil barrels, and similar goods. These he traded with the woodworking company for tons of steel wire, concrete, timber, and other goods, which he then turned around and resold. In this way, wheeling and dealing at will and always on the lookout for a profit, he earned 7,600 *rmb*, which he shared with Manager Lu.

"When Criminal Liang's activities were uncovered by the manufacturing and commerce departments of Shuangshui County, he took fright and escaped to Zhanjiang [in southern Guangdong]. There, with the aid of an introduction from the speculator Fu Rixin, he was hired by a neighborhood cooperative factory—Diancheng City's metal products factory—to serve as their 'black market sales and purchasing agent' and 'black market authority.' In this capacity he scuttled back to Xinhui County, where he tricked Xingjiang Brigade in Sanjiang Commune into investing more than 7,000 *rmb* in his factory. When this money arrived at the metal products factory along with a load of aluminum scrap that he had purchased along the way, the unit's leading cadre praised him up and down for his enterprise.

"Not long thereafter, Criminal Liang bribed an accountant of the state-run Maoming chemical fertilizer factory, a certain Mo, into making out purchase orders in the amount of 29,400 *rmb*. Purchase orders in hand, he scurried off to Zunyi, Guiyang [large cities in Guizhou Province], and Chongqing, purchasing three lots of expensive and valuable goods and engaging in speculation in a big way. This criminal misuse of national capital was a direct attack on the nation's planned economy and undermined the foundations of socialism.

"But no matter how clever or devious criminals are, in the end they cannot escape the dragnet of the law. In late 1977 Criminal Liang was taken into custody. When he was brought to account for his crimes, he compounded his offenses by being unrepentant and by making no effort to return his ill-gotten goods, forcing the legal organization to punish him severely. He received a life sentence without possibility of parole, and was stripped of his political rights for life."

A murmur arose from the crowd at the harshness of the penalty, and the assistant police chief paused to let it die down before reading the title of the next case: "Unrepentant Resistance: The Road to Death." Another ripple of interest surged through the crowd as they picked up that the punishment in the case had been execution.

"Mo Beijie, male, 40 years old, resident of Qiaomei Brigade, Shuangshui Commune, Xinhui County, family class status middle peasant, individual class status student," the cadre went on. "From the time Mo Beijie was small, his parents fostered in him a lazy and prideful character by smothering him with love. After graduating from upper middle school, he returned to his production team to participate in labor, serving at different times as the team's work-point recorder, pig and water buffalo keeper, and credit association clerk. In 1958 he was accepted as a cadre in the Qiaomei Brigade's credit association, and was sent to the association's northeast station to serve as its accountant and cashier. But Mo Beijie did not engage in serious political study and abandoned thought reform, and the small-producer mentality of the household into which he was born began to assert itself. He gradually turned toward the life-style of the capitalist class, greedily seeking after eating, drinking, and other pleasures of the flesh. As early as 1965 he had embezzled a total of 900 *rmb* [$600] using a forged account book in order to build himself a house. He had fallen into the black pit of crime.

"Criminal Mo's embezzlement activities became more and more flagrant with time. By underpaying interest and pocketing the difference, purloining individual household savings accounts, 'swallowing' long-term enterprise loans, pilfering from the production team's maintenance funds, and various other schemes, he had by July 1976 embezzled a total of 21,350.46 *rmb*. He often went about saying, 'Get drunk this morning on this morning's wine; let tomorrow worry about tomorrow's sorrows,' the philosophy of the capitalist class. He cultivated a flashy style and pretended to be rich and generous, spending money with wild abandon. Several youthful idlers and loafers became his boon companions, and he often invited them to the commune teahouse, where they gorged themselves on food and liquor at his expense. Worst of all, he used money and presents as bait to entice and debauch women in order to satisfy his depraved desires. Thus he passed a life of extreme luxury and lasciviousness.

"Criminal Mo's deviant life-style had early alerted the masses that he was embezzling large sums of public money. During the 1970 'Strike One, Oppose Three' movement, evidence brought forward by the masses led the commune to undertake a patient effort at reeducating him. But instead of making a clean breast of things, Criminal Mo deceived the commune by pretending to repent and was treated with leniency. In his heart he had not accepted the opportunity he had been given to reform his wickedness into virtue, but had only changed his methods and become more cautious in his crimes. However, 'A cover-up cannot be maintained for long: there will come a day when the truth will out' [quotation from Chairman Mao].

"In 1976 the brigade held a movement called 'Basic Party Line Education,' and the revolutionary masses again accused Criminal Mo of thievery and provided numerous clues. The Party committee of the commune ordered him to come completely clean, but again he secretly resisted the investigation by pretending repentance while offering a lot of deceitful excuses. In the face of overwhelming evidence of wrongdoing, he produced only 700-odd *rmb*, swearing that he had 'held nothing back.' In order to save him, he was given another opportunity to reform himself. He was permitted to return to the credit association station and continue working, with the understanding that he would repay the money he had stolen. But Criminal Mo's greed was too deeply rooted in his character. He again took advantage of his position to forge false transfer slips, embezzling an additional 500 *rmb*.

"Mo Beijie embezzled public money over a long period of time and in large amounts, seriously damaging the process of socialist economic construction and creating a bad influence among the masses. Although the Party organization repeatedly tried to reeducate and save him, he refused to mend his ways, throughout displaying not a shred of regret or true willingness to reform. In the face of irrefutable evidence, he still tried to confuse and beguile the Party with deceitful arguments. Not only did he not make an honest confession, he also refused to make reparations for the money he had stolen. While in custody and under investigation, he even tried to escape the reckoning of the masses by taking phosphorus, but his suicide attempt was unsuccessful. Criminal Mo's thought was totally corrupt and dissipated, his crimes were great and evil, and the circumstances of his case were extremely serious. Stubbornly resisting to the bitter end, he was mercilessly controlled by the state."

On that note the evening's reading of Communist morality plays ended. The police chief stood up, briefly admonished the villagers to respect collective property, and called the meeting to a close. The peasants quickly dispersed.

The underworld of crime syndicates and corrupt cadres, illegal profiteering and embezzlement, underground factories and illicit shipping companies that was paraded before me that evening seemed a parodic inversion of the image of a crime-free state of honest workers and upright cadres that Beijing has tried to project abroad. That PRC officials prefer to deny the existence of these serpents in the socialist Eden, given communism's claim to moral and social perfection, is hardly surprising. According to Marxist-Leninist doctrine, crimes of property are a disease of capitalism, and the persistence of corruption after the establishment of a socialist state was an ideological embarrassment that grew ever more acute as Chinese socialism approached middle age. But while putting the best possible face on Chinese society for foreign observers, particularly during the Maoist years, Beijing was also waging a protracted campaign inside China against the spontaneous entrepreneurial and acquisitive instincts of the Chinese people.

In this struggle the PRC has relied mainly on periodic anticorruption movements to reeducate people in socialist economic ethics. In recent years these have taken the form of mass meetings like the one I witnessed, held in every village, factory, and office in the country, where political tracts stamped "for internal use only" and featuring potted case studies of crime and punishment are read to massed listeners. Between movements, local-level departments of public security keep up a stream of admonitory

The central room in a village home complete with ancestral tablets and Mao poster

Young village men gathered around the central table for evening tea and conversation

A Chinese man sorting dried bakchoi, *a Chinese cabbage*

Below: Preparing for a feast: cleaning fish

Eating lunch

*Peasant woman with her
two grandchildren*

Young man shopping for vegetables in a local rural market town

Peasant woman at home preparing turnips for the family meal

Above: Peasant dwelling

A village man picking up the family rice ration

A young girl at work collecting grass for the fishponds, using a carrying pole

A man drawing water at a village well

A village girl doing the family wash

posters listing recent economic crimes and the sentences handed out in each case.

But neither the meetings I attended nor discussions with peasants convinced me that they had digested the hefty helpings of socialist do's and don't's periodically dished out to them. The propaganda was treated more as a form of light entertainment than as food for thought. Often, posters weren't even put up by harried local cadres bombarded by endless waves of directives and recurrent required reports. And whatever these efforts to reeducate the Chinese masses have achieved, it remains true that the lower levels of the public security apparatus, especially its commune and county branches, devote almost all of their attention to thefts of state property, corruption, and illegal trade.

Nothing more heavily underscores the seriousness of Beijing's continuing problem with corruption than the swift and terrible nature of the punishment meted out to those who have committed serious economic crimes for which they show no remorse. Mo Beijie's immediate execution for embezzlement was not an isolated case: economic crimes have been punishable by the death penalty from the founding of the People's Republic. Because such cases are rarely reported in the press, it is impossible to know with any precision how many Chinese are sentenced to death for corruption, but the number of people "mercilessly controlled" each year is surely in the tens, and may run into the hundreds during the heat of an anticorruption movement.

Since 1980 PRC newspapers have broken their long silence on underground operations and have begun publishing accounts of criminal wrongdoing, even reporting an execution or two. But even today they typically report only individual cases of theft and speculation—an embezzling accountant, a large-scale theft of state property, an official charged with graft—and have not zeroed in on the crime syndicates which account for the larger operations that can net the criminals tens or hundreds of thousands of *renminbi* and make serious inroads into the state-controlled economy.

Neither do the newspapers reveal the range of corruption, which is so all-inclusive that Chinese I knew contended that almost anything is available for the right price. In Guangzhou a young taxi driver told me that it took 800 *rmb* to get a job as a driver, a fee that included the training necessary to pass the driving test and obtain a license. Peasants in the Pearl River Delta related to me that it took a payoff of 600 *rmb* to transfer an individual's household registration status from peasant to worker, after which it was possible to move out of the village and to live and work in the more comfortable surroundings of a county or commune town. A workman told me that he had made a gift of a small tape recorder, worth about 300 *rmb* at 1980 black market prices, to get a permanent job in a commune-run electric motor factory, and that it had been well worth it because, although he was still classified as a peasant, he would never have to go back to the fields. I found that it is even possible to purchase an escape from China. An itinerant peddler revealed to me that the equivalent of 3,000 *rmb* in gold or Hong Kong currency only would buy a guaranteed passage to urban Hong Kong, complete with a guide and a change of clothes upon arrival. Although the escape parties were sometimes captured on the Hong Kong side, he went on, this never happened on the Chinese side because the smugglers bought off PRC border patrols to ensure that their human contraband passed safely over the border.

Even at the mundane level of the delta communities I visited, I found corruption in the form of bribes, thefts, and kickbacks to be pervasive. Each of the anticrime movements of the seventies netted hundreds of small-fry thieves in every village, whose crimes were usually pilfering petty amounts of collective property, a bunch of bananas or a stick of sugarcane, but who occasionally raised their sights to stealing sacks of grain or hard-to-replace agricultural implements. Small-scale graft by collective cadres in the countryside has become a way of life, with a small gift of cigarettes, food, or liquor necessary to secure an authorization to build a house, buy a bicycle, or arrange to work in a brigade enterprise. In the countryside as well as in the cities speculators do a thriving business in TV sets, tape recorders, and electric fans, not to mention the universal petty commerce in the rationed goods—cloth, oil, grain, and the ration coupons themselves—that nearly all dabble in on occasion.

The overall dimensions of illicit trade and corruption in the PRC are difficult to gauge. Statistics which could serve as rough indicators, such as the number of economic criminals arrested each year, are well-guarded secrets. It is my impression that the People's Republic has probably not yet developed an underground economy on the scale of the Soviet Union, where each year tens of billions of rubles in goods and services flow through permanent pipelines of illegal entrepreneurs, speculators, and thieves to all levels of Soviet society. In part this is because corruption in the PRC, with the possible exception of Guangdong with its long commercial history and proximity to 'Hong Kong, is not yet as thoroughly commercialized as that in the older Soviet state. Many, if not most, transactions still take the form of trading favors— two packs of cigarettes for a movie ticket—with no cash changing hands. A more important limiting factor on the size of the PRC's underground economy is poverty. Few of the peasants and workers who constitute the overwhelming majority of China's population have the wherewithal to trade in major black market items, though it is common for them to engage in penny-ante trading for basic items. The main consumers of black market goods and services are more affluent middle- and lower-level cadres and their families, who number in the millions but constitute only a minute percentage of the population as a whole.

Corruption, theft, and illegal collective and private enterprise in the People's Republic are the unavoidable byproducts of a stodgy economic system that assigns a low priority to the production of consumer goods, attempts to channel nearly all commerce through its own wholesale and retail network of state stores, and even rations the basic necessities of life. The short-changed consumer has no recourse but to grease the balky mechanism of supply where this is possible and turn to the black market where it is not. The result is a flourishing demand for all manner of bootlegged goods of uncertain origin, including not only scarce luxury items and expensive manufactured goods but also basic necessities like grain and cloth. Even favored state and collective enterprises find occasional purchases of raw materials outside of sluggish and inefficient official channels indispensable aids to meeting production quotas.

But though the socialist economic system has proved fertile soil for its growth, corruption's seeds were sown by ancient Confucianism, an "our gang" ideology which stressed the importance of human relationships over objective law or standards. Under the Confucian code of conduct, individuals tied by kinship and social bonds were duty-bound to help one another—a moral imperative that resulted in nepotism, favoritism, factionalism, and a host of other venal-sounding practices that were not regarded as corrupt in the traditional Chinese cultural milieu at all. Only the omission of Confucian proprieties was considered opprobrious, so much so that the Chinese said that "a person who does not repay a favor does not understand what it means to be human." Thus commerce followed old-boy networks where deals were predicated on personal ties and customarily clinched with kickbacks. And appointment to office amounted to a license for venality, with officials expected to be on the take. The ideal career pattern of aspiring officeholders was several years as a mandarin spent amassing a fortune, followed by early retirement to a country estate to enjoy it.

While graft and corruption may have been held to moderate levels in the first years of the PRC as a new generation of Chinese rallied to the call to build a "New China," they thereafter took off on an upward trajectory that was only partly checked during the Cultural Revolution and has still not peaked. Corrupt functionaries openly receiving gifts and trading favors, the demoralizing effect of this official graft on public scruples, the lack of opprobrium attached to thefts of state or collective property—a category that includes almost everything—and the relaxation of formerly rigid economic controls since the end of the Cultural Revolution have all contributed to this upswing. But Chinese friends maintained that it is the pent-up materialism of the postrevolution generation that accounts for much of the continuing spread of underground activities. "People have been asked to sacrifice for so long—for the Great Leap Forward, for the Cultural Revolution, and now for the Four Modernizations—that many just don't care anymore," a high school teacher told me. "They want their material life to improve now. So they use connections and buy and sell on the black market."

———————

One of my first personal encounters with corruption came a few days after I first moved into Sandhead village. The pleasant spring weather that had greeted me on my arrival had changed to the bitingly cold northwest wind that blows at intervals throughout the winter down to Guangdong, and after a night spent huddled under a thin quilt, I decided that a thick cotton comforter of the type that is standard winter bedding in China was in order. As a newcomer, I thought it best to ask a friend to go to the state-run village store ("supply and sales store") in my stead to make the purchase, but he replied, rather mysteriously I thought at the time, that I had better go in person. Arriving at the centrally located store, the only outlet in the brigade where peasants could purchase cloth, plastic shoes, thread, kitchenware, and other sundry items, I looked about but saw no comforters on display. I asked the clerk who had come bustling over to serve me, ignoring the half a dozen other customers lined up to make purchases, if there were any comforters for sale. She looked inquiringly at her supervisor, who nodded curtly, and turned without a word and disappeared into the back of the store. She emerged a moment later, her arms embracing a bulky bale of cotton. The fourteen catties of cotton comforter came sans cover, held together only by a mesh of string which enveloped the pad like a fishnet. At the government-set price of 1 *rmb* a catty, the bill came to 14 *rmb*, which I paid without ado and started home.

On the way I found myself, even more than usual, the center of attention. All eyes were on me and the bulky bundle I was carrying. Acquaintances sang out cheerfully, "So you bought yourself a comforter," as if it were a great joke. I began to understand their interest when, halfway home, the sight of me and the comforter stopped two gray-haired, black-suited peasant women in their tracks. "Look what the American is carrying," I overheard one say to the other. "And the clerks in the store have been saying that they are out of comforters for four months now!"

My friend, who had clearly been prepared for this turn of events, told me later that day that the sight of my purchase had caused a minor run on the store, as a couple of dozen people crowded up to the counter asking for a comforter, only to be told that there were none. One man, he related with great relish, had stormed out in a huff saying that "you sell to the American but you won't sell to Chinese." This was too much for me, and I made to return my new purchase, only to be deterred by his pleading.

"That is the way things work here," he explained, taking the comforter from my grasp and putting it back on the plank bed. "Do you know that saying, *Gaogan sung shang men, zhonggan zhou-houmen, laobaixing qiuqiu ren?*"

I caught the literal meaning of the sentence, roughly "High-ranking cadres have front-door deliveries, middle-ranking cadres go in the back door, while ordinary people ['old hundred names'] beg," but failed to see the connection with the comforter and said so.

"What we mean by this saying," he went on in the unhurried fashion of the peasant, "is that the *gaogan* have everything they need directly provided them. Middle-ranking cadres use connections, influence, or bribes to buy things. This is called going in the back door. The rest of us have to go beg friends or relatives for favors." She paused to let that sink in before continuing. "The clerks in the supply and sales store always keep a few of each item on reserve. When they are out of stock, they like to have a few left over in case a cadre comes in to buy, or so they can do a friend a favor. They sold you a comforter because they figure you are important, like a cadre."

This was my first, accidental encounter with *zhou-houmen*, the most important term in the extensive Chinese lexicon of illicit trade. *Zhou-houmen*, which literally means "going in the back door," is the Chinese equivalent of "under the table" or "on the side," and refers to any transaction that is not officially sanctioned, from the use of influence to make a difficult purchase (as I unwittingly did) to trading favors and out-and-out bribes. In a system where money and ration coupons together are often not enough to purchase perennially scarce goods or obtain necessary services over the counter, the back-door route is often the only course left to those who do not belong to the privileged elite.

What opens the back door is a connection, in Chinese a *guanxihu*—a special relationship with someone who has entrée to the state supply system. Truck drivers and chauffeurs who work for the state, for example, have an ample supply of gas ration coupons, which they trade or sell to more closely rationed collective units or to the small but growing number of urban owners of imported motorcycles and Shanghai-manufactured mopeds who are otherwise limited to 15 liters of gas a month. The purchasing clerk of a factory, enterprise, or institute is an even better person to know, for he can buy in essentially unlimited quantities goods that are closely rationed for private purchasers. "Purchasing clerks always buy extra when they go shopping," a bespectacled factory accountant explained to me. "They then give the extra produce, meat, or liquor to their friends in return for favors. Or they sell the stuff outright." But the most valued *guanxihu* are with employees of the state-operated retail trade sector, who have direct access to the entire range of manufactured goods distributed through that sector.

So essential are such *guanxihu* for even the most trivial purchases—tickets to the movies, a pack of better-quality cigerettes—that Chinese consciously cultivate extensive networks of connections as a necessity of life. Often based on a preexisting relationship as kin, co-workers, classmates, or fellow villagers, useful bonds of friendship are forged by formal reciprocal calls at Chinese New Year's and mutual invitations to family feasts at weddings, funerals, and births, as well as by frequent informal visits and gift-giving. As one employee of a rural People's Bank branch noted wryly to me, "A gift increases the revolutionary sentiment between two individuals." ("Revolutionary" has become the ultimate expletive in the PRC, debased to mean nothing more than good, while "counterrevolutionary," it goes without saying, is the ultimate invective, the evil opposite of its root.)

The instrumental use of relationships, a practice deeply rooted in traditional Chinese mores, has become even more blatant since the revolution brought the marketplace under state control. The immediate, almost instinctive reaction of a Chinese who wants to make a purchase or obtain a service is to seek out an acquaintance with the appropriate connection. These networks of favor ramify with incredible complexity, often involving second- and third-hand transactions, the intermediaries creating obligations and carrying debts that they will settle gradually over time.

A sense of the all-pervasiveness of contemporary corruption can be gained through the realization that even the mere existence of a relationship by blood, marriage, or friendship with someone who is in a position to do a favor is considered to be *prima facie* evidence for the fact that such favors are done. There is simply no question in anyone's mind that you make use of every available connection to purchase scarce goods, curry favor, finagle permission to build a new house, wrangle a better job assignment—in short, to engage in back-door machinations. And the truth of the matter is that nearly everyone does.

All of the Chinese I spoke with admitted to at least an occasional underground transaction, even though these are technically illegal. "There is no way that the Party can stop such exchanges," a friend explained to me. "After all, it is just friends doing favors for each other. The average person says to himself, 'What am I afraid of, sure I'll trade a bottle of Maotai for a pair of shoes.'" While these exchanges, often involving goods valued at no more than a few *renminbi*, seem inconsequential by Western standards, this is not true in China, where against the backdrop of the general poverty they take on not inconsiderable dimensions.

But back-door transactions can also reach proportions sizable by any standards, as I found out at the end of my first six-week stay in the Guangdong countryside when I paid a call on Qi Maoji, a balding engineer related to a Hong Kong acquaintance of mine. I had already decided to return to Sandhead three months later to carry out a community study and confided my plans to build a house in the village to him.

"There is no way that you can build a house in three months," he said, shaking his head. "It takes years to build a house here because materials are rationed and scarce." But then he paused thoughtfully, running his hands through his closely cropped hair, and suddenly brightened. "I have a friend in the provincial building materials department," he said. "He might be able to help out."

The next evening I returned to Qi Maoji's apartment and was introduced to Comrade Lin, a distinguished-looking and well-dressed cadre in his middle fifties, obviously someone well up in the hierarchy. After dinner he got down to business.

"How large a house do you want to build?" he asked. I explained that I wanted to build a small two-story house and gave him the dimensions of the building site that I had arranged. He took out an expensive foreign-made pen and made a few quick calculations in a small notebook.

"You will require 32,000 bricks," he said shortly, "plus concrete, steel wire, wood, and glass. The total price is 5,200 *rmb* at subsidized government prices. Otherwise it would be 50 percent more. I will give you a requisition document authorizing the building materials storage depot in Southeast County, the closest depot to where you will be building, to issue this amount of construction material to your friends in the countryside. Once the material is in hand, if the weather holds up, your house can be completed in a matter of weeks." Then he paused and looked significantly at our mutual acquaintance.

"Comrade Lin is interested in getting a Japanese diesel van for his division," Qi Maoji revealed, setting forth the terms by which I would receive the materials.

Cadre Lin quickly picked up his friend's opening. "You see, there are currently over eighty people in my division, but we have only two cars. We badly need more vehicles. We make frequent trips, many to quite remote parts of the province. We have a quota for another Chinese-made van to be delivered a year from now, but that won't solve the half of our problem."

I had, in six weeks in the People's Republic, heard frequent tales of favor trading, and I knew something of back-door deals in bicycles, radios, and electric fans, but the size of this transaction startled me. After Comrade Lin had left, Qi Maoji reassured me that the exchange was nothing out of the ordinary. "All of the Hong Kong companies that have dealings with the government of the PRC are engaged in similar exchanges. It is against the currency regulations, but officials just ignore this. And the whole exchange is very simple. Comrade Lin will write a letter to the Guangdong provincial committee on overseas Chinese affairs and state that there is a patriotic overseas Chinese who wishes to donate a van to his division. Once they approve it, and they always do, they will issue an authorization for the van to be imported without duty. And after the van actually arrives, it is a simple matter for my friend to release the building materials. It happens all the time."

"But what's in it for Comrade Lin personally?" I persisted.

"He will have first use of the van whenever he takes a business trip," he answered and added, smiling, "The van will be his personal *qiao*," referring to the litters borne by servants that past dynastic officials customarily traveled in.

I politely bowed out of the proffered illicit exchange, but the proposition stuck in my mind, and I soon found out from Hong Kong businessmen who had ties with the mainland that my experience was anything but unusual. "You were lucky," a pudgy clothing manufacturer I struck up a conversation with on the Guangzhou–Hong Kong hydrofoil commented after I recounted my experience. "You could refuse their offer. To me they make demands. There is nothing I can do about them except give in. In order to start a garment factory in Nanhai County near Guangzhou, I had to give gifts to officials from six different

provincial departments." He testily rattled off the names of the
departments that he had been forced to deal with in this fashion
and the TV sets, tape recorders, and watches that had gone to
officials in each, before going on. "Every time a problem comes
up with the work force, or with production or with delivery, it
is more of the same. PRC officials have an insatiable greed for
Western goods." He lamented that this extortion was one of the
main reasons why, a year after his factory had come on the line
and despite the cheap labor and easy terms offered by the provincial government which had led him to invest in the first place,
he was finding it difficult to break even.

I caught a glimpse of how these transactions look from the
other side, that of the cadres on the take, a few weeks later. A
Hong Kong businessman, planning to raise fish for the Hong
Kong market, had signed a contract with the municipal government of the border town of Shenzhen to excavate a large number
of ponds, and had contacted Dragon's Course Commune, his native place, for men skilled in fish farming. The "capitalist" (as
the commune cadres rather condescendingly called the entrepre-
neur for short) required forty men in all, and offered to pay each
a salary of 140 *rmb* a month, an unheard-of sum several times
average local monthly earnings. Commune cadres pointed out
to him that it was forbidden to hire labor directly, and that the
payroll would have to be administered by the commune. The
result of further negotiations was that for its role in purveying
the necessary labor the commune was to receive a Japanese-made
van and skim 1,000 *rmb* off of the monthly payroll. This, at least,
was the publicly acknowledged part of the exchange.

I heard from friends that back-door bargaining had netted
the commune cadres considerably more—three TV sets, six portable tape players, and two items that were to raise eyebrows all
the way from the commune to the county seat: two Kawasaki
150-cubic-centimeter motorcycles. By coincidence I visited the
foreign affairs cadre on the day the goods arrived. I stepped into
his office to find it piled high with boxes of Sanyo and Tatung
electronic equipment, with the two spanking new motorcycles
forming the center of the unintended display. Off in a corner
the half a dozen leading cadres of the commune were talking in
excited voices. As they saw me, they fell into an embarrassed
quiet, like so many little boys caught with their hands in the cookie

jar. Realizing that I had stumbled onto the conference to divide the spoils, I fumbled for something to say. "My, there certainly is a lot of stuff piled up in this room," I blurted out, and instantly regretted it. The cadres went rigid and exchanged nervous glances. I left quickly.

I was never able to ascertain the exact distribution of the bulk of the booty I had seen that day. The TV sets and tape recorders simply disappeared into the homes of the cadres involved, and I heard from others that several were quickly resold on the black market. But as to the disposition of the motorcycles there could be no question. The Kawasakis were frequently to be seen careening about the dirt roads of Dragon's Course Commune, or roaring off to the county seat 30 kilometers away. Astride them, unsteady at first but quickly taking the measure of this new contraption, were the Party secretary and assistant Party secretary of the commune.

As the above examples suggest, it is ironically from among the ostensible guardians of the state economic and political order, particularly middle- and lower-level cadres, that most of its worst and repeat offenders come. Although no segment of PRC society, with the exception of the privileged class, is exempt from the necessity of occasional back-door forays, cadre corruption occurs on a Brobdingnagian scale that dwarfs the activities of relatively poor and powerless workers and peasants. While nearly everyone cultivates connections useful for back-door trade, bribes clerks for scarce items, and trades on the black market, cadres have the reputation of maintaining the most far-flung back-door networks, paying the largest bribes, and making the most expensive black market sales and purchases.

The most enterprising operator I knew personally in the PRC was a cadre. This genial middle-aged brigade official had pulled wires and somehow sent all three of his daughters, aged 15, 16, and 18, to the Portuguese colony of Macao near Hong Kong, where they found work in garment sweatshops. The three sisters' earnings totaled less than 200 *rmb* a month, scarcely enough to cover ordinary living expenses, but they lived together with the exceptional frugality practiced by mainland Chinese, renting a little room with wooden bunkbeds where they slept and cooked their simple meals of steamed rice and vegetables in an electric rice cooker. By dint of this extraordinary economy they were able to save the 350 *rmb* necessary to purchase and pay customs duty on a black-and-white TV set every three months or so, at which point one of them in rotation would make a trip back to Dragon's Head Brigade and present the TV to their father.

I found out about their father's traffic in TV sets accidentally. I was attending to some business in the market town when Uncle Min, as he is known to his fellow villagers, spotted me and came over.

"The brigade would like to borrow your van tomorrow," he said, sporting the avuncular grin that had given rise to his nickname. "We have some business to attend to in Linrong City." Having no plans to use the van the following day, I agreed, telling him that I would send my driver over to his village the next morning.

On the evening of the following day, my driver returned the van's keys to me and said, "Guess where we went today."

"Linrong," I said absentmindedly, for I was engaged in writing down an interview.

"And guess what we did in Linrong," he went on drolly. Pausing only long enough to make sure that he had my attention, he continued. "Uncle Min sold a TV set to a factory worker for 800 *rmb*. He makes 450 *rmb* on each set that his girls bring home, and this was his seventh set."

"Eighth," corrected my cook, who was well up on local village gossip.

"Seven, eight, what difference does it make," my driver said admiringly. "He has already made enough money to build a new house." And this was true. I had gone to Uncle Min's housewarming two weeks before. By mid-1980 when I left the commune, according to the calculations of envious fellow villagers, Uncle Min's daughters had thus demonstrated their filiality a total of nine times. It sounded like a Chinese version of a folk tale about a wicked stepfather, and in my notes I bemusedly entitled it "The Tale of the Three Filial Daughters," but it was a true-life story.

Cadres' corruption is not limited to trafficking in the black market on the side, but includes frequent, far-reaching, and direct abuses of their position and authority. Bribe-taking is common and comes in all forms from accepting gifts from toadying underlings to out-and-out influence peddling. On several different occasions I heard Chinese friends complain that their superiors expected gifts to accompany any special requests, instancing not only such substantial considerations as a good work evaluation or a new job assignment but also such petty dispensations as a half day off to take care of personal business or special timing of a yearly vacation.

So common—and effective—is this bribery that the first advice offered to anyone with a work-related problem is likely to be to give the boss *"liang ge mantou yi bao yan"*—an expression which literally means "two steamed rolls and a pack of cigarettes," but which by extension means any of the goods used to buy the favor of a superior. The actual coinage is considerably more complicated, including foodstuffs, liquors, tobacco, and tea, the only requirement being that the coinage be consumable. Aside from leaving little evidence of their passing, presentations of food and similar goods have the additional merit of permitting the pleasant fiction that they are not bribes at all, but merely gifts, because it is considered uncomradely for members of the same unit to give or receive cash bribes among themselves.

This is a gentlemanly nicety that is not observed when the comrades in question are from different units and have no other connection. The standard put-off line of the PRC bureaucrat, that a request needs "research," has become a standing joke about official avarice. *Yanjiu,* the Chinese word for research, also happens to be a homophone for "cigerattes and liquor," which in turn are symbols of the bribes that help smooth a bureaucrat's researches as he processes applications. The list of bribe-taking situations is endless. If a PRC resident wants permission to live and work in an urban area, an exit visa to study abroad, or the restitution of a position lost during the Cultural Revolution, he must frequently pay off a cadre in the office concerned to push through his case. Even routine requests for larger quarters and the like stand little chance of approval unless an official in the relevant department is induced to take a special interest in the matter.

Much expense can be avoided if the petitioner has a connection that can be tapped. "Things are a lot more convenient if one knows people in the unit one is doing business with" is how one brigade Party secretary with long experience put the matter to me. "In fact," he continued, "it is not simply a matter of convenience. If you don't know someone, it is often impossible to get even routine matters taken care of unless you give them a *hongbao* [payoff]. This is simply the way business is done in China," he concluded, "and probably the way it is done throughout the world." He looked at me for confirmation, and I nodded without conviction.

Officials also abuse their authority in other ways. As administrators and managers of communes and county-level departments and enterprises, these powerful functionaries use their combination of political and economic clout to illicitly allot to themselves a scaled-down version of the special privileges of higher leaders. Despite its illegality, such mimicry is pervasive. Lower-level cadres are usually housed in government-subsidized housing posh by local standards. I remember visiting one commune in the Pearl River Delta and noticing six single-family residences under construction in the wings of the park-like area behind the commune headquarters. I was nonchalantly told by one of the work crew that the homes were intended for the six ranking members of the commune Party committee and their families. Although the houses would not have found buyers in the United States and in any event would have failed to meet basic building code regulations, they impressed local peasants on several counts. Whereas the walls of adjacent peasant homes stood mere inches apart, those in the new cadre subdivision were separated from one another by a good 15 feet, leaving room for a patch of grass and a small garden. The two-story houses were also large enough to allow the cadres the luxury of living one to a room instead of sleeping crowded together in a single bedroom like many peasants. Moreover, they were built with local government funds and would cost the cadres nothing in rent. But what, above all, dazzled the locals was that the homes were essentially complete only two months after groundbreaking. Accustomed to building their homes in slow motion while scrounging for the necessary concrete, wood, bricks, and glass to continue construction, the peasants shook their heads in amazement at the sheer speed with which the cadres' homes went up. One young market town youth did note that the groundbreaking for the new commune movie theater, originally scheduled for that fall, had been pushed back until the following spring. The reason that the commune committee had given for the delay, he recalled with amused resignation, was "a shortage of building materials."

Commune and county cadres also share the same fondness for feasting at public expense as *gaogan,* a weakness that they indulge in the countryside at *chalou,* or teahouses. The word "teahouse," which conjures up visions of a small cafe with a handful of tables and rustic decor, leaves one unprepared for the new collectivized reality of this venerable Chinese meeting ground. Typical of the new proletarian style, the teahouse I visited most often was a plain, box-like building four stories in height constructed of whitewashed concrete. No mere coincidence had led to its construction immediately across the street from the commune headquarters, for I found that its drab, characterless exterior housed not one teahouse, but two: a lower teahouse on the first two floors for peasants, and an upper teahouse on the top floor for local officials.

The first and second floors were nothing more than cavernous halls, broken only by the pillars that rose every few paces to support the heavy concrete slab ceiling above. At all hours of the day their expanse was crowded with clusters of men mostly in black peasant garb, sitting on backless stools in groups of five or so around the eighty small, unfinished wooden tables that filled the halls. These tables are packed in so tightly together that what little space remains is totally taken up by each table's rim of peasants, who sit with their backs nearly touching their neighbors' at adjacent tables, making passage difficult. There are no waiters; rather the customer is left to fend for himself in a kind of reverse cafeteria style. He first pays for his order at a counter near the entranceway and then takes the receipt to the kitchen, where he picks up his order after a short wait. The system works better than might be imagined because of the simplicity of the menu. Normally only spareribs (from which all but a few shreds of meat have been carefully trimmed off) or fried pork fat is available, along with one or two kinds of greens. On the one occasion I attempted to eat in this lower teahouse, I was literally pushed upstairs by a matronly attendant, who told me in a booming voice, which could be clearly heard despite the din of conversations and scraping chairs, that "you don't want to eat down here. It's unsanitary and the food is no good." I meekly followed her lead upstairs, but not before I checked out the impact of her message on its unintended audience. The peasants unconcernedly continued eating and chatting after an announcement that would have had most Americans bolting from the teahouse.

After passing through the third floor, which serves as a hostel and is divided into small bunkrooms, I emerged into the very different atmosphere of the fourth floor. The entire center section of this floor is taken up by an inoperative fountain and its surrounding pool of stagnant water. (The pump ordered never arrived.) There are eight round, banquet-sized tables placed at intervals around the room, miraculously covered with plastic tablecloths printed with large floral designs. The metal folding chairs have backs, and the china service, when it arrives, has a pleasant floral pattern, though it is already missing many corners from rough washings by peasant hands. The menu in the upper teahouse always includes chicken, fish, and lean pork and sometimes duck and eel as well. There is a waitress to take your order, and sometimes, if he is not too busy, the old cook will appear in person to discuss the day's menu and recommend a dish or two. On any given day at lunch only two or three of the tables will be occupied, these by blue-jacketed or white-shirted commune cadres. The leading cadres of the commune put in frequent appearances, often in the company of an official from a county office who has come to the commune on business. They dine on a meal of baked eel, steamed freshwater fish, and pork strips fried with vegetables, swilled down with glasses of beer or rice liquor. All this is to ordinary peasant fare of steamed rice and chopped salted vegetables what a meal at Twenty-One is to a TV dinner. While by American standards the restaurant is decidedly greasy spoon, it is a world away from the crowded, dirty pandemonium of two floors below.

While ordinary peasants are not directly forbidden to enter the upper teahouse, as they are the more select clubs of the *gaogan*, there are several subtler exclusion mechanisms that serve to keep them in their place. The prices are so high, at 3 to 5 *rmb* per dish, that only commune and brigade cadres, who can charge the expense to their unit's account, can afford to eat there regularly. Nevertheless, villagers would probably still occasionally splurge on a meal with friends were it not for the exclusive, club-like atmosphere of the place. On the two occasions I invited peasants to join me for lunch in the upper teahouse, their presence occasioned amused stares from the cadres at adjoining tables, as well as evident disdain from the waitress. With the heightened class consciousness of those who serve the powerful, she treated me with extra solicitousness while completely ignoring my companions. My indignation at all this was not shared by my friends, one of whom shrugged, with an Uncle Tom–like acceptance of their lot, "We peasants don't know how to eat in a place like this."

Those Chinese I spoke with about cadre abuse of power and corruption were in the same way more resigned than indignant, most often seeing it as an intrinsic part of the social order and the way of the world. At most, better-educated Chinese expressed a kind of subdued cynicism brought on by the enormous gap which they saw separating officially proclaimed morals and the venal reality of things. Ordinary Chinese, and especially villagers, tended to view official corruption as not immoral at all—for it involves no activities that they would have scruples about engaging in given the chance—but merely unfair, because the cadres are able to profit so handsomely and effortlessly from their public positions.

"Everyone is out for themselves, especially cadres," I heard more than once. My reaction, that surely some cadres must put the interests of the public ahead of their own, was dismissed as naive by all except the cadres themselves. When I protested one rural woman's contention of universal cadre corruption as too sweeping, she retorted by telling me about the exodus of cadre offspring that had occurred in her native brigade of Heaven's Gate (and throughout central Guangdong) in 1978. At that time the tiny Portuguese colony of Macao had briefly opened its gates to mainland immigrants, setting a quota of several tens of thousands, and Guangdong Province had printed up the allowed number of emigration forms and distributed them down the administrative hierarchy of prefecture, county, commune, and brigade. "By the time meetings were held at the team level to announce the emigration program, the forms were all gone," she recalled. "The cadres at each level had 'confiscated' them for their own family members."

Still smoldering with resentment that the "cadre kids" had been allowed to go abroad while her own could not, she testily ran off the names of the dozen cadres from her brigade and the numbers of relatives that they had gotten out of China this way. After a pause, she added, "Only one cadre, Guohan, didn't go along. In fact, he even stood up at a brigade meeting and denounced the rest of the cadres for sending their sons and daughters to Macao. So the other cadres offered to let his younger sister apply for a factory job. But he replied angrily that his sister only had four years of schooling and was not qualified for a factory job."

My tentative appraisal that here was a cadre working for the public good (*wei gong*) was, however, quickly quashed. "Even Guohan is out for himself," the woman retorted. "You ought to see his house. It is filled with gifts—furniture, pictures, china, and so on—from urban youth sent here from Guangzhou during the Cultural Revolution.* You see, Guohan used to be in charge of our brigade's urban youth. A lot of them gave him gifts so that he would approve their applications to return to the city. He didn't refuse them."

———————————◆———————————

Those who might think that the above portrait of pervasive cadre corruption is overdrawn should consider that it is not only the humblest Chinese who complain about official venality but also the highest. Strongman Deng Xiaoping has repeatedly blasted corruption within the government and Party. In late 1980, for example, he charged that cadre ranks were rotten with those who offered personal favors and accepted bribes. Deng's worry is that widespread corruption is acting as a brake on his Four Modernizations program, and he seems bent on curbing such abuse.

Some recent inroads into corruption have been made, primarily by conceding the legitimacy of certain economic activities formerly beyond the socialist pale. Individual entrepreneurial activities in the agricultural, retail, and service sectors, ruthlessly extirpated by Maoists as "poisonous weeds of capitalism," have been legalized. Small-scale private enterprises in the area of retail trade and service are now permitted, and hundreds of thousands of family-run teahouses, restaurants, noodle stands, and small shops have sprung up at crossroads around the country. Peasants can now sell their produce, eggs, and fowl openly in reestablished

* The rustification program under which millions of urban youth were sent down to the countryside is discussed in Chapter 5.

rural markets instead of, as during the Cultural Revolution, in secret. This relaxation of the formerly blanket ban on private enterprise, although designed primarily to reinvigorate an ailing socialist economy, has decriminalized much underground activity and brought it into the open. But while some corruption was redefined out of existence, that which remains on the wrong side of the law appears to be on the upswing.

The imperative for underground trade in basic goods has weakened, but other sectors of the black market, particularly that involving imported goods, flourish as never before. Ironically, it is the overambitious advertising of the Four Modernizations that has provided much of the impetus for increased corruption in this area. The beckoning promise of a better life that has been held out to the Chinese people by the regime creates wants at a time when China is still scarcely able to meet basic needs. As a result the demand for consumer durables has soared, giving rise to a black market even in mass-produced goods such as bicycles (1980 production, 10 million), which speculators buy for a purchase price of from 100 to 200 *rmb* and then sell for 30 to 50 *rmb* over that.

But much of the recent surge in consumer demand centers on Western goods, on products that the PRC's economic system hasn't the technology, resources, or interest to supply at an acceptable price and quality, and is closely related to increased contact with the outside world. Members of official delegations return home laden with color TV sets and four-speaker tape players. Hong Kong residents bear gifts of sewing machines and rice cookers back to China for their stay-at-home kin. Overseas Chinese make hard-currency purchases of the Chinese and foreign-made luxury goods on sale in the Friendship Stores to give to their cousins and uncles. Many of these goods are then resold on the black market. Because of its proximity to Hong Kong the problem is worst in Guangdong, but the foreign-made electronic goods hand-carried through customs at Shenzhen are traded to all parts of China by canny Cantonese and find a ready market everywhere. Current PRC rules on economic exchanges allow the sale of personal possessions but strictly forbid profits on the turnaround. The public security apparatus may not approve of a family that immediately resells a gift rice cooker at black market prices, but takes action only against repeat offenders. Rather, Beijing has tried to stop this triangle trade at the border, in 1979 restricting the number of electrical appliances and electronic goods that a Hong Kong resident or an overseas Chinese could bring in to one item a year. Hefty import duties have also been imposed; in late 1981 they reached a staggering 300 percent of the market value of the import. Tariff levels have had to be raised to such levels so that PRC factories can compete on an equal basis with black market goods and begin to reduce their own overstocked inventories. No more need be said about the shoddy quality of PRC-made consumer goods. Although these tariffs were primarily designed to protect local industry from outside "legitimate" competition, choking off the burgeoning black market trade in foreign-made TVs, tape recorders, and other electrical goods and appliances at its source was also a consideration. In closed Party conclaves threats have even been made to register all such items, confiscating those whose owners cannot produce both a custom's receipt showing that import duty has been paid on their possession and a satisfactory explanation of how they came by it.

Obviously because the problem has been getting worse, the People's Republic on April 1, 1980, followed the lead of other Communist countries and set up a separate currency system for the use of foreigners and nonresidents. Where formerly the Friendship Stores, which carry the best in the way of Chinese manufactured goods, accepted only U.S. or Hong Kong dollars, they now take only *waihuijuan*, or "foreign currency certificates." Predictably, instead of being the solution to Beijing's black market blues, the certificates have become part of the problem: by 1981 the underground exchange rate for certificates had equilibrated at 14 *rmb* for 10 *waihuijuan*.

Government and Party cadres are on the cutting edge of this soaring corruption. The relaxation of economic controls has given an additional autonomy to lower-level officials that some have exploited for personal gain, awarding themselves bonuses and extra allowances, for example. At the same time the previously guaranteed right of workers to openly criticize their superiors by putting up big-character posters has been written out of the most recent constitution. I once asked the assistant head of a commune factory about the practice of accepting payment for the right to work in a factory. I had expected him to deny that it existed, but instead found that I had hit a nerve. "I hate that practice," he exclaimed, "but everyone does it now. Before the modernization program few cadres dared to accept bribes. Gifts, maybe, but not bribes. They remembered the 'socialist education campaign,' or the posters that people used to put up criticizing those in power for corruption, for abusing their power. Now no one says anything. They just go out and do the same things themselves."

The Deng regime realizes that it faces a huge and growing problem, and has unleashed a barrage of propaganda to try and contain it. After maintaining a discreet silence on official peccadillos during the Cultural Revolution, the state press has begun lashing out against some of the more obvious abuses of power. In 1979 a "Party rectification" movement to correct the work attitudes (favoritism and influence peddling) of officials was held. Such efforts, though producing their requisite number of scapegoats, seem to have had little overall effect. Each of the PRC's entrenched bureaucracies protects its own, and the most that a well-connected official can expect for even flagrant violations is a reprimand administered privately within the Party. Cadre corruption is likely to prove intransigent.

With the tawdry example of officials hawking favor and bartering their way to a better life, the regime's demands for austerity and honesty from the rest of the population for the sake of the modernization program are likely to go unheeded. However successful Beijing is in ultimately curbing the consumer appetites of its organization men, many ordinary Chinese now see modernization and cadre corruption as two sides of the same debased coin. As one worker observed to me, "The main beneficiaries of the Four Modernizations program thus far have been the cadres." He went on to tell with the characteristic cynical humor of mainland Chinese the difference between the Four Modernizations program for cadres and that for the masses.

"For well-connected cadres," he said brightly, "the Four Modernizations provides a modern TV set, a modern tape recorder, a modern wristwatch, and a modern hand calculator."

"And for the masses?" I asked.

"For the masses," he went on, "the Four Modernizations means hearing about modernization, talking about modernization, thinking about modernization, and gazing at modernization from afar."

5

Childhood: Learning to Be Chinese and Communist

The more students learn, the stupider they become.

Mao Zedong, 1958

A school's work is to change students' thinking.

Mao Zedong, 1974

It would have been difficult to find a country that more revered education than traditional China. Alone among agrarian states, China boasted schools filled with hopeful young scholars in all villages of any size. No historical figure was held in higher regard than Confucius, China's patron saint of learning and the source of much of the ancient wisdom that formed the curriculum of the traditional school. He was revered so much that at the beginning of each school year the village pupils and their parents would hold a special ceremony in his honor. Temples dedicated to Confucius abounded in the countryside, and it was here that the mother of a young boy just starting school would come to petition the Sage on her son's behalf, offering incense, candles, and prayers that he might be successful in his studies. The written word was a symbol of power and its study a near-sacred undertaking, for only those literate in the classics could compete in the world's earliest civil service examinations. Scholarship was the sole road to highly valued—and highly lucrative—government service.

Thus it came as a surprise to me, a short time after taking up residence in the countryside, to overhear Sandhead villagers speaking ill of education. To hear the descendants of good Confucians saying "Study is useless" (*jiaoyu wuyong*) was like hearing a practicing Catholic dismiss Mass as a waste of time. I had expected the outward trappings that surrounded study in traditional times to have been shorn away by the incessant attacks on superstition, and thus anticipated the absence of Confucian temples and rituals, but I was quite unprepared for the "10,000-foot fall" in the prestige of education itself. In China's villages today, studying, once one of the most highly regarded of endeavors, is now one of the lowest, and teaching, once a high-status occupation, now ranks among the lowest. The "venerable preceptor" of as recently as twenty years ago has become one of the "stinking nine"— nine categories of enemies of the Chinese revolution whose noxious ranks include reactionaries, counterrevolutionaries, landlords, and others of their ilk, bad company to keep in revolutionary China.

The lofty regard in which rural Chinese held "book-learning" was still intact in the early years of the People's Republic. Students crowded into schools in unprecedented numbers as the country enjoyed its first period of nationwide peace in twenty years. It remained possible, as it had been during earlier dynasties, for an able village youth, poor though he might be, to achieve a higher education and a position in government solely on the basis of scholastic merit. In fact, opportunities for government service had never been greater, as the rapidly expanding Communist bureaucracy recruited millions of new cadres during the 1950s. All this served to maintain, even enhance, the perception of education as a route to upward mobility.

The human face of this mobility can be very moving. An old man in his seventies who had been an itinerant cloth peddler in Equality Commune before the revolution told me pridefully of his daughter, Huang Yuexiu, who had done well enough on the 1958 college entrance examination to be sent to Beijing to study at a petroleum engineering institute. Later, on a trip to Guangzhou, I had lunch with this tall, stately female engineer, and she told me about her college life. She had gone to the national capital and hit the books with a vengeance, living a spartan existence worthy of a novitiate—or a dedicated revolutionary. "I lived in Beijing for five years and never saw an opera or a movie," Huang Yuexiu told me. "I and my classmates were too busy studying. We used to stand in line for hours at stretch for a seat in the institute's library, and once seated would stay until the library closed at midnight. At mealtimes we would take turns going to the cafeteria to quickly wolf down a bowl or two of rice so that there would always be someone guarding our seats in the library. All of my time in Beijing was spent either in class or in the library, and this was true of my classmates as well. We were the first wave of students to complete high school and college after the revolution, and we were studying not just for ourselves but for the nation."

Huang Yuexiu's description of students fired by a patriotic, collectivist ardor seems rousing enough to those used to the laid-back, me-first coolness of American secondary and college students, yet Chairman Mao was far from satisfied. He apparently felt that it was all too easy to be enthusiastic for the revolution on a full scholarship to a university, and suspected those who went on to higher education of harboring more selfish goals, such as careerism and elitism. They would, after all, be guaranteed employment by the state upon graduation, assigned to one of fifty-odd ministries and bureaus. Mao had a different set of aspirations he wished to impress upon China's youth, not only upon the small minority attending the nation's universities and colleges but upon those in secondary and primary schools as well. He wanted them to come to grips with rural life and manual labor, and to cease regarding education as a means to enter officialdom or, in the case of rural youth, as a way out of the dirt and Tobacco Road drudgery of the countryside. "The more students learn, the stupider they become" was how Mao described the education of the time. In his opinion what was needed was to make education relevant to rural life, and during the Great Proletarian Cultural Revolution he set out to do just that.

In the Pearl River Delta the first reaction to Mao's 1966 call for an educational revolution was a burning of the books. Sand-head students, following instructions from somewhat enthused, somewhat confused teachers, assembled in the schoolyard and cast their textbooks onto bonfires. When classes began again after several months of political meetings, lessons had to be written out on blackboards for the students to transcribe into their notebooks. Despite the obvious inefficiency of this laborious process, which reduced the speed of a child's progress in school to a scrawl, it was not until late 1969 that a new set of textbooks appeared.

The distinguishing characteristics of these slender volumes were a cover picture of Mao striking a heroic revolutionary pose and a stirring quote from the Chairman's Little Red Book, *Quotations from Chairman Mao,* on the first page. Less noteworthy were their contents, which, following Mao's dicta, had been simplified, politicized, and rusticated. All this did not save them from being incinerated in their turn in early 1974 when the "Criticize Confucius, Criticize Lin Biao" movement began. *All* books were now declared to be "dead knowledge," and bonfires blazed up again in the schoolyards. Peasant parents viewed these proceedings with increasing chagrin. "For a time it seemed like we were buying textbooks for our children just so they could be burned," one middle-aged mother and primary school teacher recalled with a grimace.

Although the students were again without books, this time it mattered less, for everyone now knew that the classroom was not where it was at. Rather, the schools were to "open their doors" to the rural world, and peasants were to take charge of the education of the young. Although they had little in the way of formal education, the new peasant preceptors had considerable experience in farming, and it was this farm lore that they passed on by word of mouth to the younger generation. Discussions of mathematical concepts were replaced by lectures on the use of the abacus. English was eliminated in favor of open-field discussions on the application of pesticides and fertilizers. Students went to hear peasants talk of growing rice and sugarcane, of raising pigs and fish. Recalling this period, one pigtailed girl in her middle teens gushed that "school was a lot more fun than it is now because we were only in the classroom maybe two or three days out of the week."

But if the students enjoyed the new education, its sheer superfluousness boggled the minds of village parents. Their children had been performing chores from the time they were old enough to manage a carrying pole, and already had considerable exposure to the facts of agricultural life at an age when children in Western countries had trouble taking out the garbage. Following graduation from school, a life-long apprenticeship to agriculture awaited them, which would in time teach them all they wanted or needed to know about farming. Yet here they were splashing along the edges of fish ponds listening to a fish farmer hold forth on the art of raising fish, or gathering around a sow that had just given birth to a litter of piglets while an old peasant discoursed on pig pediatrics. "Lifting a rock to drop it on one's own foot" was how one peasant graphically described such "open door" education to me.

Village parents were further dismayed when Mao directed that all schools throughout China, rural and urban alike, start farms and factories to provide pupils with the class-consciousness raising and character-building experience of good, hard work. Such a policy was not without value in the cities and towns, where a small school farm on the outskirts of town could provide urban children with an opportunity to enjoy country air and exercise. In the countryside, where children already had great gobs of fresh air and hours of exercise everyday, it made little sense.

It was not just that the schoolchildren were too busy between field trips and fieldwork to learn much that rankled peasant sensibilities; it was the work itself. Village parents came to see the schools as exploiting their children's labor. He Shenfu, a 45-year-old peasant whose four children had all been in school during the closing years of the Cultural Revolution, spoke for many of the villagers when he rasped resentfully, "I sent my children to school and paid their tuition. All for what? To carry buckets of mud for the school sugarcane? To cut grass for the school fish pond?" Many parents reasoned rightly that they would be better off, and their children no worse off, if they took their children out of school and put them to work at home or in the collective. Their children could learn the same things they were learning in school and help the family economy at the same time.

Mao's Cultural Revolution campaign to make education relevant to rural life succeeded only too well. With classrooms abandoned for open-air exercises in pulling weeds and toting mud buckets, teachers replaced by illiterate peasants who lectured on raising sugarcane or reeling silk, and books discarded in favor of "living knowledge," education became rural life in miniature. School was turned into a kind of dude farm, where peasant children played at being, of all things, peasants. In the eyes of frugal peasants struggling for subsistence, education had become an exercise in redundancy—"painting legs on the snake," in the Chinese metaphor. Even worse, it had become uneconomical.

Mao Zedong's primary concern was not the prestige of rural schools, but their political function, which he bluntly described in 1974 as changing students' thinking. The Deng coalition has moved away from this "the more, the better" attitude toward political conditioning that marked the Mao years, in part because the expansion of instruction in the sciences and mathematics related to the modernization program has placed other demands on the curriculum. Classes in politics have been reduced from three periods a week to two, and the amount of time devoted to work and political activities has been cut back even more drastically. Even so, education retains a pronounced ideological bent.

It is not just that students from primary school to university are required to sit through courses called "Politics" in which the leading role of the Party, the dictatorship of the proletariat, and the current political line are drummed into them. Communist ideology spills over into other courses as well. Lower middle school students studying Chinese language and literature are issued textbooks that consist mostly of essays from Mao's hand, many of which are overtly political in content. History is also taught in the Marxist mode, with particular emphasis given to earlier peasant rebellions, which are interpreted to the students as glorious precursors of the inevitable triumph of the socialist revolution.

But no course of study in Chinese schools is more in thrall to ideology than English. It may come as a surprise to those who regard the study of a foreign language as an implicitly humanistic endeavor, but in China English is taught without reference to the society and culture of the countries where it is spoken. Instead the course cleaves faithfully to the ideological straight and narrow. The textbooks used read like children's books of Maoism in English translation. In one lesson in the lower middle school textbook, children are described listening happily and attentively to an old peasant recount the hardships of his life before the revolution (a Communist ritual); in another, Chinese schoolchildren are depicted as going merrily off to the school farm to engage in edifying manual labor; and so on. Recently, textbooks at all levels have been expanded to include lessons on the languages of mathematics, physics, chemistry, and agronomy, the thought here being to launch students on their way to understanding scientific English so that they can contribute to the Four Modernizations, themselves the subject of a lesson or two. The path may enter the forest from a different point, but it ends in the same ideological bog.

The effect of such a skewed education is predictable. Once, while in the county town of Dali, I was accosted by a student from the local normal college who was eager to practice his English. His ordinary conversational ability was limited to a greeting, an inquiry as to one's health, and a question about one's origins. Then we were off into politics. "China is building socialism," he revealed to me. "The program for the Four Modernizations will make China into a strong socialist country." I replied politely, evincing an interest I by no means felt for his programmed recitation. "The Four Modernizations are"—here he took a deep breath before wading slowly into the sequence of memorized polysyllables—"industry, science and technology, agriculture, and military."

Wanting to lead him away from his memorized text, I seized the initiative as he was trying to recall his next English sentence to ask, "Do you think China will be able to modernize?"

The orthodox answer, the one which is repeated with monotonous regularity in the official press, would have been "China will be able to modernize by the year 2000." But here my conversation partner's punch-card loquaciousness could apparently not carry him over his doubts, and he replied slowly and honestly, "I don't know."

One reason for the failure of this heavy-handed effort to successfully program a blind love for the Party, state, and official ideology into the heads of hundreds of millions of young Chinese is overkill. I found it impossible to engage even intelligent upper middle school students, much less ordinary village youth, in political discussions. Even asking them about the current line—which they know backwards and forwards from constant exposure in the classroom and out—elicited merely smiles and shrugs of disinterest. Saturation politics had not worn them down into an uncritical acceptance; it had numbed them into a yawning indifference.

Occasional reports in the Chinese press of students informing on their parents' backward thoughts or counterrevolutionary actions to school or other authorities seem to be nothing more than Communist fairy tales, at least in the countryside. Communist leaders may wish that they ruled over a people that put their love for the Party before their own parents, but the peasants of the villages I visited could not recall even a single case where this had happened, and were furthermore convinced that it could not happen. "No child would be that unfilial to his parents," one peasant remarked.

I did stumble upon one special case, though. It involved the son of a landlord, a young man in his early thirties called Ouyang Guofu, whom I was surprised to find holding a post as a minor commune cadre. He confirmed that his situation was quite unusual. "I am the only commune cadre from a landlord family. My bad class background was overlooked by the commune revolutionary committee because my thoughts were considered to be relatively advanced." I soon found out from local residents what his "advanced thoughts" had consisted of. It so happened that at the onset of each new political campaign Guofu's actions were predictable: he would stand up during a mass meeting and denounce his father, at length and in the most abusive terms possible. That he was willing to do this accounted for his rise within the commune, but it also caused him to be held in total contempt by the villagers. "He lies, cheats, and is underhanded," an old peasant said scornfully when I asked him about Guofu. "It is best not to have anything to do with him." As far as I could judge on the basis of a year-long acquaintance, Guofu was a forthright and honest person. All that mattered in the villagers' eyes, however, was his unfilial behavior—his betrayal of his father— which the villagers could neither forgive nor forget, and which they saw as proof of his total lack of moral character. It was one thing for *them* to criticize his father, Landlord Ouyang, and in the past they had frequently done so, but for the man's own son to do so was going beyond the bounds of propriety, and permanently discredited him in his native village.

What made the case difficult to judge was that Guofu's father had fled to Hong Kong in 1949 and so had not suffered either personally or socially from his son's attacks. Not only that, but he had taken a second wife after a year in Hong Kong and started another family, conveniently forgetting that he had a wife and three small children in the village. In thirty years they had not received a single letter, remittance, or message of any kind from him. Whatever it had been that had turned Guofu against his father, it had not been merely political indoctrination.

Given the lack of respect for learning and the belief that the schools are not introducing notions subversive to family values, it seems natural that the first day of school passes without parental anxiety or fanfare. No nervous moms giving last-minute admonitions to study hard and listen to the teacher lead neophyte first graders down the alleyways to school that morning. No tense gaggles of parents cluster outside the classrooms, worried about their youngsters' reaction to the school environment, fearful that they will not be able to adjust properly. No ceremony or celebration, Confucian or Maoist, is held to mark the beginning of a child's education. Rather, the village 7-year-olds make their own way to the nearby school, and are soon at work on their first lessons. Their parents, for their part, go to work in the fields as on any other day. Having equipped their offspring with the necessities—textbooks, notebooks, and pencils—and paid his or her first semester's tuition, they leave all other concerns to the teacher. Going to school is an expected step in a child's life as he or she reaches 7 or so years of age, and its demands dovetail nicely with those made by parents.

Until that age, Chinese children live in a permissive world in which their physical wants are catered to by protective parents, and they are generally given their own way. Not that rural Chinese dote on children. Babies are not romanticized as lovely little toys to be coddled and fussed over, but are apprehended as helpless little beings that it is necessary to feed, care for, and otherwise nurture to the age at which they are fit to become members of the family and of society. One American baby can reduce a roomful of otherwise normal adults to cooing, fawning infantility. Chinese babies don't cast the same spell over their elders. Men generally ignore infants, except to quietly hold their own on occasion. Women are more drawn to an infant, but even they rarely address it directly, cooing and clucking as matrons in the West instinctively do. Rather, they talk to the mother *about* her child, commenting on its weight and color, asking after its health. Even after the toddler stage, adults interact very little with children. Of children of 6 or less it is said that they "do not understand" (*bu dong shi*), and so they are not told stories, not taught how to count or write simple characters, and certainly not encouraged to ask questions. For the same reason, they are rarely disciplined, their every error being excused on account of their supposed ignorance. The idea of young children as persons in their own right would just amuse rural Chinese, who are concerned to keep their off-spring plump, warm, and healthy but otherwise allow them to do as they please.

Day care centers, though a fixture of the model commune and factory circuit and generally available to urban children, turned out to play but a minor role in child rearing in the country-side. Although collective day care centers had been started by the hundreds of thousands during the Cultural Revolution by order of the central government, most of these had been quickly closed by the late seventies as unsuited to rural conditions. In a typical example, while a decade ago South Isle Brigade in the Pearl River Delta had such centers for each of its twenty-four teams, the only one left in operation by 1979 when I visited the brigade was that belonging to Team 6, a large team of some 400 members.

This day care center consisted of a single large room in a building that had formerly been the ancestral hall of the same branch of the village clan that now formed Team 6. Twenty chil-dren, ranging in age from 1 to 5, were kept there, watched over by two women. The barn-like interior of the center had been whitewashed, floored in fired clay, and was reasonably clean, but was barren. The only splash of color in the room was made by two large poster portraits of Mao and Hua pasted up on an end wall, both Chairmen beaming down on their young subjects with identical expressions of pleasant, empty benevolence. The room was without tables or chairs, the only furniture being four make-shift wooden cribs in a corner for the youngest infants. Nothing in the way of toys or other play equipment was available.

My questions about artwork, singing, organized games, nap periods, and simulated work activities perplexed the two young women in charge. Ordinary young peasants, they considered themselves first of all fortunate to have been released from field labor for the easy duties of the day care center. It was not expected of them that they should structure their charges' daily stays or try to teach them anything. Their job, they told me, was to ride herd on children too young to be trusted on their own. The main thing was to keep the children from wandering out the entrance-way and falling into the canal that the hall fronted on.

The kids were entirely on their own, little kinetic balls of energy bouncing about and rebounding off one another without adult direction or purpose. Thrown back on the devices of their own imaginations, they formed play groups and dissolved them spontaneously, much as small children play at home around busy mothers whose attention is distracted by household chores. The women in charge were oblivious of selfish behavior—although the absence of any toys kept property disputes to a minimum. Discipline was limited to a firm hand on the backside, and this was administered sparingly, usually only to those who broke the cardinal rule against wandering outside or who behaved very badly, striking another child or continuously creating distur-bances. It all seemed hardly likely to create good socialists.

I had brought along my camera to get shots of the children at play, but I had no sooner taken my first photo than one child, frightened by the flash, ran to a corner of the room and began a terrible, frightened howling. No one—neither the women in charge nor the other children—made any move to comfort or reassure him. Rather, they all stood back at a distance of about 8 feet and laughed at him, the children busily adding insults about his childish behavior as well. I don't know if this temporary ostra-cism and collective punishment made any impression on this 5-year-old boy, who appeared to ignore his tormentors and howled all the louder, but it moved me to approach him and tell him in low tones not to be afraid. This the women found amusing also, indicating that they themselves rarely gave such succor. But in general, I doubt if this little human zoo, which is more typical of the nursery schools that do exist in the countryside than the ones foreigners are taken to see, had any effect at all on the kids. Rather, it was just a little child station, where peasant women could check their children on the way out to the fields and pick them up again in the evening on their way home.

The majority of rural Chinese children never set foot in a nursery, but are raised by Amahs—grandmothers—from birth un-til the time they start school. Since most of these old women reached adulthood before the revolution and are in addition illiterate, they have been little affected by the changes that have overtaken China over the past thirty years. They raise their little grandchildren in the same way that, a generation before, they raised their own children, in a very traditional, family-centered fashion.

Once little boys are thought old enough, at 5 or 6 years of age, to play without supervision, they are allowed to escape from the watchful eye of their Amah (or they are no longer sent to the nursery, an expense that peasant parents are glad to be free of). They form ragtag gangs of half a dozen or more boys and, except for meals, are rarely home during the daylight hours. They can be seen running free around the village alleyways, playing in front of the ancestral halls or in the schoolyard. Little girls stay closer to home, usually following their grandmother through the daily round of chores, imitating her work in play as children do.

All this changes when the child reaches 7 or so. Parental indulgence gives way to a world of rules and expectations enforced by suddenly stern and demanding adults, who prove surprisingly quick to discipline a child who does not behave in accordance with his new status. The family I lived next door to had two boys, an 8-year-old and a 6-year-old. Despite the closeness in their ages, they might have been ten years apart for the way they were treated. The younger brother's frequent tantrums were ignored; the older was spanked if he so much as yelled. The younger often received special treats like meats and pastries from his mother; the older waited in line for the leftovers. Moreover, the younger was totally exempted from the chores which occupied his older brother for half an hour or so every afternoon after school. The difference arose not from favoritism, but because, while the younger brother had yet to reach childhood's end, the older was already of the age where he was expected to understand what was expected and acceptable (*dong shi*).

Since children cross the threshold into what may be called personhood at about the same time that they start school, teachers are natural allies of parents in demanding proper behavior. One reason parents have no qualms about giving their offspring over to be educated is that the values of obedience, diligence, and respect for authority demanded in the classroom are also those expected in the home. In class most of the teachers are still very Confucian in their strictness with their students. Especially the lower grades are ruled with an iron hand, with students upbraided and shamed in front of their classmates when they are caught playing or daydreaming in class. From my house adjacent to Sandhead primary school, I could often hear teachers shrieking at their little charges, telling them to stop talking in class, to pay attention, to learn their lessons, to sit up straight, and a hundred other admonitions. The impressions that students take away of their early years in school are impressions primarily of fierce and demanding teachers. I once received a visit from a local second-grade teacher, a slight, deferential woman, on the short side even for a southern Chinese. After she left, my assistants, two of whom had been in her class over a decade earlier, told me that this little wisp of a woman was a high-handed terror in the classroom, and remarked with nervous smiles that they still felt uneasy in her presence.

While tongue-lashing is an approved part of the curriculum, the use of the hand or rod, that mainstay of the Confucian order, is strictly forbidden. When a male teacher in Southhead lower middle school struck a first-year student with the flat of his hand, a blow which sent the boy home with a headache, it was treated as a major infraction. The teacher was forced to write a confession admitting his error in striking the student and read it before a school-wide assembly. He was also ordered to visit the boy's home and offer a personal apology to the head of the household. More conservative teachers saw all this as an overreaction, however, and argued that since the 1950s, when the use of corporal punishment was forbidden, students have grown increasingly hard to manage.

Certainly the perfectly ordered urban classrooms that foreign visitors are taken to see bear little resemblance to rural reality. Chinese country schools have problems in discipline that parallel in many respects those in schools in Western countries. Chinese children too play hookey, are tardy, fail to do homework assignments, talk in class, and break school regulations. Even though smoking is officially forbidden, I have come across boys as young as 7 or 8 puffing away on an unfiltered cigerette in a corner of the schoolyard.

When my assistant, Joceline Lau, and I administered a questionnaire to schoolchildren in grades 2 to 7 in Sandhead Brigade schools, we quickly discovered that the students cheated rather brazenly, glancing openly at their neighbors' papers. It was only by repeatedly telling them that on this test there were no right or wrong answers, that they could answer whatever they wanted to, and by keeping them under constant surveillance that we were able to keep copying from undermining the whole attempt. Teachers' reactions ranged from acute embarrassment to honest admissions that cheating on exams was endemic. "It's the only way that many students can pass," one seventh-grade teacher shrugged in explanation. "I have several students who can barely read, and many others who do not prepare for exams or do their homework."

But I really got an idea of the extent of the problem at the end of my month-long stint as an English teacher. I had spent the month prepping third-year middle school students in basic English grammar for the upcoming province-wide upper middle school examinations, and I wished to see how much progress they had made in that time. To say that they had not done well on the test I had given at the outset would be an understatement. The average score had been 22 out of 100, and there had been numerous exam papers turned in blank except for the student's name. On the final, although there were still two or three blank exams, a full dozen out of my thirty-four pupils had scores in the eighties and nineties, and I congratulated myself on the improvement. My satisfaction vanished the following day, though, when a good friend who was the mother of one of my students paid me a visit. She asked me, scarcely able to repress a grin, if I knew why the students had done so well. I shook my head, and she then proceeded to tell me that the night before the examination a group of my students had broken into the teachers' office where I had left the blank tests and had stolen several copies. They had then stayed up until dawn puzzling out the correct answers, coming to class with these written down on little crib sheets. "This has happened before," she revealed, "so most teachers take their test papers home with them. Of course you didn't know because you are new." She concluded by cautioning me not to let slip that I knew about the cheating because otherwise "the principal and the school would lose face."

For all this, there is less overt classroom misbehavior than in many American schools, less talking behind the teacher's back, passing of notes, throwing of spitballs, or wafting of paper airplanes. And problems serious enough to be considered crimes, such as drinking, vandalism, and theft, are practically nonexistent in the countryside. The discipline problems in Chinese schools are not truculent, unruly, and rebellious students, but disinterested, unmotivated, and stolid ones.

I recall vividly my first period as visiting English instructor. When I appeared in the doorway of the classroom, the students leaped to their feet and, with a verve that would have done credit to an Imperial German gymnasium, sang out in unison, "Good morning, teacher." They then stood suspended by their desks waiting for the order to be seated, which I gave as soon as I overcame bemused surprise. This attention-on-deck opening was deceptive, though. I soon discovered that my new students did not respond to questions with a military snap, but slowly, hesitatingly, or not at all. They proved to be respectful but passive, obedient but dull, with little interest in learning. I even had students who fell asleep during pronunciation drills, a remarkable accomplishment given the deafening decibel levels we reached. Even those who managed to stay awake chanted their drills in a peculiarly restrained, docile fashion, with none of the restless, unruly energy that American teachers unleash to their peril. In contrast to group exercises in the U.S., where there are usually students who lead the group, deliberately shouting at the top of their lungs or, anticipating the next sentence, bursting out slightly ahead of turn, these students maintained a lifeless togetherness even when reciting their loudest.

The students' failure to take an active part in the learning process was frustrating for me as a teacher, and made it difficult to gauge their progress. Even when totally confused by some new vocabulary item or grammar rule, instead of asking me to explain it further, they would simply plow through the material as best they could. And not once after class did a student come up to me with a question. This was not just shyness around a new and foreign teacher either, for other teachers confirmed this student trait. In America classes often end with a question-and-answer period; in China they end with the bell and the teacher's dismissal. When released, the students spilled out of the classroom without a backward glance or thought.

One reason for student passivity is that education in rural China today, as in traditional times, is mostly memory work. This begins in the lower grades of primary school, where much of the time and energy of youngsters are spent learning how to recognize, remember, and write thousands of Chinese characters, a dead lift of memory roughly equivalent to the memorization of hundreds of multiplication tables. But the emphasis on drill, drill, and more drill does not end here, but carries over into the upper grades. The courses in physics and biology taken by lower middle school students are taught by the textbook method, as if the sciences, like politics, were mere rote dogma to be pronounced and memorized, not subject to confirmation or denial through the use of the microscope or test tube. This stress on rote learning over critical thinking is further reinforced by examinations, which nearly always consisted of simple fill-in-the-blank-type questions. Even in upper middle schools subjective essay questions—thought questions—never appeared on exams, and multiple-choice questions were rare.

The practice of teaching in the imperative doubtless owes something to the tradition of the strict Confucian preceptor, but it has been powerfully reinforced by successive political campaigns, especially the Cultural Revolution, when a casual classroom comment at odds with the prevailing orthodoxy was enough to get a teacher criticized, confined, or even sent to labor reform. "Teaching is a dangerous activity," teachers began to whisper among themselves, and sought to protect themselves by going strictly by the book, offering no commentary and brooking no discussion. The teachers I observed "dished it out" after the peremptory fashion of Marine drill sergeants, and the students, like new recruits, "took it." Indeed, instead of encouraging their students to think for themselves, teachers actually rewarded conformity. The highest grade in a fifth-grade exercise in composition went to the following essay: "Our government is a dictatorship of the proletariat under the leadership of the Party. The Communist Party is the glorious leader of our country. The People's

Liberation Army protects our great homeland." The teacher praised this string of slogans masquerading as an essay for its "correctness of thought."

The Ministry of Education closely controls what students learn, primarily by its monopoly on the writing and publishing of textbooks but also by its detailed annual directives concerning what subjects are to be taught in each grade and the number of hours per week to be spent on each. There is no room for electives in this fast-paced curriculum, which for seventh graders in 1980 included courses in math, biology, geography, history, physical culture, Chinese, English, and "labor," in which students spend one morning each week, usually Saturday, working on the school grounds. As in other aspects of life in China, individual preferences play no part in the educational process. Mass education in China is the academic equivalent of its subsistence standard of living: the institutions are able to serve up the basics, but no choices or desserts appear on the menu.

Partly because of shoestring budgets, partly because the state plan does not make provision for them, extracurricular activities do not exist. Rural schools have no athletic teams and hold no intramural or extramural basketball or table-tennis competitions. The numerous clubs—chess, language, scholarship, athletic—that exist in American junior and senior high schools find no counterpart in rural Chinese schools. My assistant, a graduate of Hong Kong's school system, was so dismayed by the total lack of activities for students in or out of the classroom that she wrote a long letter to the local commune education office suggesting that extracurricular activities such as clubs and outings be organized for the students, and that in-class sessions be livened up by encouraging student participation and by holding calligraphy competitions and playing mathematical games—all things that are done in Hong Kong. A few days later I encountered the cadre in charge of commune education in the local market town. Taking me aside, he told me that although he appreciated my assistant's suggestions, it was impossible to implement them. "Parents don't want us to keep students after hours," he said, "even for activities that their youngsters enjoy. They want them home after school to help out with the chores. As for organizing activities in class, we are having enough trouble just teaching the regular course material in the time allotted. How can we take time out for other activities? And if we deviated from the approved ways, or organized clubs, or whatever, the county education office would hear about it. We might be subject to criticism or placed on report," he admitted with rare candor for a Chinese official. "I like my current job. I don't want to be transferred to some small primary school somewhere to teach third graders."

Reflecting the meager resources of the peasants who built them, school facilities in the countryside are at a bare utilitarian minimum. Students are out of the elements, with a tile roof over their heads, but the typical classroom has no ceiling and an earthen floor. No elaborate air-conditioning systems here. The same windows that provide ventilation in the oppressive heat of June and September also stand open to the north wind in winter. To close the shutters would plunge the classroom into near darkness, for it is not wired for electric lights. It is equipped with a blackboard (in the original sense: a board painted black), a lectern for the teacher, and row upon row of simple, flat-topped desks of unpainted, unvarnished wood. These are constructed in pairs, as if taken from an American schoolhouse of an earlier era, with a two-man backless bench for seating. School libraries do not exist, even in so modest a form as a book corner in an occasional classroom. Outside there is a small open area used for school assemblies and calisthenics. A basketball, a soccer ball, and a ping-pong table or two, with a "Bring your own paddles and balls" policy, are the usual extent of a school's athletic equipment.

Even seemingly affordable conveniences are missing. There is not a single mechanical pencil sharpener in Sandhead primary school; rather, the children all carry little pen knives to sharpen the ends of their stubby, eraserless pencils (and carve the characters of their names into their desktops). Except for half a dozen Thermos bottles of hot water in the school office used to make tea for the teachers, there is no potable water in the school. A Chinese student must wait until school lets out to quench his thirst. School toilets there are, two little thatched huts built on stilts over the school's own fish pond, but they are used mostly by teachers. "Fat water should not be wasted on the fields of others," parents say, prudently instructing their school-aged children to empty their bowels only into the family pot.

Boys of school age keep their hair cropped short, and girls wear braids of varying lengths, but this is more rural custom than school regulation. Custom also dictates that unmarried girls not wear jewelry, which indicates adult status and is first worn by women on their wedding day. In fact, youngsters of either sex rarely wear anything in the way of bracelets, rings, and watches, which are beyond peasant means. Unlike Chinese children in the Taiwanese countryside, who go to school neatly outfitted in navy blue uniforms, including cap, black leather shoes, and Day-Glow yellow book backpack, in mainland China school dress is catch-as-catch-can. It would be hardly possible to mandate uniforms for over 200 million schoolchildren, supplies of cotton cloth being so limited that they must be strictly rationed. Still, poverty imposes uniformity of a kind. Girls and boys alike come to school bare-headed and often barefoot, clothed only in pants and shirt. These are cut square and styleless out of rationed cloth—solid blues, greens, and grays for the boys, a lighter print for the girls—and are often patched and worn from long wearing. Only a few children have book bags, these stitched together out of cast-off PLA canvas, but since children's thin, paperback textbooks altogether make a stack only about 3 inches high, they can easily carry them to school clutched in one hand.

The warm, balmy weather of spring and autumn in South China makes few demands upon the children's dress or upon the school as a shelter, and during the sweltering months of summer the children do not have to attend school; as in the U.S., there is a three-month-long summer vacation which runs from mid-June to mid-September. But except for three weeks at the Chinese New Year, the children are in school throughout the winter, and during these months they suffer. Winters are relatively short and mild in Guangdong, with periods of merely cool weather alternating with periods of wet cold during which the temperature hovers a few degrees above zero degrees centigrade. Because such periods usually pass quickly, rarely lasting longer than a week or two and because field work continues throughout, Sand-head peasants do not resort to the thickly padded cotton over-clothes worn by Chinese in more northerly regions. Schoolchildren cope with the cold by adding on extra layers of thin summer garments, until they resemble walking cabbages in the leafy profusion of collars of various shapes and sizes sprouting from their necks. But they have no gloves for their hands, and only sandals or cloth slippers for their feet, and the extremities suffer during long hours at a school desk. With the windows left open for light, there is a steady draft of chill air flowing through the unheated classroom. The children sit hunched over their desks, their feet curled up under the bench and their hands thrust inside their clothing, looking like rows of little two-fisted Napoleons. The right hand—for all Chinese are right-handed—occasionally appears to write or carry out some other essential task, only to disappear again inside the shirt at the first opportunity. Congealed, numbed fingers have trouble even holding a pencil, much less making meaningful ideograms with it, and penmanship declines dramatically.

Such prolonged exposure to cold combined with forced inactivity can have more serious consequences as well. Ah Fang, a lively 11-year-old, used to come home from school stamping her feet and blowing on her hands, laughing that it had been so cold in school that day that the students had had trouble walking home after class. At first I dismissed this as childish exaggeration, but later heard from one of the local barefoot doctors (a kind of paramedic) that many schoolchildren actually did suffer from a mild form of trenchfoot during the winter months. This illness, called locally "turnip foot" because of the bloated, discolored appearance of affected feet, is caused by the moist cold of winter months and makes walking very painful. After an afternoon sitting at their desks, it was all many children could do to gimp home on their benumbed or aching underpinnings.

Yet the surprising thing about Chinese rural schools is not that they are backward and ill-equipped, but that they exist at all, at least in poorer areas. Although larger, wealthier villages like Sandhead have always had schools, today the children of even isolated hamlets have an opportunity to attend a local primary school for several years. Currently as many as 90 percent of all children of primary school age are actually in school, more than double the percentage of thirty years ago. The magnitude of the educational effort required to achieve this advance becomes clear from the numbers: in 1978 there were 200 million students in China, 146 million in primary school and 64 million in secondary school, receiving instruction from over 9 million teachers.

Contrary to PRC claims, this success in bringing schools and teachers to China's backwaters owes at least as much to the efforts of local villagers as it does to Beijing. Not that Beijing planned it that way. By 1954 the central government, after the fashion of socialist states everywhere, had established a monopoly on education, and the administration of all primary and secondary schools then in operation had passed to the Ministry of Education. Teachers, many of whom had formerly been hired by rural villages and towns, became employees of the state. But these ambitious steps—involving a financial burden 2 to 3 percent of national income—so strapped the government that plans to rapidly expand the numbers of primary schools and teachers beyond this initial level had to be shelved, and many districts remained without schools. Even rural communities in areas that already had primary schools at the time of the revolution found their facilities bursting at the seams a few years later as the baby-boom children of the postwar period came of school age. In Sandhead, as throughout China, the percentage of school-age children attending school actually declined during the late fifties over what it had been a few years before.

Mao Zedong must be credited with pointing out that there was only one way out of this dilemma: a return to the tradition of local village responsibility for education. In a policy about-face, villages were encouraged to build schools using local funds and materials and to staff them with teachers hired from among the local population. During the late fifties and throughout the sixties, rural schoolhouses numbering in the tens of thousands went up in remote villages from Shenxi (Shensi) Province in the northwest to Guangxi (Kwangsi) Province in the far south. Typical of more prosperous settlements, Sandhead constructed a second school to relieve crowding in a converted ancestral hall. No exact figures are available, but perhaps half of Chinese schoolchildren, or 100 million students, today sit in classrooms built by their local communities and are taught by teachers paid by the collective rather than the Ministry of Education.

Cost-sharing was intended by Mao to be only one of a set of policies designed to integrate education more closely into its rural setting. But following his death in 1976 and the downfall of his leftist supporters not long thereafter, the more radical innovations in education that he inspired were abandoned across the board. By 1979, field trips had been eliminated, political study and labor assignments cut back. Peasant instructors had given way to professional teachers, and farm lore to courses in physics, chemistry, biology, and English. It became possible to hold back students where formerly everyone was promoted. Grades and examinations, once rejected as undemocratic, resumed their earlier importance. Education in China had backtracked to the policies of the fifties.

The reason for this policy reversal is China's modernization program, toward which end the whole educational system has been ordered into doubletime. Students are now expected to learn characters at nearly twice the leisurely pace of the Cultural Revolution period. The principal of a rural primary school in Zhongshan County of Guangdong told me that his students used to only have to learn 800 characters by the end of the second grade, 1,500 characters by the fourth grade, and 2,000-odd characters, enough to read a newspaper, by graduation at the end of fifth grade. "Now the rate has nearly doubled," he said worriedly. "My students will have to master 1,500 characters during grades 1 and 2, an additional 1,500 characters during grades 3 and 4, and over 3,500 by the time they graduate. I don't know how many of them are going to be able to do it."

Not only has the pace of education quickened, but at the same time the going has been made more difficult. Because of its centrality to modern science and technology, no course of study has been toughened more than mathematics. While the first post-Cultural Revolution mathematics textbook for fifth graders was only a little over 100 pages long, the new text is over twice that, and goes well beyond the simple multiplication, division, decimals, and fractions of the old to include algebraic concepts, number sets, and other elements of the new math. In a revealing reversal of the American experience, it was the teachers, not the parents, who were upset by their inability to grasp the new math. Especially the teachers hired by the collective, most of whom graduated from the same primary and lower middle schools that they now teach at, were nearly as baffled by the new math concepts they were called upon to teach as their students. They had no choice but to bluff their way through the material as best they could.

But if the teachers are often hard-pressed to keep up with the hell-bent-for-leather pace of post-Mao pedagogy, many students simply have no idea which way to run. I attended an eighth-grade class in mathematics in Sandhead Brigade's lower middle school in which the teacher carefully copied out on the blackboard what lesson 20 of the text said about certain algebraic equations while the students dutifully copied down same. That evening I watched 14-year-old Ah Ling struggling to get the correct answers to the lesson's problems by simply plugging in numbers. It was clear that for all she knew, she was playing an odd, complicated, and unenjoyable game at the teacher's insistence, one which had no real significance at all.

With promotions from one grade to the next no longer automatic as they were during Mao's time, but contingent on meeting the new academic standards, many students have failed to measure up. One rural school teacher I fell into conversation with on the Henan ferry into Guangzhou told me that he had been forced to keep back 40 percent of his fifth-grade pupils in each of the previous two years. "There is a county regulation which states that a maximum of 3 percent of students may be held back, but the schools in my area have not paid any attention to it since 1978," he revealed. "How can we? If we really promoted only those students who actually learned the new material, we would have to hold back 90 percent of our students."

Many of the current difficulties arise from the suddenness of the shift in educational policy, and should ameliorate with time. Students attending lower middle school are, like their harried teachers, still paying the price for the earlier neglect of serious education. When they were in primary school, they were spoiled by an easy course of study and undemanding teachers, those same teachers who now describe them, accurately if somewhat unfairly, as "lazy and unmotivated." These students are wrestling with new material that they are academically unprepared for, as if they had enrolled in a trigonometry course without having first taken algebra, or had skipped a grade or two. Younger children now beginning primary school, who will be exposed to the new curriculum from the first, should have considerably less difficulty with it. After all, according to older teachers, the new curriculum is only moderately more difficult than that in effect before the Cultural Revolution, which was more or less successfully taught in the countryside for a decade or more.

But the problem goes deeper than the transitory shock of a

sudden return to the basics after a decade of loose radical experimentation. Peasants who twenty years ago had an idealistic reverence for education have been disabused of this notion, and take little interest in their offspring's progress in school. Teachers in the early fifties who threw themselves into their work, even giving up their free time to hold special classes for the illiterate and help with the land reform, are often demoralized and apathetic. The young, not unexpectedly, mimic the lackadaisical attitude of their elders.

Even Americans critical of overly achievement-oriented education would find Chinese rural schools too lax for their liking. Homework, limited to an hour a night to leave time for chores, is often not done at all by students who know that their teachers do not bother keeping records of assignments completed. Exams come only infrequently, only two or three times a semester in the average course, but students do not worriedly cram for them; and when the corrected exams come back, they simply glance once at them and put them away, with none of the groaning or preening that one hears and sees in an American or Taiwanese classroom. Neither do Chinese teachers trouble to write the grade distribution, or even the average, on the blackboard so that students may gauge their performance against others in the class. As might be expected given the general unconcern with academic achievement, grade reports occasion little anxiety or pride in students or parents. I once saw a man sign his fourth-grade son's report card (required in China as in the U.S.) and hand it back to him without so much as glancing at it. The boy, it turned out when I looked over his grades, had done well in several subjects, especially math, where his grade was in the mid-nineties, but not a word of praise passed this father's lips. When I related to him that many American parents rewarded their children for such high grades with a gift of cash, this man could only laugh incredulously at rich foreigners who spend their money to no good purpose.

These attitudes are much less amenable to change than textbooks and curricula, for they are rooted in the reality that rural education does not lead up and out of the village. The new system is self-consciously elitist, focusing its efforts primarily on the bright few and concentrating its resources in a nationwide network of special academies called "key-point schools." These academies, closed during the egalitarian Mao years, are not only leagues above the minimal schools of rural areas; they are also much better staffed and equipped than ordinary urban schools. To those gifted or powerful enough to gain entrance, they offer a top-notch education and a more than even chance to continue on to college. But for the majority of students this school system within a school system draws off resources and locks up opportunities that would otherwise have been distributed more fairly. The ultimate effect of this system will probably be to further rigidify China's already crystallizing class structure of cadres, intellectuals, workers, and peasants. The sons and daughters of cadres and the resurgent intelligentsia will dominate the key-point schools, worker offspring will attend ordinary urban schools, and those of peasant stock, handicapped by their out-of-the-way location and their utter lack of influence, will go to village schools.

Whatever its long-term consequences, the establishment of key-point schools has already adversely affected education in the countryside, especially at the upper middle school (senior high school) level. As scarce personnel and material resources have been channeled into upper middle key-point schools in cities and larger towns, the number of classes in commune upper middle schools has been cut back, and some schools have been closed entirely, reducing opportunities for village youth to obtain the Chinese equivalent of a high school diploma. Thirty-one of the thirty-four third-year lower middle school students I taught English to in the spring of 1979 were at work in the fields by the end of that year. Only three did well enough on the difficult entrance examination to be granted admission to the commune upper middle school. This is about average for rural China as a whole, where only about one in every ten lower middle school graduates is able to attend one of the upper middle schools located in commune or county seats. The possibility of going on for further study at a university, college, or advanced technical school following graduation from upper middle school is even more remote. Of the over 100 students of Equality Commune's upper middle school who took the 1979 nationwide college entrance exam, the equivalent of America's SAT, only four successfully passed this hurdle. Since two of these were later disqualified, one for health and the other because he was the son of a former rich peasant, only two of the four were actually able to enroll in college that fall. The rest of the upper middle school graduates of peasant origin were returned to the villages. The odds against even one of the students in my class going on to college were, I calculated, something on the order of fifteen to one. With avenues out of the countryside closed to students, and even commune upper middle school graduates sent back to their native villages upon completion of their schooling, education continues to be a steppingstone to nowhere.

The sharpest blow to rural education has come from an unexpected quarter: the liberalization of agricultural policy by the Deng leadership. To increase agricultural production, peasant families have been allowed to market their private plot produce in free rural markets, engage in handicrafts and other sideline occupations, and lease collective fields on a seasonal or yearly basis. Since these are, unlike collective labor, all activities that children under 16 can participate in, parents have become increasingly reluctant to keep their children in school as they grow older and stronger. The percentage of school-age children in school actually declined in the countryside between 1978 and 1981, especially for children of lower middle school age. The school that I taught at had three classes of first-year students, two classes of second-year students, and only one class of third-year students, reflecting the high attrition rate as children reach their teens.

I received a graphic demonstration of the close connection between rural economics and education one spring day when I went to the fields to watch the planting of the peanut crop. Formerly cultivated collectively, this short-term crop has been given over to cultivation by individual peasant families. The small plots had already been distributed by the time I arrived, and the peasants were bending to their task of preparing the soil for seed with considerable energy and enthusiasm. The borders of the plots were not clearly marked, for the peasants were unwilling to lose even the few inches of earth necessary for demarcation, but their general location was nonetheless unmistakable. Each plot was being worked by a family unit, a father, mother, and anywhere from one to four youngsters, who had been drafted to help with the planting. The classrooms stood empty.

As this example suggests, in agrarian China the transformation from consuming child to producing adult is as simple as quitting school. This decision is made by the family, not by the student as in the West, and it is made with the needs of that larger unit primarily in mind. The point at which children are taken out of school varies from household to household. Wealthier or larger families usually wait until near the end of lower middle school, while poorer families, or those with no older children to help out at home, generally end their childrens' education with graduation from primary school, although even earlier student withdrawals are not uncommon.

Monetary considerations were clearly uppermost in the mind of a neighbor of mine who told me one evening when I stopped by for tea that he had decided that his son was old enough, at 13, to work in the fields. "Books and tuition are expensive," the father began to explain to me. His son's small, dark face remained expressionless. "He's not doing well in school. He has no chance to go on to high school. This way he can help out at home." He paused to take a gulp of tea and then said with finality, "A peasant doesn't need to study a lot of books."

For all its problems, the current emphasis on academic achievement has one undeniable advantage: it provides a solid grounding in the fundamentals. Children who graduate from primary school under the current curriculum will, by dint of drill and memory, have learned basic written Chinese and mathematics, and will have been exposed to the natural sciences. In making formal, factual education again respectable, the program has also won the guarded support of teachers. One primary school principal I came to know well spoke for many of his colleagues when he said, "For the first time in many years we can concentrate on teaching." He went on to say that it was a relief not to have to "slap our own faces" anymore, a reference to Maoist policies that were inimical to formal education and professional teachers. Even the attitude of students, though still a problem, has improved somewhat over the last several years, he pointed out. The result of all this is that much more real learning is accomplished in Chinese rural classrooms than was the case a few years ago.

But while there can be no doubt that the new education is teaching primary school children the three R's, it is also force-feeding older students much knowledge of more questionable value. China can afford to send only a tiny fraction of its middle school students on to college and yet, in an appalling waste of human resources, compels them all to go through the same college-prep curriculum. For the 99 out of 100 rural youth who must return to the collective farm at the end of middle school, learning the calculus and memorizing the periodic table of the elements are cryingly pointless exercises.

I wound up concluding that Deng and Mao were both right: China must have well-educated scientists, technicians, and managers to modernize, but it also needs to enlist the educational system in the effort to improve rural life. The current program sacrifices the interests of peasant and working-class children to those of an educational elite essential to technological progress. Though it can be attacked as unfair, which it blatantly is, it will probably succeed in reaching its goal of spurring China's modernization. The same cannot be said of Mao's experiment. Its egalitarianism lent it a certain superficial attractiveness, but right to the end it remained more sloganized vision than practical program. The destruction of education as an enterprise that it brought about benefited no one, least of all those Mao had set out to equip with useful skills—the peasants.

The extent of Mao's failure was brought home to me one Sunday afternoon during a conversation with a teacher from Sandhead Brigade primary school. She was a professional and demanding taskmaster, like all good teachers very close to many of her students. On that particular afternoon a bright-looking, attractive girl of nineteen, who had been a student of hers during the Cultural Revolution, came calling. We had been talking of the effect of the Maoist innovations on students, and to make her point the teacher gestured at this girl. "Take Ah Ming, for example. She knows absolutely nothing. She went on all the field trips, watched the poor peasants draw pigs on the blackboard, listened to lectures on sugarcane blight, and learned nothing." Here she laughed—and the girl laughed artlessly along with her—before concluding, "She might as well have not gone to school." The girl nodded and, without the slightest embarrassment, seconded what her former teacher had said: "I can't even help my younger brother, in the fourth grade, with his homework."

This peasant girl, living in a rural village, faced with a life of domestic drudgery and field labor, will not be overly handicapped by her intellectual retardation. Equally important, neither she nor her family originally cherished any expectations concerning her education, and all are satisfied that she is at least minimally literate, a claim that neither of her parents can make. But where frustrated dreams and ambitions are present, such a situation takes on the real dimensions of a family tragedy, as I learned one day in conversation with a cadre who held a position of some rank in the light industry department of the provincial government. He had always hoped that his son would be able to continue on to college, especially since he himself had a college degree. From grammar school on, however, the boy's education was repeatedly interrupted by political campaigns. He was in primary school during the worst period of the Cultural Revolution, in junior high school at the time of the Lin Biao affair,* and attended high school at the time of the Gang of Four episode. He received in all only ten years of education, having attended the abbreviated and simplified course of study of the Cultural Revolution, and upon graduation was sent down to the countryside along with millions of other youths to labor as a peasant. His father was able, as an establishment figure of some rank, to arrange for his son's transfer back to Guangzhou after two years. From 1976 to 1979 he supported his son while the young man prepared for the college exams. He bought textbooks imported from Hong Kong and even obtained a tutor for the boy, until recently a practice frowned upon. Despite all this, the boy flunked the entrance exams twice in succession, failing by a wide margin to achieve the minimum passing score. After the second try the father, with a heavy heart, arranged a job for his son, already 24 years old, as a worker in a provincial factory. "My son was not stupid," this cadre told me in an anguished tone of voice. "It was just that he was taught nothing in the schools. The highest grades were always given to those with the correct political thought, and school was frequently canceled or devoted to political meetings. He learned little in ten years of school."

* Lin Biao, who rose to become Mao Zedong's "closest comrade-in-arms" during the early stage of the Cultural Revolution, was behind an abortive plot to assassinate Mao in 1971. Lin died in a plane crash while attempting to flee to the Soviet Union after the plot was discovered.

6

Youth: Coming of Age in the Cultural Revolution

The Red Guards were first deceived and then made use of, turned into cannon fodder only to become scapegoats in the later period [of the Cultural Revolution]. . . . The sending of young students up to the mountains and down to the villages is camouflaged labor reform.

Lin Biao, 1971

It was a muggy midsummer day in Guangzhou, and the beginning of the lichee season. I stopped to buy a catty of the succulent, apricot-sized fruit from a roadside vendor, engaging in the customary mock-serious haggling over the price. I talked him down from 1 *rmb* to 90 *fen*, although I knew if I had been from Hong Kong, I probably could have gotten the fruit for 80 *fen*, and guessed that a local could have shaved the price 5 *fen* or so more.*
As I turned away with my purchase, a young woman, one of the crowd of the curious that the minidrama of my purchase had instantly attracted, spoke to me.

"Your Cantonese is very good. Are you a student?"

"Sort of. I'm in China as part of the cultural exchange program between the U.S. and your country," I replied. After a pause to let her absorb this, I continued lightly, "I'm studying you Chinese."

* There are 100 *fen* in 1 *rmb*.

133

She finds this amusing, and by unspoken agreement we turn away from our little knot of onlookers and begin walking down Liberation Road, talking as we go. She tells me that her name is Zhou Wenfang, that she is the daughter of a cadre, and that she is 21 years old. I had thought she was older, for she is tall for a Cantonese and, though not overweight, is more sturdily built than most. Her heavy black hair, unusual in this city of pigtails and pageboys, falls in loose waves down to her shoulders, attractively framing an oval face with strong, regular features. She wears a simple but nicely tailored blouse and a pair of cream-colored, hip-hugging slacks. She could be a tourist from Hong Kong except for one flaw—plastic sandals, the ubiquitous summer footwear of mainland Chinese women, that stand out in pink and garish contrast to her otherwise faultlessly Western attire. I am the first foreigner that she has ever spoken with, she says exuberantly, but then falls into an embarrassed quiet, evidently struck by the incongruity of our meeting.

After we walk a few steps in silence, I mention an event I heard about that morning from another youthful friend. "Is it true that a dozen people were arrested for dancing recently?"

"Not really for dancing," she answers, relaxing a bit. "About twenty young people went to a restaurant near the Culture Park for dinner. After they finished, they turned up the volume of the tape recorder they had brought along, cleared a space among the tables, and began dancing. The police were called, and arrested them for disturbing the peace and interfering with other people trying to eat. What surprised everyone was that they were detained for nearly two weeks before being released. After all, they had only been having fun."

"In Guizhou," I say, "I saw three couples dancing in a public park to music from a small tape recorder."

"Dancing is not prohibited," she responds. "Recently factories, at least collective-run factories, have begun holding dances sometimes. Of course, they don't let the young people dance the way they want. The only dances permitted are ones where the partners hold hands like the rhumba and the tango. It is strictly forbidden to dance without holding hands. The dances are always held on Saturdays when they won't interfere with the next day's production."

I am reminded of junior high school sock hops that used

to have the same rule about holding hands, but don't want to break into Wenfang's explanation.

"Private parties are strictly forbidden even on Saturday night," she continues, "but they are still held all the time. Someone brings a tape recorder and a few tapes, and they gather in the living room of a friend's house and dance. People are afraid to turn the music up too loud, though, or to dance too vigorously. If the police catch you, they fine the family who lives there 30 *rmb*. This is a pretty steep fine, about a month's pay for most of my friends. Everyone usually chips in a few *renminbi* to pay it. The police say that such activities keep young people up late at night and sap the energy they need for the next day's production. We young people are to 'dedicate our lives to the Four Modernizations,'" she said, mockingly repeating one of the favorite slogans of the current propaganda campaign touting the Four Modernizations. "Work is what is important to the state. They want everyone to eat dinner at 7 P.M. and then go to bed every night by 9."

As nearly as I could judge, most youth in urban China adhere closely to Wenfang's hypothetical schedule, though not out of consideration for the state's production plan. Recreational activities are largely limited to outings and the movies. An outing can be anything from a day-long excursion to a nearby lake or mountain to a simple stroll through a city park in the afternoon. But the buses back to the cities and towns stop running in early evening, city parks tend to close at dusk (reportedly because of problems with overardent lovers and security), and movie theaters let out their last showing usually before 10 P.M. With so little in the way of public entertainment, gathering with a few friends for a party at home seems natural and harmless enough diversion, but private initiative here, as in other areas of Chinese society, is closely restricted. Official disapproval seemed to me counterproductive, though, since the most exciting aspect of these fairly tame get-togethers, according to Wenfang, was the thrill of surreptitiously sharing forbidden fruit. Naturally, dancing is a phenomenon restricted to more worldly-wise urban youth. Most rural youth wouldn't know a two-step from a tango, much less have the social presence to overcome their embarrassment at engaging in any activity in public with a member of the opposite sex.

The Deng regime has an attitude toward pop music that can

be best described as ambivalent—not banning it, as during the Cultural Revolution, but not encouraging it either. There is no homegrown popular music; what passes under this label consists largely of tinnily recorded marches, folk songs, and operatic pieces. The closest thing I saw to a rock group in China was an informal string quartet from the recently rehabilitated Guangdong Provincial Orchestra that got together for jam sessions at home and played pieces by modern composers whose scores had been purchased in Hong Kong and laboriously copied by hand. Even this they considered daring, for, as they never tired of telling me, during the Cultural Revolution "decadent" Western music was outlawed, and many musical instruments were destroyed.

Popular music gets carried in on cassettes from Hong Kong through customs, and once in China, it is rerecorded onto empty cassettes using portable tape players. Demand is so heavy that this retaping is often carried to the point where not only the words but the tune threatens to lose itself in background noise. The most popular tapes are not Western rock stars, who are still relatively unknown in China, but Taiwanese singing stars like Feng Feifei, Qi Yu, and Deng Lijun, whose music the Guizhou park couples I came upon were dancing to. Despite the ideological gulf that separates the mainland from Taiwan., the Beijing authorities may feel less threatened by Deng Lijun's tame and rhythmic love songs than by the anarchic, subversive sounds of a group like the Rolling Stones. Urban youth seem more comfortable with music from Taiwan as well, partly because it is sung in Mandarin. But, suggesting the still vast cultural differences between city and country, even Deng Lijun proved too advanced for some Equality Commune girls that I played her music for. After listening to her tape, they rendered a unanimous verdict: "The music is all right, but we don't understand it." One little miss of 14 then piped up with "We peasants prefer traditional Cantonese opera." And prefer it they did. The Cantonese opera tapes that I had brought to the village with me were constantly being borrowed and retaped by villagers young and old, while my Mandarin music tapes sat untouched on my shelf.

Like music, other dimensions of China's nascent youth culture also vary from city to country and worker to peasant. Whereas in the West, youth of all social backgrounds and educational attain-

ments dress in jeans, listen to rock music, go to see "Raiders of
the Lost Ark," and drink Coke, in China few truly cross-class
symbols of youthful status exist. The low wages of employed
youth, modest or no parental provision for allowances to the unemployed among their number, and an anemic consumer sector
that ignores the young mean that in China there is little on either
the demand or the supply side equivalent to the youth market
in the West. Teenagers and young adults are still more important
in China as producers than as consumers. They have little cash
to spend on soft drinks, cosmetics, and clothes, and there is nothing in the way of products targeted especially at youth available
on the open market. Only the offspring of the privileged and
affluent, those who can travel abroad or have access to the special
elite stores, have been able to adopt the trappings of Western
youth culture. Only in this class will you find girls who regularly
wear make-up and have their hair done, and youth of both sexes
who dress in imported Western clothes instead of the shapeless
jacket and baggy pants of Maoist fame.

At the next level are youth, like Wenfang, whose fathers are
lesser but still important functionaries and who can afford higher-
priced, nonrationed cloth and a private tailor to fashion pants
and shirts with a Western flair (although Wenfang did hers at
home on the family sewing machine). Girls of working-class background who can't manage a whole ensemble will content themselves with a brightly colored blouse with a frill or two on the
sleeves and collar. For them, permanents, at 4 or 5 *rmb* a sitting,
and a face cream ("face frost"), at 2 *rmb* for a 3-ounce jar, are
luxuries to be indulged in only on special occasions.

Peasant girls hope for little more than a plainly cut shirt made
from one of the half a dozen cotton prints on sale in the state
sales store in their village, which resemble the flour-bag patterns
worn by an earlier generation of American women. Young village
women naturally avoid the somber blues, blacks, and olive drabs
of rationed cloth, which they will have to adopt soon enough
upon marriage. The Guangdong peasant girl with her dark skin,
straight hair, and sturdy body outwardly has little in common
with the pale, slender, and permed daughter of a high-ranking
Beijing family.

The lowest common denominator of youth culture is a pair
of sunglasses. In what may be the PRC's first nationwide fad,

youth from Siquan to Shanghai are wearing shades. I have seen
sophisticated Guangzhou youth on evening promenades along
Chongshan Road affecting wraparound shades, and roughhewn
peasant youth on the dusty main street of a remote mountain
market town at noon sporting square-cut sunglasses. Even a poor
peasant youth can save the 2 or 3 *rmb* that the cheapest sunglasses
of heavy black plastic are hawked for at little roadside stands,
and the more affluent can choose among a wide range of tints
and styles carried by department stores in the larger cities which
go for 10 *rmb* or more a pair. They are donned by university
students, factory workers, and commune peasants, and are equally
popular among men and women, although rarely seen on anyone
over 30. Those in the older age brackets shake their heads at
the shuttered youth for blindly worshiping the West. In disdain-
fully referring to them as *jia huaqiao,* or "phony overseas Chinese,"
these critics of the shade craze may have pinpointed its significance.

Consisting of a little subdued pop music, clothes that are
slightly less conservative than their elders, and these ubiquitous
sunglasses, the tangible elements of China's emerging youth culture are as impoverished as the country itself. However unimpres-
sive these faint outer manifestations may seem to those from the
West, they are singularly striking after the ironclad proletarian
conformity of earlier years. But what makes it truly legitimate
to speak of youth in the generic sense is a shared sense of identity
among this generation of Chinese youth, a state of mind that
was forged in the common crucible of the Cultural Revolution.

———————◆———————

The Cultural Revolution was the formative experience of Chinese "Youth." It not only provided the social milieu in which
an entire generation completed their individual transformations
from children to adults but also was the catalyst that created Youth
as a separate span of existence between puberty and maturity.
In the West, Youth as a stage in individual social development
emerged out of the gangling years of late adolescence as a special
estate around the turn of this century. In China, it was not until
the middle sixties with the onset of the Cultural Revolution that
a condition called Youth existed for contemporary Chinese who
were suddenly neither children nor adults.

Unlike previous student movements in China, which had involved only a tiny fraction of the nation's youth, the Cultural Revolution affected nearly all. The only reasonably close parallel in recent American history would be the social convulsion caused by the Vietnam War. But the Vietnam War protests sprang primarily from the college generation, and it was young people from 18 to 28 who marched with placards and pumped their fists in the air. The Chinese Cultural Revolution differed in that it affected nearly all segments of the population. Primary school children held political meetings and "struggled" classmates with questionable family backgrounds, children of junior and senior high school age searched people's homes for Western clothes, books, and other bourgeois contraband, high school students associated with different political factions fought in the streets with clubs and chains, and college students and young workers in some areas graduated to armed clashes. The Cultural Revolution was also of much longer duration than the Vietnam War protests, lasting until 1977 (although the violent phase ended in 1969), so that even adolescents in their early teens have impressions of the turmoil.

They were China's post-civil war generation, probably the largest pack of progeny that prolific China had ever produced, numbering over a hundred million strong. These baby-boomers, like youth everywhere, were instinctive free spirits, empty vessels for the thought of Chairman Mao and willing foot soldiers in his political struggles. To be sure, workers and bureaucrats fought battles in Wuhan, Liaozhou, and other cities in the name of Mao, but it was the young who formed the bulk of his legions, carried the Chairman's standard the highest, aggressively dominated the political stage, and enthusiastically acted out Mao's ambition to establish more than a semblance of communism in China in his own lifetime. The first years of the Cultural Revolution were a kind of children's crusade. But when Mao's children began developing minds of their own and threatened to usurp the stage, Mao quickly acted to rein them in.

In 1969 the army, under Lin Biao's direction and with Mao's connivance, reasserted control, rounding up the most active groups of Red Guards and shipping them off to army farms for what was essentially reeducation through labor. In the years that ensued, as their younger brothers and sisters came of age, they too were sent to the countryside in what by now had been blown into a glorious campaign to purify China's urban youth by sending them to the uncorrupted countryside to learn from the poor and lower middle peasants. China's backwaters, in their turn, were to be enlightened by these graduates of urban lower and upper middle schools, who were optimistically billed as "educated" youth. In the decade after 1968, 17 million young people were rusticated to the countryside. If the first act of the Cultural Revolution had been a vivid, exciting drama of Reds and revolution, the second was a dark still life of young urbanites frozen as peasants.

The regulations that governed the sent-down youth program stated that participation was to be voluntary, but only the semblance of choice was actually maintained in many cases. According to one young woman who had graduated from upper middle school in 1971, at the school she had attended the process resembled conscription more than recruitment. After several days of meetings at which participation in the down-to-the-countryside movement was represented as every student's obligation to Chairman Mao, the Party, and socialism, application forms were passed out to the assembled students. "The school Party secretary told everyone to write down that they wanted to respond to Chairman Mao's call to go down to the countryside, learn from the poor and lower middle peasants, and participate in socialist construction," she recalled. "He even wrote it out on the blackboard." Most students complied, especially during the opening stages of the program. For those who didn't, a powerful net of coercion and control was cast about them and drawn ever tighter. At school, they were pressured by ardent Communist Youth League activists who stressed their socialist obligations, and were required to attend arm-twisting sessions where they were told that they would not be assigned jobs in the city and so would have no future there. Their parents were spoken to by Party cadres at work about their children's "backwardness" and received visits at home from members of the local neighborhood committee and the police, who intimated that the child's household registration would be transferred to the countryside upon graduation regardless of whether he agreed to go or not and that his ration coupons would then stop. In later years even these measures, severe though they were, proved insufficient to exact obedience as stories of the hardships that early groups of youth had encountered in the country-side began to circulate in the cities.

The transition from school to work is a difficult one for adolescents to make under the best of circumstances, since it occurs for most when they are not yet physically or emotionally mature, but it is hard to imagine worse conditions under which to grow up than those that the sent-down youth of China were plunged headlong into. Early waves of youth beached on the distant shores of Xinjiang (Sinkiang), Dongbei (Manchuria), Inner Mongolia, Qinghai, and Ningxia, grim and inhospitable places that had not been settled in earlier times by the Han Chinese, despite the Malthusian press of population growth that had wedged them into every other colonizable geographical niche, because their climate was too extreme, too dry or too wet, too hot or too cold, or their soil was too poor or too rocky. Even the arid deserts of Xinjiang could have been farmed with sufficient capital investment and technological ingenuity, but colonies of cast-off youth were set down in this wilderness with little more than encouragement, base rations, and the resources of their own numbers. Even today, a dozen years after their founding, many of the camps still scrabble out of the desert barely enough for their own provisions.

As the decade wore on, the destinations of sent-down youth were neither army camps nor isolated settlements, but rural collectives in China proper. Here the newly minted "peasants" faced a shock almost cultural in depth. Not only were they unaccustomed to the daily grind of manual labor, the poor living conditions, and the skimpy diet of rural China; they additionally had to learn a local dialect and adjust to peasant conservatism and social traditions. Patient counseling could have reduced the trauma, but this was not forthcoming. There was nothing to prepare the youth for their sudden transformation from urban students to rural farm hands. The only meetings that were held before their departure stressed their political role in the countryside, not practical problems of adjustment. One day they were simply trucked out to the countryside. The next their initiation into fieldwork began.

Work is what forges the man from the boy. Ideally it admits him to a social circle, linking him closely with not only his peers but also people of other ages and ranks; it gives him an economic role in the community, which grows more important with time, and it allows him to achieve financial independence, which is the anchor of his self-respect and the precondition to setting up his own household. Work in the countryside as a sent-down youth fell disastrously short of this ideal. The students left the cities with fanfare and were greeted in the villages with silence. The abstract entity entitled the "poor and lower middle peasant" that they had been told they were to learn from often proved disappointing in the flesh. They saw the peasants as conservative, provincial, superstitious, and uncultured. The peasants, taken aback by the abrasive mannerisms and strange ideas of these urban youth, viewed them with suspicion. Although the youth had been told that their assignment was for life, they regarded themselves not as members of the community, but as temporary sojourners, an attitude that was shared by the villagers and strengthened by the young peoples' living usually not with village families, but in hastily erected huts with their own kind.

Their social marginality was also a matter of economics. The short stints of manual labor that many urban students had done in school factories and farms had hardly prepared them for the rigors of rural life. Physically immature youngsters toiled alongside hardened peasants—and found that they could not keep up with the pace of work. "When the educated youth first arrived, they were just children," a cadre in Guangdong Province who had worked with the youth told me. "They were only fifteen or so, so homesick that they would cry themselves to sleep at night. They had little strength or experience. We collective cadres had to make special arrangements for them. We gave them light tasks that even they could do, such as tending water buffalo or herding ducks and geese. These are jobs that are normally reserved for peasant children younger than the educated youth. A lot of cadres complained. We had to treat them like little treasures."

But it was not just the coddling that the youngsters had to be given that the peasants in general resented, but the drain they represented on community resources. Production teams soon discovered that it cost more to keep these outsiders minimally housed, clothed, fed, and healthy than their labor was worth. This meant that at the year-end accounting many youth were in debt to the team, having drawn more in the way of grain, other crops, and cash from the team than they had coming to them. Remittances from parents made up the difference for some youth; the annual bonuses and extra rations of cloth that they later began to receive from the central government, which was trying to contain peasant and parental resistance to the program, helped others. But the debts of not a few had to be carried year after year by the production team that they had been assigned to.

As "educated" youth, they had been told that they could make important contributions to socialist construction in the countryside. In truly backward areas, some of the high school graduates may have contributed to the community they joined by serving as elementary school teachers, barefoot doctors, and team accountants. In regions with substantial minority populations their presence in positions of responsibility would have further sinicized tribal minorities and thus brought them closer to Beijing's orbit. But the Chinese heartland had little use for their services, and the youth in turn were too busy just staying alive to contribute much. One young woman from the city of Kunming spent six years in the southern hills of Yunnan in a village whose sole water supply was a stream a mile and a half away. One of her daily tasks was to trek to the stream and fetch two wooden buckets of water back to her hut. One she would use for cooking. The other was for her sponge bath, a daily necessity in that tropical area. It was an exercise in water conservation. She would first use the water to wash and rinse her head and hair, then scrub down her body and reuse the water a second time to rinse off; finally she would recycle the now murky water again to clean her feet. It then went to the pigs. She recalled life in the village as an endless round of like chores.

As the youth matured, some began to pull their own weight, but to the end few had the means to marry, even as they reached their middle twenties. Their presence came to be grudgingly accepted by the villagers, but their generally low labor ability, unmarried status, and urban ways prevented them from ever earning their respect.

Most youth came to regard this banishment from their urban birthplace to some impoverished backwater to work as a peasant with the same horror that an American youth would feel if ordered into lifetime service as a bracero, and never ceased hoping that they would one day be reassigned to the city. The fortunate were able to manipulate family connections to arrange an urban transfer and employment within a year or two after they arrived in the countryside. Others, as their rural internment lengthened, despaired of waiting and took matters into their own hands. Some, especially in Guangdong, attempted to escape to Hong Kong. Others made their way back to their urban birthplace and took up residence illegally, even though this meant trying to live without a job or rice ration. A third group obtained a transfer back to the city by bribing local cadres into approving their release, which allowed them to transfer their household registration legally back to the city, so that they could qualify for employment and ration coupons.

My initial doubts about the feasibility of this last course were laid to rest by a Beijing youth who used his own case by way of example. He had originally been assigned in 1972 as a sent-down youth to a brigade in the old Communist base area near Yanan in China's northwest. By 1979, not only had the youth he had come with long since departed; even those who arrived as late as 1975–76 had managed to return to Beijing, many of them by paying off brigade and commune cadres. He finally wrote in desperation to his none too well-off family for a loan of 300 *rmb*, the best part of a year's income, and set about making liberal dispensations to local cadres. The first 50 *rmb* went to the brigade Party secretary, who then interceded on his behalf with the commune cadre in charge of educated youth: "Ah Guo has been with us for nine years. He has worked hard during this time and learned much from the poor and lower middle peasants. Is it possible to arrange for his transfer back to Beijing?"

"This question requires research," the commune cadre had replied indifferently, using the Chinese code word for a polite refusal. Any request that needs research is dead, or at least dormant. But that night Ah Guo went to plead his case personally to the commune cadre with several cartons of cigarettes and a bottle of liquor, and received a sympathetic audience. "This thing that you want is possible," he was told, "but the process will still be a very difficult one." Nevertheless, they quickly came to an agreement. Two nights later, Ah Guo delivered a red envelop containing 75 *rmb* to the cadre, who handed him a document stating that he, Ah Guo, had served the poor and lower middle peasants well and was being transferred back to Beijing to care for aging parents. He was instructed to get the brigade to stamp his papers and then go directly to the county United Front Office responsible for sent-down youth. "You have no papers from Beijing, but I think that you can nevertheless persuade the responsible comrade," the commune cadre told Ah Guo, repeating the word "persuade" twice as the Chinese do for emphasis.

Ah Guo packed his few belongings and the next morning caught a bus into the county seat. He first tried a direct assault on the United Front Office, but this was easily repulsed by a bored clerk: "We can't let you go. You have no supporting documents from Beijing to prove that you have elderly parents to support." He nevertheless took Ah Guo's release papers, worth 140 *rmb*, for "research." Undaunted, Ah Guo spent the rest of the afternoon purchasing the favored gifts of Kaoliang and East Wind cigarettes, and that evening paid a call on the cadre in charge of the United Front Office. This man proved intractable. Not only was he unmoved by Ah Guo's modest prestations, but he actually managed to sound indignant over his efforts to return to the city. "How can we release you?" he asked Ah Guo. "The commune was incorrect in releasing you. This is in violation of the spirit of the regulations governing the sent-down youth program." He insinuated that Ah Guo's proper place was to stay and continue to learn from the poor and lower middle peasants.

Despair engulfed Ah Guo. "Why am I so ill-fated as to encounter one of the few cadres who isn't willing to bend the rules?" he thought to himself, and made to go. "Of course," the cadre continued, beckoning him to remain seated, "I can understand your desire to 'develop.' You want to go back to the city and a good factory job. You want to get married, have children, and buy a TV set, a bicycle, and a tape recorder." Smiling at Ah Guo, he added, "I sympathize. I would like to own a tape recorder myself."

Ah Guo was jolted out of his gloom by the cadre's comment but remained perplexed. "A tape recorder," he thought to himself. "Where can I find a 'ghost' tape recorder in the hills of Shensi? And even if I could find one, it would cost at least 200 *rmb*, and I only have 160 *rmb* left." He decided to simply give the cadre his remaining cash immediately, keeping aside only 20 *rmb* for his train fare. He discreetly placed the envelop containing the cash on the tea table and left.

The next night, he again visited the cadre. "Why didn't you come earlier?" the cadre said to him, offering him a cigarette and a glass of Kaoliang almost simultaneously. "I was hoping to invite you for dinner." He affected the mock-scolding manner that Chinese reserve for those whom they want to convince of their sincerity. Ah Guo knew then that he had probably given about 50 *rmb* too much, but consoled himself with the thought that he would soon be on his way back home. He arrived in Beijing a week later, release papers in hand, and had no difficulty reregistering at the police station two blocks from his home. He told me that in order to return as a bona fide resident of Beijing, he had in all spent 320 *rmb*, a sum that it had taken him over a year to earn back. When I raised an eyebrow, Ah Guo insisted that his case was by no means unusual. "A lot of my friends bought their way back to Beijing," he said. "It cost many of them even more than it did me."

Most of the educated youth had been released from their rural purgatory by 1980, and the "up to the mountains, down to the villages" program had been put on ice by the Dengists, but not before the tripartite experience of the Cultural Revolution—marching in the streets as Red Guards, work in the countryside as sent-down youth, and the final ignominious return to the city—had made a profound impression on this generation of Chinese youth.

Mao had consciously set out to create a generation of revolutionary successors, imagining youth (and nearly everyone for that matter) to be so many "blank sheets" on which his "thought" could be indelibly etched. Perhaps the act of becoming a Red Guard temporarily ended the search for identity by substituting a prefabricated one, but over the longer run, Mao's encouragement of youthful revolt had the unplanned and paradoxical consequence of creating solidarity among agemates, which was further strengthened when they were sent down together to the countryside. There, during long hours stooped over transplanting rice seedlings and while sitting around on dull village evenings, the youth had time to work out where they stood in the Maoist scheme of things.

It had been made clear to them that Mao, who had earlier wanted them to become revolutionaries, had now decided that they were to become peasants. But they found their new role as apprentices to the poor peasants hard to reconcile with their recent past, when they had been heralded as the pioneers of a new world. From contemplating the great issues of revolution and liberation, struggle and death, faith and despair, they fell to the lower plane of a daily struggle for existence. It was not primarily the hard work, the Tobacco Road dreariness, of rural existence that they couldn't accept, though, but this as the sum total of their future. As a limited, transitory stage they would have endured it; as a permanent way of life it was intolerable. However glorious this role was made to sound in slogans, in fact it came to appear to many youth as nothing more than a modern-day version of the traditional punishment meted out to dissenters: banishment to distant and backward regions of the Celestial Empire. With the easily aroused guilt of youth they discussed among themselves what they had done wrong, and questioned where they had failed. They did not lose their confidence in Mao in a sudden flood of disillusionment, but gradually, through an imperceptible erosion, the way beaches disappear. Lin Biao spoke for many when he wrote, "The Red Guards were first deceived and then made use of, turned into cannon fodder only to become scapegoats in the later period [of the Cultural Revolution]. . . . The sending of young students up to the mountains and down to the villages is camouflaged labor reform."* Or as one bespectacled youth, a former Red Guard who spent six years as a sent-down youth, put it more succinctly, "Mao betrayed us." This generation of Chinese did not have an easy time growing up, but, with the resilience of the young, grow up it did. Out of its collective experience was born Youth, not as a special and privileged stage of life as in the West, but as a bitter and disadvantaged one.

Beginning in 1977, because of the continued resistance of the youth and the dissatisfaction of the peasants, the Party rescinded mandatory rustification for recent graduates and, within two years, repatriated most of the sent-down youth already in the countryside back to the cities. While the program remains formally in force, it has in fact been all but discontinued. The end of the Cultural Revolution (now put at 1978, when the last

---

* Quoted from the famous "571 Engineering" plan concocted by Lin Biao and his son in 1971, when Lin Biao was still Mao's designated successor, for the overthrow of Mao Zedong. An edited version of the plan can be found in Dick Wilson, *Mao: The People's Emperor* (London: Hutchinson & Co., 1979), pp. 429–30.

of the leftists were finally ousted) and the down-to-the-countryside program marked a watershed of sorts for urban Chinese youth, who are now allowed to stay in their home towns. But while solving one set of problems, this has exacerbated another.

The rustification program had reduced urban unemployment during the years it was in force, but now with the return of millions of youth the problem became worse than ever. Not only did work assignments have to be found for the normal annual complements of middle school graduates, but the flood of returnees also had to be somehow occupied. Only a tiny fraction of the returned youth and recent graduates were able to continue on for a university education; most hoped to find gainful employment in a state enterprise or office.

Beijing has long experienced difficulties in putting its youth to work, although it has never revealed the exact dimensions of unemployment. Not only does Beijing not publish statistics on the jobless rate, but also the Chinese characteristically refuse to admit that their economy has come down with the "capitalist disease." In China, idle youth are not said to be unemployed, merely "waiting for job assignments." In spite of official stonewalling, a sense of the overall dimensions of the problem may be factored out of official reports. The *People's Daily* reported in a 1981 article on the population problem that from 1957 to 1979 an average of 3.25 million persons a year had been employed in nonagricultural positions in state-run industry and government. But this accomplishment pales before the sheer number of youth coming of age each year, which an article in the 1981 *Liaoning University Journal* gave as 17 million for 1977, and 25 million a year from 1978 to 1981, for a five-year total of 117 million. Assuming that 85 percent of this number were employeed in agriculture, there were still 17.5 million youth lining up for state employment during this period. The state would have had to place 3.5 million youth in jobs each year, or well over the average of 3.25 million, just to avoid rising unemployment in this group. But even this would not have solved the jobless problem, for to the five-year figure of 17.5 million must be added an additional number of youth returned from the countryside, perhaps as many as 10 million in all. Even optimistically assuming that the state provided work for half of the returnees, there would still be 5 million able-bodied youth out of work, or perhaps 5 percent of the urban labor force.

While not high by the standards of the industrialized West, such a jobless rate is catastrophic for a country with a socialist economic system. Unemployment of such magnitude is unprecedented for post-civil war China, where the government has generally preferred to pad work rosters. This panacea has been attacked by Deng, however, who is determined to shake down the inefficient economy he inherited and increase both production and worker productivity. As a consequence, the problem of unemployment, which had already reached worrisome proportions by the late seventies, shows no sign of abating in the eighties.

As in the West, youth between the ages of 18 and 25 bear the brunt of the unemployment plague. The problem has become so severe that Beijing has taken the ideologically distasteful step of allowing, even encouraging, youth to become self-supporting. Returned youth can be seen selling Popsicles in front of factory gates, hawking peanuts and pastries in city parks, and manning small noodle stands and mobile bicycle repair shops along the main streets of market towns. The more enterprising have organized small collective industries in their neighborhood manufacturing an assortment of toys and trinkets, catering to consumer demands that the revolution, engaged in the vastly more important task of socialist construction, has disregarded. Except for the occasional success story, such odd jobs, while staving off absolute penury, are hardly sufficient to achieve economic independence. Without a unit to provide housing, most of these youth can only continue to live with their parents; without the prestige, security, and other benefits, of government employment, many have difficulty finding a spouse. And in any event the hundreds of thousands of youth who are self-employed are but a fraction of the jobless.

Although job assignments, when they finally come through, are "iron rice bowls" carrying life-long tenure, the wait can be excruciatingly long. While only 13 percent of the unemployed in the U.S. are between jobs for more than six months, youth told me that middle school graduates are often idle for a year or more after leaving school and that many reurbanized youths are still unemployed after three years in the cities. Neither do those "waiting for a job assignment" receive a cushion of unemployment assistance to tide them over their vigil. Such benefits are unknown in socialist China, where families are expected to assume the burden of supporting a jobless youth, although he does continue to receive his regular ration coupons from the state.

Since in most families both parents work, jobless youth can and do make a contribution of sorts to the domestic economy. Wenfang did all of the shopping and cooking for her father, mother, and older brother, and I met other youth who carried the full load of housework. But most families cannot afford indefinitely to feed an extra mouth and provide pocket money. While a bus ride costs only 5 *fen* and the movies only 20 *fen*, over time even these paltry sums can mount up to strain domestic finances.

Financial strains there may be, but there is no question that the family not only will continue to support a youth indefinitely but will also accept his situation. No parental tempers flare over his idleness, for everyone, including the youth, knows that the matter of his employment is largely out of his control, and he is seen as a victim of the system. Still, he cannot help but rue the drain on the family resources that his joblessness entails. He feels unworthy because he is without the means to express his deeply felt obligation to his parents for having brought him up, for in China filiality is still measured mostly in *renminbi*.

As their period of enforced and enervating idleness lengthens, the young are by stages discouraged, dispirited, demoralized, and finally alienated. The strains that this puts on the fabric of urban society are familiar. Alcoholism has increased, even though by Chinese standards there is no such thing as a cheap drunk, and urban vandalism and crime have risen sharply as youth have vented their frustrations and sought an income by other means. Perhaps most troubling to the regime, increasing numbers of youth are questioning the superiority of socialism on the irrefutable grounds that their joblessness has debunked its claim to provide social justice through full employment.

The work assignment that finally comes down does not necessarily spell the end of the youth's discontent, for it will be made almost solely on the basis of the state's need. Not only will little account be taken of the youth's interests; even the effort to match skills to available jobs that will be made in placing graduates of high schools is usually minimal. A waitress in the new cafe attached to the Dongfang Hotel countered my comment that her work in an air-conditioned, nicely decorated, slowly paced environment was attractive by saying shortly, "It was not what I wanted." Without prompting, she went on to tell me that "I have always wanted to be a nurse. When I was in the countryside as a sent-down youth, I served for seven years as a barefoot doctor. I would have taken anything in the medical field, but they said that there was nothing open and sent me here instead. They told me I had no choice. The work is easy enough here," she shrugged, "but it is meaningless."

As the waitress's case suggests, if the proffered position is even marginally acceptable, the young person will resignedly accept it, for not only is it difficult to reject a work assignment, but the attempt to do so can mean another period of idleness as long as or even longer than the one he or she just endured. Wenfang told me that she had received orders to report to work at a neighborhood-run sewing collective six months after she graduated from high school at 18 but had turned the work down, telling the state employment office that she would wait for an opening at a state unit. She was still waiting three years later.

Outwardly at least, rural China has less of a problem with employment. Anyone who reaches his sixteenth birthday can brush the characters of his name on a tablespoon-sized tag of wood and hang it up on the work assignment board of the team that his family belongs to, thereby obligating the team head to find work for him to do. Yet for many youth, work as a field hand is so unattractive that they participate in collective labor only with the greatest reluctance, preferring to do odd jobs at home and wait for their "chance"—an opening in a commune or collective enterprise. Among these are graduates of the commune senior high school and PLA dischargees, who generally regard fieldwork as beneath their status as "educated" youth and "Liberation Army" men. Provision for nonagricultural work is made for some, but many are simply returned to their villages. Altogether, there are several dozen youth in Sandhead Brigade who for these various reasons have been unemployed for up to five years, including the former head of the commune high school's Communist Youth League (CYL) branch, who graduated from high school in 1975.

These long spans of frustrating though voluntary unemployment have predictable consequences. Three of these idle youth, including the former CYL branch secretary, were apprehended by the brigade police in early 1981 as they were poaching fish from collectively owned ponds. Each was forthwith fined 50 *rmb* by the police chief, and all three were held at the security defense committee headquarters until their families had paid the fine and they themselves had produced an acceptable written confession of wrongdoing.

All things considered, the crime rate among youth is still much lower in the countryside than in the cities because even the very young understand that antisocial acts are freighted with social consequences in the compact world of the village. For this reason, offenses are commonly committed against property rather than persons, and most often property that is public rather than personal. Another factor holding down rural crime committed by youth is that even the most rambunctious youngsters suddenly find themselves saddled with grown-up responsibilities at the age of 16 when most begin work. After a punishing day of such activities as spreading buckets of mud weighing 50 pounds each over mulberry fields as fertilizer, few have the reservoirs of restless adolescent energy that lead to serious delinquency.

The one potentially violent crime that happened to me in China smacked more of youthful high jinks than deliberate violence. I was driving the road toward the famed resort city of Guilin, having spelled my driver at dusk for the last three-hour stretch into the city. Night had come quickly. About an hour outside of Guilin, a trailer parked on the right-hand side of the road came into the sweep of my headlights. In a moment we were up to it. I had caught a sense of vague, shadowy motion behind the trailer, so I gave it a wide berth, swinging far to the left. All at once, the night exploded. The road lit up momentarily as if a flare had been fired, and I heard a heavy whomp next to my ear. Etched on my retina was the image of a group of men, six in all, who had been standing in the lee of the trailer. I instinctively hit the brakes, but my driver yelled at me not to stop.

"What in the son of a turtle's egg was that?" I shouted, lapsing into the vernacular.

My driver, looking as grim as I was shaken, explained that groups of youth frequently lurk on the edges of roads at night and throw bottles, rocks, and homemade cannon crackers at passing trucks. "It's just a game with them," he said. "They do it because they're bored."

"But they could have broken our windshield," I gulped, still shaken.

"If they just break your windshield or dent your fender, you can consider yourself fortunate. What we drivers really worry about is taking a shot in the head and having a possibly fatal crash. That's why most drivers keep their windows rolled up even on stuffy nights."

I quietly rolled my window up.

Trucks are inviting targets for casual vandalism, my driver went on to explain. There can be no reprisals from the driver, who, outnumbered five or ten to one, can only curse and continue on his way. But there was more to the matter than just opportunity, for I had learned in conversations with country youth that the very mobility of drivers aroused envy. To illustrate his point, one youth repeated to me the jingle *Zhongguo zhiye you san bao, siji, yisheng, zhuroulao,* which literally means, "There are three guaranteed occupations in China—driver, doctor, and butcher." "A butcher gets all the meat he can eat," the youth explained, "a doctor gets free medical treatment, and a driver gets to travel all over." A driver's license is a kind of internal passport, for with it one can travel across provincial boundaries, visit areas where there are no rail or bus connections, and check into hotel rooms throughout China without the travel permit otherwise necessary. Truck drivers represent the freedom and opportunity that sedentary rural youth yearn for, the chance to go to the cities, to travel without restrictions, and the chance to work with machinery instead of their bare hands. This contrast fuels the resentment that occasionally ignites in rock-throwing incidents.

For the most part, though, this resentment over their rural lot does not ignite into crime or violence, but smolders quietly, evident only in a certain grim hopelessness and fatalism that seems incongruous in those so young.

When I asked Ah Ming, a 19-year-old Sandhead girl with a demure manner and chocolate almond eyes, about her future and her ideals, I was astonished at the vehemence of her reply. "What future? What ideals?" The words rushed out, her eyes growing hard. "Ideals, aims, and ambitions are like shadow bubbles. All the time I am hard at work, laboring from morning to night. What can I do? As we Chinese say, I submit to my fate [*ting tian you ming*]. In the beginning my breast was full of eagerness to participate in labor. But the numerous bad aspects of this society, without my willing it, made my red-hot ardor grow cold.

Where is the youth who doesn't have ambition? Where is the youth who doesn't have aims? You want to fly, but it's hard to fly; you want to leave, but it's hard to leave. It is like a healthy person suddenly going blind. They don't let you know anything. In fact, the will of the people doesn't change anything. All we can do is go silently along with the push of fate."

"Life is really very frightening," she continued despondently. "It is true that no one in this world is ever able to do everything that he wants. But whether the life of a person imprisoned in a cage is bitter or sweet is obvious, isn't it? There seems no way out of this bizarre place. I have thought several times about escaping to Hong Kong, but each time I give the idea up. I think, 'I am a girl. How could I bear the difficulties I would encounter?' " Ah Ming was unusual only in her eloquence and candor, for I heard numerous other rural youth echo the same sentiments of political alienation and personal anomie.

Since the overthrow of the Gang of Four, young villagers in large numbers have also reached Ah Ming's conclusion that they should attempt to reach Hong Kong or Macao. In Sandhead Brigade alone, nineteen villagers tried to escape to Hong Kong in 1979. In the first nine months of 1980 this human wave gathered further momentum, and over thirty attempts were made. With a tenacity that would have made Horatio Alger proud, some youngsters who did not at first succeed continued to try again. The brigade record for escapes is held by a gutsy youth who has four attempts, two by land and two by sea, to his credit. He is currently serving a six-month sentence in the county detention camp, where he is said by villagers to be plotting attempt number five.

But the recent upsurge in escape attempts does not merely represent the action of a disgruntled few. By 1978 the desire to emigrate had become widespread among the young. During the winter of that year, the colonial government of Macao announced that substantial numbers of mainland Chinese would be allowed to immigrate. The reaction of rural Chinese was immediate and strong. In Sandhead, more than 800 people—10 percent of the local population—applied at the local level (though only fourteen people were in the end allowed to immigrate by Macao authorities). Since the applicants were mostly young peasants between the ages of 16 and 30, this means that slightly over half of Sandhead's youth opted for emigration.

That more would-be migrants don't actually act on their ambitions and make their way to Macao or Hong Kong on their own is a consequence of the difficulties of the crossing, which are formidable. The flood of refugees in recent years has led the authorities to increase border patrols, and to assign regular army units to comb areas formerly the responsibility of the local people's militia. Hu Sheng, whose close-cropped hair bears witness to his recent stint in a labor camp, told me how his escape attempt ended with him in the hands of the People's Liberation Army. There had been four of them in on the attempt, Hu Sheng himself and three others, all born and raised in the small peasant community of Shangli, all young men in their early twenties and unmarried, and all "know-heart friends," as the Chinese call intimates. They had made plans and preparations throughout the winter of 1979, gathering intelligence from the unsuccessful about possible routes and crossing points, and sewing small canvas knapsacks and purchasing army surplus canteens for the hard biscuits and portable water they would need on the way. They were ready by February, but a snap of cold weather led them to postpone their attempt for several weeks. Finally, on a balmy day in late March, the four youths began their short odyssey by catching the early bus into Guangzhou. There they purchased train tickets to Zhangmutou, 40 kilometers away from the Hong Kong border and the last station on the Guangzhou-Kowloon line where they could disembark unmonitored. They arrived at Zhangmutou in the early evening and, after dinner, struck off southward under the cover of darkness toward the mouth of the Pearl River. Avoiding the roads and rail line, by dawn they had penetrated well into the 13-mile restricted border area. They slept in the thick hillside underbrush during the following day, taking turns standing watch. At dusk they set out again, hoping to cross over the border that night. A heavy cloud cover made it difficult to find their way, though, and by daybreak they were still several kilometers short of the border. Their venture ended two hours later when they were apprehended by one of the many army patrols that constantly sweep the border hills.

They were held at the border region for three days before being returned to their county seat for sentencing by the local people's court. They were first confined in the county detention center, but after their three-month sentence was handed down, they were transferred to the more pleasant surroundings of a commune-run labor camp. Hu Sheng told me that originally there had been only one detention center in the county, but that by 1978 the number of prisoners had so outstripped the capacities of this facility that the county had ordered its constituent communes to set up their own labor camps to cope with the overflow. The increase in numbers came primarily from youths captured during escape attempts and the lengthening of the minimum sentence for such attempts from three days to one month, according to Hu Sheng. By 1980 this Gulag Archipelago in miniature held nearly 1,000 prisoners, of whom 300 were in the county center and the rest distributed among the ten commune-run camps. Hu Sheng pronounced the county detention center to be overcrowded and unsanitary, describing in bleak terms how everyone slept on the concrete floor because there were no beds, and how sanitation facilities for several dozen inmates consisted of a single chamber pot placed in a corner of each large open cell. In contrast to these bleak conditions, commune camps had plank beds and outside toilets. But the main advantage of the commune camp, to hear Hu Sheng tell it, was that the rice rations were adequate. Prisoners held in the county camp, he told me, receive only two bowls of rice a day and are continually faint with hunger. Food is so scarce that cooperation gives way to selfishness. Food packages brought by families for imprisoned members often cause conflicts as ravenous inmates struggle for a share of the spoils. Compared with this surly selfishness, relations in the commune camps are cooperative and cordial.

Hu Sheng and his companions spent their time in the camp laboring in the commune orchards, doing work not unlike that they had done all their lives, and time passed swiftly. They completed their sentences in June 1980 and were released into the custody of their brigade's security defense committee (zhibao hui). There matters ended. Brigade authorities levied no fines, imposed no extra labor, and required no self-criticism sessions, not even for the two youth in the group who were Communist Youth League members, but simply allowed them all to return at once to Shangli. There neighbors and friends applauded them for their effort and commiserated with their failure. Hu Sheng himself said straight out to anyone who would listen that he did not regret their attempted escape, only that they had been captured. He shrugged off his period of confinement at hard labor by saying, "As peasants, we have to work hard everyday anyway, and mostly have only rice to eat. What is so hard about conditions in the labor camps? Besides, even if you are caught, you only have to spend a few months at hard labor. If you succeed, you have a lifetime of good fortune [*fu qi*]." But most surprising to me was the reaction of a senior brigade official, a man with twenty-five years of service as a Party member and cadre. "If I were young, I would try to escape to Hong Kong myself," he told me as we discussed this problem, "but now I would go only if I could do so legally."

In other brigades, the youths' ordeal does not end with their return; instead they are often punished a second time for the same escape. In New China Brigade, this double jeopardy takes the form of corrective labor, self-criticism, and fines. The security defense committee assigns returnees to perform day labor with the brigade under its supervision for a period of time ranging from one day to two weeks depending on how long they have been absent from the brigade. The committee also holds self-criticism sessions where the would-be escapees atone for their crime by making oral and written confession. The latter is a particularly trying experience for village youth, but only because some find it hard to articulate their thoughts in writing, not because of abstract questions of conscience. The less adroit often agonize through several drafts before they can admit their wrongdoing in writing clearly and coherently enough to satisfy the local police chief.

Even more intimidating to New China Brigade peasants is the 2-*rmb*-a-day fine that is imposed on the families of those absent from the brigade without permission. Starting from the day a youth disappears, this fine continues to mount until the day that (1) the youth returns to the brigade, which means that it continues to accrue while he is incarcerated, or (2) the family receives word, usually by telegram, that the youth is safely ensconced in Hong Kong. Failure is the more common outcome by far, and in this case the family goes into debt to the brigade for sums ranging from 60 to 300 *rmb*. This amount, which will take months or years of privation to repay, constitutes a kind of criminal value-added tax on the sentence decreed by the county court.

As unfair as all this seems, since the youth are in effect being punished twice for the same infraction, things were even worse in the recent past. Brigades formerly ran their own labor camps, where those judged guilty of some crime—besides attempted escape the most common were theft and gambling—by the security defense committee were imprisoned for up to a month or more, performing forced labor during the day and attending mandatory self-criticism sessions in the evenings according to a fixed schedule. A former prisoner recalled that he and others were frequently harassed by camp guards (that is, committee members), who threatened to "break the rice bowls" (cut off the rations) of lagging workers. "Don't think that we'll still let you eat if you don't do more work," he was told. It was only in 1978 that brigades were told to abolish these little penal colonies, and even now they retain the authority to assign day labor without pay to those they judge to be miscreants.

The majority of brigades follow the government in treating successful escapees as Hong Kong residents rather than local criminals. The prevailing attitude was summed up by a Southsand Brigade official. "The way we see it here," he said, "if you have enough ability to escape, then good for you." Other brigades are not so magnanimous, and have on their own authority imposed sanctions. For those whose native villages have marked them for retribution, a successful escape not only brings the longed-for beginning of a new life but less happily marks the beginning of a lengthy period of exile.

Until recently, young New China Brigade members who had escaped to Macao and Hong Kong were afraid to return for fear that they would be forced to stay on in the brigade. At least twice in the late seventies, the security defense committee had confiscated and destroyed the Hong Kong identity cards of visitors, making it impossible for them to leave China. In late 1979, New China Brigade expatriates in Hong Kong decided that their effective exile from their home village was intolerable and sent an emissary, chosen because he had a brother on the security defense committee who had guaranteed his safe passage, back to the brigade with an offer: if the brigade would affirm their right to return to the village on visits and pledge to stop persecuting their families on account of their escape, they would present the brigade with a new 2½-ton truck. The Party secretary agreed to these terms, and the bargain was struck. A month later, all thirteen of the brigade cadres in high spirits made the day's journey down to the border town of Shenzhen to take possession of the truck and receive their eight expatriate benefactors. The following day, the expatriates, with a twist on the prodigal-son story, celebrated their return with a forty-table feast for relatives, friends, and the guests of honor, the baker's dozen of brigade cadres. Since that time, other illegal emigrants have returned home to New China Brigade with no ill effects.

Escape rates continued to rise over the period 1978–80 despite beefed-up border patrols and overlapping punishments levied by state and village, despite China's mobilization to modernize and new liberal policies in agriculture, and despite—this was the most puzzling of all to me—improving living conditions. From 1978 to 1980, as a result of a production incentive program, family incomes from the collective increased 30 percent in Sandhead Brigade and achieved comparable gains in other delta brigades.

This was anomalous because in the sixties and early seventies the escape rate was a kind of "misery index," mirroring how well or poorly the regime was meeting basic subsistence needs. When conditions worsened, people risked escape; when conditions improved, people stayed put. The escape rate rose during the "three difficult years" of economic belt-tightening which followed the Great Leap Forward and fell thereafter. Escape attempts reached an unprecedented high in 1971–72 as leftists pushed an agricultural policy—"Learn from Dazhai"*—which they hoped would further communize the countryside but which in fact led living standards to drop precipitously because its nondiscriminating egalitarianism undermined peasant incentive to work. As this policy was gradually eased from 1973 to 1977, earlier in Sandhead than elsewhere, incomes rose, peasant diets improved, and the number of youth endeavoring to escape decreased. In Sandhead no attempts were made at all from 1975 to 1977, a striking turnabout from the earlier situation. But in 1978, the pendulum began

* The movement was named after a small, impoverished production brigade in the Chinese northwest, at the time much vaunted for its collective spirit.

inexplicably to swing back. Despite gradually improving conditions, which had previously served to dampen the escape rate,
the number of attempts soared.

The living standards of Hong Kong residents have increased
at a much faster rate than those of mainland peasants over the
last three decades. In the early fifties, it was not uncommon for
Hong Kong youth to return to China to study and work. In many
cases politically motivated, they chose to make the then modest
economic sacrifice that such a move demanded. As Hong Kong
stabilized and began to develop in the 1950s, so did China, but
more slowly, so that Hong Kong entered the ranks of industrializ-
ing "countries" in the 1960s while China remained among the
poorest of nations. Then came the "lost decade" of the Cultural
Revolution. While China's economy stagnated in the midst of
political chaos, Hong Kong completed its transformation into a
modern industrial city and entrepôt. The relative difference in
living standards between capitalist Hong Kong and Communist
China is currently as great as that between the United States and
Mexico, across whose joint border this disparity has set in motion
a riptide of illegal immigration only too familiar to Americans.

Though the economic differences have long been substantial,
it is only since the beginning of the Four Modernizations program
that China's outward reach for technology and capital has inadvertently brought the outside world within the grasp of Guangdong
peasants. Rural Cantonese are much better informed about conditions in the colony than they were before the downfall of the
Gang of Four in 1976. In line with the renewed government policy
of encouraging visits, remittances, and capital investment by overseas Chinese, the number of Hong Kong and Macao residents
visiting China has increased rapidly, many paying their first visits
to their ancestral villages in decades. The increased contacts that
have resulted have brought home Hong Kong's affluence to the
countryside as never before.

The returned emigrant's every move is calculated to impress
his relations near and distant that his long sojourn abroad has
been successful. He will in the first place arrive laden with gifts,
chief among which are Japanese-made television sets and tape
recorders. Then, shortly after his return, he will invite hundreds
of his former village fellows to a deliberately ostentatious feast

where they will be treated to expensive dishes of chicken, duck, and pork that seldom grace their own tables. Finally, he is often to be seen strolling about the village paths in his Western-style business suit, smoking an American-brand cigarette and brandishing a Japanese-made watch. Villagers come away from this performance either impressed with his success or shaking their heads over the surprising fact that he, too, succeeded.

Most unsettling to the villagers is the return of more recent migrants who have only been absent from the village for a few years. They are called, with the resentful admiration of those who knew them when, *xin fa cai*, or *nouveau riche*. These formerly down-at-the-heels peasant youth, now virtually indistinguishable in dress and manner from long-time Hong Kong residents, are compelling first-hand evidence that wealth awaits all who escape to Hong Kong.

The television sets that these visitors munificently bestow on their relatives provide visual confirmation of Hong Kong's prosperity, and stimulate without satiating. A youth who saved for two years in order to buy a bicycle is astounded by the sight of Kowloon streets filled with private automobiles. A family that spends a month's earnings on an ordinary radio is stunned to learn that in Hong Kong a month's income would buy them a color TV set. The mainland viewer is dazzled not just by the material prosperity of Hong Kong but also by its cultural ambience. The urbane, cosmopolitan vitality of Hong Kong indicts by contrast the staid monotony of village life, with its dawn-to-dusk drudgery and dearth of entertainment. It brings home to village youth the emptiness of their lives and prospects while at the same time suggesting an alternative to their earthbound fate. Indeed, programs from Hong Kong serve almost as a television university, priming and prepping young viewers to make the plunge from the rustic, low-key, and communal life of the village to the fast-paced, Westernized, individualistic world of urban Hong Kong.

But all of this would have little impact were not the current crop of young adults something of an alienated generation, bored with politics and cynical about their leaders. Without heroes or ideals, they are ripe for cultural conquest by the West.

The propaganda counteroffensive undertaken by the Guangdong authorities has been clumsy and ineffectual. Apparently alarmed by the influence that Hong Kong television exerts on the young, the powers that be announced in June 1980 that such broadcasts were off-limits. Instead, people were urged to watch PRC stations, which one friend described as so boring that even his 3-year-old daughter, who would sit and watch Hong Kong programs by the hour, promptly disappeared elsewhere to play when he switched to the Guangzhou channel. The official press has also published featured articles on former escapees who became disgruntled with life in Hong Kong after a time and fled back to the fold. These repatriates are quoted holding forth on the "high" cost of living, the "high" unemployment rate, and the "high" incidence of crime, the Westernized life-style, and other "problems" that patently have less to do with modern Hong Kong than with their own short and troubled stays there. In any event, these reports have likewise failed to reach the young, since newspapers are available only in collective headquarters and are generally read only by the politically active, a category which includes few youth.

But what above all leads the youths Westward is not primarily seditious foreign influences or political disaffection, but the Four Modernizations. Contradictory as it may seem at first glance, China's own program for the modernization of agriculture, industry, science, and the military may have to bear the brunt of the blame for the increasing numbers of young Cantonese peasants attempting to escape to Hong Kong. Material progress, especially if that meant a better life for the masses, fell into disrepute under the assault of the Maoist ideologues. During the long years of the Cultural Revolution, political goals were paramount, given priority even when they conflicted, as they frequently did, with economic development.

The Four Modernizations legitimized demands for a better life, intimating that it was better to be rich than Red. Materialist cravings that only a few years ago would have been grounds for self-criticism as bourgeois consumerism are now permitted and accepted. The political activists of the 1960s and 1970s have become the expectant consumers of the 1980s. After the revolutions endured by the Chinese people over the last few decades—the Communist revolution and the Cultural Revolution—they find themselves caught up in yet another, the revolution of rising expectations.

The hopes of the Chinese people were raised high by the promise of modernization. The country was gripped by excitement in 1977–78 as the pragmatists regained command and charted a course that they said would lead to a strong, modern China and offer a higher standard of living to its people. Yet little progress has been made to date in gearing up China's underdeveloped consumer economy, and the people of many impoverished regions have little likelihood of seeing improvements in their lifetime. Indeed, China's leaders by 1981 were acknowledging that it will take a generation or more to achieve the basic goals of the plan, and even longer to raise the standard of living in Guangdong and other areas to anything comparable to that of Hong Kong. The new-found tension between expectations and reality creates a creeping dissatisfaction with the way things are in Guangdong and elsewhere.

Even so, rural youth told me that they would not consider emigration, legal or otherwise, if they could move to an urban area and into a factory job. In its own inimitable fashion, however, Beijing has kept its peasants down on the farm. Official permission is required to change one's occupational registration from peasant to worker and one's place of residence from rural to urban, and applications are routinely rejected. Ironically for a society that espouses equality, social mobility is kept at extremely low levels by severely restricting internal migration and occupational mobility. This leaves the majority of Chinese peasant youths without immediate prospects in their native land, and with nowhere to turn for opportunity but outward.

Although the standard of living has been rising in Guangdong in the years since the fall of the Gang of Four, this has served only to whet the consumer appetites of those who subsisted for years on slogans. Illegal emigration is not so much a creation of Hong Kong's affluence as it is of the glaring contrast between China's continuing poverty and the outsized promises of material progress made by leaders in Beijing. Chinese youth, languishing in the countryside with inflated expectations and few immediate prospects, will continue to surge outward for opportunity until the gap between expectations and reality can be narrowed enough to stem this human tide, or until the two-day journey to Hong Kong is made as difficult as the thirty-year "New Long March" that their leaders are exhorting them to undertake.*

The exodus of Guangdong youth to Hong Kong is only one of many forms of escape prevalent among the young in China. The escape fantasies of other youth, especially those of other provinces, focus less on fleeing to Hong Kong than on deliverance to America or Taiwan, and I was often asked about these possibilities. The only question that was put to me more often than how to emigrate to America was how to learn English, which I came to understand to be no less a symptom of youthful alienation than actual escape.

Wenfang popped the inevitable question the second time we met. "Will you teach me English?" she asked, regarding me with great intensity.

"I am only going to be here in Guangzhou a few days," I replied. "I spend most of my time in the countryside."

She was visibly disappointed, but the subject of English was plainly one that fascinated her, for once launched upon it, she could not easily leave it aside.

"I want to learn English very much," she said animatedly. "We had English in school but didn't really learn it. Actually, I didn't learn anything in school during the Cultural Revolution. None of us did. All they taught us was how to shout slogans. Even my English class was devoted to learning the same slogans in English. I can't even carry on an ordinary conversation. Last year I studied under a tutor. We used a Hong Kong textbook, *English Essentials.* Do you know it?"

I had to admit that I didn't.

"I paid 10 *rmb* a month to the tutor for eight hours of group

* Shortly after I left China, the British administration of Hong Kong announced stern measures to curtail the inrush of illegal immigrants. The "touch base" policy, under which an immigrant who made his way into the urban center of Kowloon or Hong Kong was home free and could openly apply for an identity card and permanent residence, was rescinded. Replacing it was a policy of immediate repatriation: from November 1, 1980, all illegals captured were returned to China without exception or delay. By making it more difficult, though still not impossible, for successful escapees to settle in Hong Kong, this policy will, with time, probably reduce the number of attempts.

tutoring a month. This went on for eight months, but stopped because the other students dropped out. I have just signed up for a course in English in night school," she went on, taking out her student card and showing it to me. "The course is 8 *rmb* for half a year."

Yet for all Wenfang's enthusiasm for English, she had no clear idea of how she was going to put her language skill to use after she succeeded in acquiring it. "Maybe I can get a job here in which English is required," she said without real conviction, "or maybe I can go abroad to study." In other parts of Asia such as Taiwan or Japan these would have been reasonable goals that stood an excellent chance of being realized. But in China, as Wenfang knew better than I, skills aren't marketable because work assignments are handed down by the state, while opportunity for study overseas is so limited that it requires genius or official connections to go. There seemed something unreal in Wenfang's determination, which she shares with millions of her generation, to learn English, until I saw it was an end in itself. Studying English may open no doors of opportunity, but it is still an enchanted key.

Like her agemates, Wenfang knows only scattered bits and pieces about the West, but she more than compensates for her ignorance by an aching enthusiasm for this El Dorado of plenty. Studying English gives her satisfaction, even if it is unlikely to prove the first step in leaving China and making her way to the U.S., for it allows her to reach out in an almost tangible way to the outside world. The current English craze, though less dramatic a demonstration of disaffection than escape, is no less a renunciation of the PRC status quo.

The most striking manifestation of the ideological alienation of this generation of Chinese youth is their unabashed materialism, especially coming as it does so soon after the Cultural Revolution period when youths appeared to be dedicated by the millions to idealistic social and political goals and values. A mere decade later, a self-centered ethic of pleasure-seeking and materialism seems to have sprung up full grown, and scant evidence of the once strong commitment of communal goals is evident. Although much of the Chinese population seems to have come down with a bad case of bourgeois acquisitiveness since 1976, the youth have been the most seriously afflicted. One pretty young woman, whose Cultural Revolution experience created in her a lasting love-hate relationship with politics, told me that she found many of her contemporaries neither attracted to nor repelled by issues that troubled her, but totally indifferent. All they talk about, she said, is gossip at work, next weekend's outing, and possible girl-friends or boyfriends. Although herself critical of the grim years of the Cultural Revolution, she deplored the current one-sided concern with consumerdom where all that matters is whether one has a watch on one's wrist, a Shanghai bicycle in one's entryway, and a Japanese tape recorder on one's chest of drawers. "Young people are so materialistic because they have no *jingshen* rewards or *jingshen* life," she insisted, using a Chinese word that means cultural, spiritual, and intellectual life (as opposed to physical life). "They turn to materialism because they have nothing else."

What she meant was not just that cultural life in China is anemic, though this certainly is indisputable, nor was she referring to the fact that the limited numbers of books published, plays staged, and movies produced are all injected with heavy doses of the prevailing orthodoxy, though this too is all too evident. Rather, she meant that youth who have rejected the prevailing orthodoxy face a pauperization of the spirit, because there are no cultural, spiritual, or intellectual alternatives available. Youth who have ceased to believe in communism do not necessarily come to oppose it, because that would require them to develop a competing ideology, but tend instead to escape to the here and now of social and material concerns.

This falling away from Communist ideology is revealingly decried by PRC propagandists as a loss of faith. Just as Western religions demand of believers that they give their hearts to God, so does the CCP require of youth that they "give over their heart" to the Party. But youth have lost confidence in the Communist Party, seeing Party members at all levels motivated more by self-interest than by a desire to "serve the people," and they no longer believe in the socialist system, whose much-vaunted superiority seems to exist only in the empyrean realm of theory. Even Shanghai's *Wen Hui Bao* (Wen Hui Newspaper) admitted in December 1980 that "certain" youth are of the opinion that Marxism is already old-fashioned, backward. If capitalism is so corrupt and is bound for extinction, the students were quoted as asking, then why is production in capitalist countries steadily increasing? And if socialism is relatively superior, then why is China still undeveloped after thirty years of socialism? Suggesting that political textbooks should be updated to answer these questions poised by increasingly sophisticated youth, the article pointed out that propaganda efforts among the youth required considerably more attention.

For all the Party's voiced concern about ideological slippage among the youth, the Communist Youth League (CYL), the organ that attends to the political indoctrination of promising youth and grooms them for full Party membership, was in the doldrums the year I was in the People's Republic. Very early on, the CYL had become a pawn in the political struggle between left and right. It was first abolished in the opening phase of the Cultural Revolution for being too elitist and reactionary, its leadership was then purged and vetted by the leftists, and it reemerged in the early seventies to propagate radical policies among the youth. With the accession of the Dengists to power, this same process was repeated, only in political reverse. A campaign to root out functionaries with radical tendencies from the organizational superstructure of the CYL began in the late seventies. This cleanup was apparently still underway in 1981, for the *Guangming Daily* reported in February of that year that the (reconstituted) Central Committee of the CYL had identified "this year's most important task of reeducating members and turning them into 'real' CYL members." The first stage of the rectification campaign had evidently been less than entirely successful, for, the report went on to reveal, "There are those who have not accepted reeducation and who do not repent of their errors, and there are others who have given the [CYL] organization a bad name. These, in the future, will be subject to punishment according to the regulations."

With the middle echelons paralyzed by the purge, local CYL branches have been left to their own devices. Most have simply stopped functioning, holding no meetings and inducting no new members, a lapse that local Youth League cadres blame on a growing indifference to politics. One frustrated brigade CYL cadre told me that her efforts to keep her local branch active had been foiled because "no one is interested in the CYL. In the early seventies," she recalled, "when we wanted CYL members to help with the sugarcane harvest or the winter vegetable crop, it was easy to mobilize them. Now if there is a problem, nobody comes forward to help. They make all kinds of excuses. Some say they are too busy with their own family's contract fields. Others say that their collective work takes too much time. But the fact is they just aren't interested. No one came to the meetings I used to call, so for the last two years I have stopped holding meetings." She concluded that there had been a real decline in collective spirit among the youth in her village.

Although many youth have turned away from the state, Party, and officially sanctioned ideology to a private, spiritual, or material narcissism, not all Chinese youth are politically alienated. For most, to be sure, the Great Proletarian Cultural Revolution experience of being misled, used, and discarded constituted an unforgettable lesson in the futility of political participation. But not a few, in reaction against the arbitrary abuse of power that had characterized the GPCR, felt called to work for democracy in China to ensure that such tragedies could never happen again. Mao may have succeeded in his stated GPCR goal of creating a generation of "revolutionary successors," though hardly in the way he imagined. Without a doubt, those who participated in the Cultural Revolution learned two things essential to conducting a future revolution—how to organize and how to fight. The irony is that these revolutionaries are committed not to the furtherance of Mao's order, but to its overthrow. Mao's true revolutionary successors are not the radical cadres that the Dengists are busily purging from Party, army, and bureaucratic ranks, who are concerned primarily with the preservation of their own power, but the activists of the Democracy movement like Wei Jingsheng, the tens of thousands who pasted up and read posters at the Democracy Wall, and the hundreds of thousands who demonstrated at Tiananmen in 1976. Mao's most important legacy to China may have been the human time bomb of this generation of Chinese youth, which may finally rip apart the bureaucratic totalitarian structure of the status quo, not in a second Cultural Revolution but a cultural restoration.

7

Sex, Love, and Marriage: Public Repression, Covert Expression

If married persons have affairs, it is the business of the public security office. Such relationships affect two families. They are a social problem and must be controlled.

Commune public security cadre, 1980

Not long before the Chinese New Year, Sandhead Brigade was rocked with the infelicitous news of a young woman's suicide. Although suicides are not uncommon in rural China, her act aroused unwonted attention because it was carried out in the sleeping quarters of a married man, one of the three doctors assigned to the local commune-run health station. Her death was of more than passing interest to me as well, for our paths had touched, albeit tangentially. Although she and I had never met, the health station where she died was located only a few steps from my house and I passed it daily. And on the several occasions I was not feeling well, I had gone there and been treated by the doctor said to be involved in the affair, a Dr. Gao.

Dr. Gao's full name was Gao Zhongmao, but he was always referred to as Dr. Gao by the villagers, who held him in high regard for his mastery of traditional Chinese herbal medicine and kindly manner. Though only 34 years old, he already had a decade and a half of clinical experience behind him, for like many Chinese

169

country doctors, he had studied medicine at a three-year, second-ary-level technical school and had begun practicing at age 18 following graduation. Before coming to the Sandhead clinic the year before, he had worked for ten years at the commune clinic in the market town, and it was there that his wife and two children still resided.

It was during the last year of his tenure at the commune clinic that he first met the young woman, Wang Meilan, who later was to kill herself. She was a 21-year-old practical nurse when she was assigned to work with Gao Zhongmao, and quickly devel-oped an unbounded admiration for this skilled and sympathetic young doctor. These feelings took on a new dimension as Dr. Gao treated her for a heart condition that she was found to have. When Dr. Gao finally discovered that his assistant had fallen in love with him, he tried to discourage her affections, gently pointing out that he was a married man with children, but she persisted and they became intimate. (A foregone conclusion, said a neighbor of mine, reciting for my benefit a local folk saying, *"Nü fang nan, yi zuo qiang; nan fang nü, yi zhi zhang,"* which means literally that "a woman resists a man's advances like a wall, but a man resists a woman's advances like a sheet of paper.") Oddly enough, it came out later that Gao Zhongmao's wife had been aware of their relationship from the beginning, but instead of pressing for a divorce from her husband or at least an end to his liaison, she apparently chose to ignore it, for she was never heard to complain about her husband's infidelity. Friends described her as a quiet, unassuming woman who was lucky to have married as well as she had. When rumors about Gao and Wang's relationship reached the main commune clinic, however, matters became seri-ous. They were criticized in a closed-door session and warned to break off the relationship, and Dr. Gao was abruptly transferred to the Sandhead health station, the one most distant from the main clinic.

In spite of their unit's opposition, which made divorce and remarriage impossible for Dr. Gao, he and Wang Meilan continued their affair. He spent his weekdays at the Sandhead station, where Wang Meilan would often visit him, arriving well after dark and leaving before dawn the next morning. Before long, Wang Meilan's erratic comings and goings had also alerted her parents to her relationship with Dr. Gao, whom she persisted in seeing despite their resistance. Nevertheless, she gradually became depressed over the seeming hopelessness of her predicament, and only her parents' timely intervention prevented an attempt to overdose herself. This led Gao Zhongmao to attempt to bolster her spirits by promising to take her on a day trip to Guangzhou. They would leave on the early riverboat to Guangzhou, he told her, and spend the whole Saturday there. Early Friday night, he fetched his 6-year-old son to the health station, which lay near the riverboat landing, after telling his wife that he was going to take the boy to Guangzhou the following morning. At ten o'clock that evening, Wang Meilan arrived. Because it was late, they turned in after only a brief conversation, Wang Meilan lying down on Gao Zhongmao's single bed alongside his already sleeping son, while Gao went to bed in the next room.

Early the next morning he was awakened by his son, who told him that "auntie was ill." He went and found that she had injected herself with an overdose of drugs the night before. She had already been dead for several hours by morning. In shock and grief, he locked his room, left his boy with neighbors, and pedaled frantically over to break the news of the tragedy to Wang Meilan's father. The older man took the news as if he had half expected it, and told Gao calmly that they would wait until nightfall and then bring his daughter back to the village, where she could be given a fitting funeral and a scandal avoided. The body was successfully carried back that night, but in the days that followed, the real cause and location of Wang Meilan's death leaked out, and the Party committee in the commune clinic decided to take action.

Dr. Gao was hauled before a meeting of the clinic staff and "struggled," that is, publicly humiliated and criticized. The primary accusations leveled against him were that he had had an improper relationship with a "comrade" and had behaved in an unprofessional manner toward a woman who had been a patient of his. He was required to recant all of his wrongdoings in a written confession. Finally, the commune clinic prepared a detailed report on his infidelity, in which he was held to have contributed directly to Wang Meilan's suicide. This report and Gao's confession were forwarded to the county public security department, and the clinic Party committee requested a formal police investigation.

Dr. Gao was taken into custody two weeks after Wang Meilan's death. He was held responsible for her suicide, though I wasn't able to ascertain the exact nature of the charges brought against him, for these were never publicly announced or posted. People close to the clinic Party committee said it was pressing for heavy punishment, and had recommended a 15-year prison term. Villagers said that it was only because of the strenuous objections of the dead girl's father, who said that Dr. Gao was a good man and had not hurt his daughter in any way, that her suicide had been her own doing, that the county court in the end reduced the sentence to only five years at hard labor.

——————◆——————

This tragic episode—especially Dr. Gao's unexpected imprisonment for his lover's suicide—underlies stern official attitudes toward sexual transgressions outside of marriage. A commune public security cadre, whose lean and astringent features gave him an ascetic look, gave the rationale for the government's reaction to Wang Meilan's suicide: "If married persons have affairs, it is the business of the public security office. Such relationships affect two families. They are a social problem and must be controlled. Young people aren't the same, so we usually don't take action."

Although premarital sex, unlike the extramarital variety, is not considered to be a crime, it is hardly regarded with favor by the mainland authorities, who take the same jaundiced view of young love that they take of all activities which are spontaneous, self-interested, and private. Any regime as bent on harnessing its population to state production plans as that which occupies Beijing must regard as anathema the spontaneous dissipation of energy that sexual activity involves. To the Party, with its revolutionary ideal of communal service to state goals, intercourse must seem the very embodiment of selfishness, for it gives pleasure to only two people. Sex is the private act par excellence in a state where any activity which occurs behind closed doors, whether the door in question leads to the bedroom or the living room, is automatically suspect.

This line of reasoning was played out to its eccentric apogee during the Cultural Revolution, when love and, by implication, sex were attacked as decadent and dissolute. In a 1979 pamphlet entitled *Love, Marriage, and Family,* an article on "How Youth Should Treat Love" describes the then prevailing attitude: "The Gang of Four espoused a feudal, Fascist ascetism. Questions of marriage and love were placed off-limits. Although they personally led lives of extreme debauchery, they donned a radical leftist guise, saying that youthful love and marriage were vulgar, low-class behavior. They even forbade literature describing love. If a work dealt with questions of love, it was accused of being pornographic and depraved."*

Although such extreme manifestations of Communist prudery ended with the GPCR, the years of the Four Modernizations have hardly been a new era in which anything goes. The reaction of the Party Central Committee to the first self-indulgent stirrings of post-Mao lovers was to demand that "propaganda concerning the proper proletarian view of love and marriage be strengthened," and articles like "How Youth Should Treat Love" do exactly that in no uncertain terms. The state's interest in love, marriage, and the family is not merely didactic, but political, for as the above article concludes, "If these matters . . . are handled well, not only will they bring happiness and well-being to individuals, they will also excite people to enthusiastically put their all into the program for the Four Modernizations."**

The revolution, which has currently assumed the guise of the Four Modernizations, is still the prime mover of all activity in China, including love and marriage. There is, after all, not much to choose from between past and present leaders in this regard. Instead of making love and marriage, the late Chairman Mao wanted Chinese youth to make revolution; instead of making babies, Vice Chairman Deng Xiaoping wants them to make modernization.

What relaxation has occurred since the late seventies in the hitherto rigidly Victorian stance of the state looks, upon closer examination, more like a simple retrogression to the less repressive standards of the fifties. Movie heroes are again embracing and bussing heroines in mildly romantic scenes that were unacceptable from 1966 to 1977, but were common enough before then. To the generation which grew up during the Cultural Revo-

---

* Guan Xin, "How Youth Should Treat Love," in *Love, Marriage, and Family* (Guangdong: Guangdong People's Press, 1979), p. 18.
** Ibid, p. 23.

lution, of course, these are scenes of unprecendented daring. The
Chinese watch movies like Americans watch football games, often
carrying on a running commentary with their neighbors. The ad-
vent of a love scene, however, immediately quiets the most boister-
ous crowd, while a kiss creates a perfect silence. This lasts only
until the lovers' lips part, though, at which time the theater erupts
in chatter as moviegoers trade impressions back and forth. A
friend of mine, searching for a way to explain this reaction, told
me, "It's as if life in China is missing something."

To the foreigner, what is most obviously missing from life
in China is any public display of affection, intimacy, or sexuality.
Not only is the Western preoccupation with sex in public entertainment totally absent, but many more innocent sights are missing
as well. Lovers strolling hand in hand on city streets are unusual
enough to attract attention—disapproving glances—from pass-
ersby. Couples in parks sometimes sit snugly together, but matters
rarely go further, and public embracing, necking, or petting is
uncommon. Demure Chinese women dress in unisex clothes that
conceal curves, do not make themselves up with lip gloss and
eye shadow, and lack any suggestion of flirtativeness in their
speech or manner. Nowhere in China does one find sex flaunted
in a deliberately provocative way.

The discovery of a land where sexual naiveté is seemingly
normal appeals to the puritan alter egos of world-weary foreign
travelers. Especially Americans, with their true-confessions attitude toward their own sex life, are charmed by the discreet silence
that Chinese maintain about theirs, and further enchanted by the
artless embarrassment of Chinese acquaintances that they casually
try to draw out. They accept at face value the total disinterest
in such matters feigned by the Chinese, and are even prepared
to believe the sermonette about throwing themselves wholeheartedly into the struggle for the Four Modernizations that their blunt
questioning (which itself violates China's public sexual mores)
sometimes elicits from the politically more astute.

The prim public façade that Chinese tradition raised about
matters of love and sex has been reinforced by a generation of
rigid Communist rule. Those who openly violate sexual mores,
especially in more conservative rural areas, risk social ostracism,
if not out-and-out punishment under the law, as I found out from

the case of Ah Ling, the wife of the South Island Brigade police chief. They were obviously mismatched, she as energetic, robust, and good-humored as he was neurasthenic, spindly, and dour. One hot summer afternoon, Ah Ling was weeding a mulberry patch on the bank of a fish pond in which a strongly built man was netting shrimp. Ah Ling and the man were from the same team, and they kept up a clipped conversation as they worked. The man finished first and came up out of the water near where she was working, his wet, clinging shorts leaving little to the imagination. At this point, Ah Ling is said to have reached out and playfully patted him on the upper thigh (by some accounts *very* high on the thigh) and to have made a remark so vulgar that no villager would repeat it to me. Now Ah Ling is well known in the village for a sense of humor at once wacky and earthy, and it is just possible that she meant all of this as a kind of joke. (One time at dinner she told me, grinning, that the mash-like mixture in her rice bowl was rice and hard liquor. I had seen village men take their rice and spirits together, and I half believed her until her husband fixed her with a disgusted look and told me gravely that it was after all only water.) The other villagers working in the fields, especially the older men, did not take what happened there as any joke, however. They were incensed. They ringed the wife of one of the most feared and powerful men in the village where she stood and reviled her as a shameless whore, a wanton bitch, and used on her other Chinese obscenities which defy ready translation. Breaking away from her accusers and running instinctively for home, Ah Ling thought that she had hopelessly disgraced herself and her husband's family. It was this social opprobrium, more than a private sense of guilt or sin, that led her to locate the pesticide that she had earlier put aside for their private plot, quickly down as much as she could without retching, and lie down on her bed to wait for the end. But relatives, upon hearing the news of her public humiliation, correctly surmised that her (and her family's) disastrous loss of "face" might lead to extremities, and she was soon discovered by them and taken to the local commune clinic.

This public standard of sexual priggishness that Ah Ling violated does not, as might be expected by analogy with Western culture, rest firmly on personal prudery. In the Chinese cultural setting, the Western view, shared by the Chinese Communists, of public behavior as a necessary reflection of personal conscience does not hold. In a sense, it can be said that Chinese scruples about sex are only skin deep. As they have throughout their long history, Chinese continue to regard the sexual urge as a natural bodily function which should be neither overindulged nor repressed, but given proper expression. Possessing a healthy regard for sex, they find decidedly odd the notion of Communist puritans that it is somehow sinful, or the hint that they should sublimate their libidinous desires by throwing themselves into the struggle for production or immersing themselves in the immaculate conceptions of Chairman Mao. There is much more to the sexual life of the Chinese in the People's Republic than commonly meets the eye or ear.

Premarital sex is surprisingly common. Many rural girls married in the last few decades have been pregnant at the time they crossed the threshold of their husband's home. Abortions performed on unwed mothers, mandated by the birth control program, are currently common enough to raise eyebrows. Extramarital affairs, like that of Dr. Gao, occur even in the countryside, even though cheek-by-jowl village life makes it hard to find the needed privacy and despite potential penalties.

More serious problems are also evident to the careful observer. Nearly every village I visited had its "broken shoe," a woman usually in economic straits, who performed sex for money or other favors. Rape is not unheard of, even in the villages, and is said to be on the rise. Young women privately complain about brash young men who make passes in public places, including one particularly detested type who wedge themselves up to victims on the perennially overcrowded buses and attempt conversation or worse. Public restrooms in suburban Guangzhou had graffiti which rivaled in originality and explicitness any I had seen elsewhere, and I once found the toilets stopped up by what turned out to be inflated condoms (freely dispersed at drugstores throughout China to encourage birth control) in the men's *and* women's restroom. By the time I left China, it was clear to me that the public repression of sex had not only not created an asexual society but in fact lay behind growing covert sexual expression, sometimes in unwholesome ways.

Contemporary Chinese courtship exhibits the same combination of public prudery and private naturalness. By Western standards, the Chinese are very late developers. For several years following their graduation from junior high school at 15 or so, youth continue to deliberately ignore the opposite sex. Rural girls working in mixed groups talk to other women and sometimes to older men, whom they address as "uncle," but avoid conversation with younger men as self-consciously as they are avoided in turn. The occasional comments directed across the sex boundary are usually group efforts, as when several youth walking to market together called out in a mockingly polite manner to a girl in her late teens as she rode by on her bike, "Older Sister Fang, can I have a ride?" This maiden bashfully pedaled past without reply, pretending not to notice them.

It is only when the girls are 19 or so and the boys have become young men of 21, that they begin to notice and take the measure of the opposite sex. Even at this age, the rules of male-female contact continue to dictate reserve, and the sexes rarely speak directly to each other. I recall one time walking up the path toward my house with a 21-year-old acquaintance of mine named Qi Gen (literally, seventh root) when a girl appeared on the pathway coming toward us. She held eyes demurely downcast until we were only a pace or two apart and then, throwing him a quick glance, called out "Qi Gen" by way of greeting. Then she was gone down the path, leaving the object of her salutation so open-mouthed with surprise that he was unable to reply. A doltish grin slowly and uncontrollably spread over his face and stayed there for the next several minutes. Later, I learned that it had been the first time that a girl had openly addressed him.

Publicly at least, matters do not go much beyond this in the countryside, where the sexes do not fraternize freely at any age. The lack of open social interaction leaves most Chinese youth without the social poise to initiate a relationship even if the opportunity to do so should arise. Instead, youth rely upon go-betweens, who are sometimes professional matchmakers but increasingly often are relatives or friends, especially if the youth in question already has a prospective mate in mind. For although youth do not converse with their agemates of the opposite sex, they are hardly oblivious to their presence, and as they grow older, they begin quietly and subtly appraising potential partners.

When my 22-year-old neighbor Ah Ying decided that one hard-working young man of 24 from a respected and, by village standards, moderately well-off family in her team would be a suitable suitor, she took the initiative. She enlisted her most trusted confidante in her cause by explaining that she had caught the youth Ah Han glancing at her several times in recent weeks and wondered what he meant by this (some things you can't tell even your best friends; there is too much face at stake). The following evening her friend sought out a male cousin of hers who was also close to Ah Han. Without mentioning her conversation with Ah Ying, she obliquely suggested that the two of them would be a good match, and her cousin agreed to broach the idea with Ah Han. The latter's reaction to the proposal was positive.

The next step in this cryptic mating dance was an evening together in the commune movie theater, the standard setting for initiating courtships. The meeting resembled more a secret rendezvous than a double date, for the two groups of sex-segregated youth arrived separately, purchased their tickets separately, and took their seats separately. But through the collusion of their amateur go-betweens, Ah Ying and Ah Han nevertheless found themselves sitting side by side. What then transpired was—nothing. There were no whispered conversations, no popcorn passed familiarly back and forth, and certainly nothing as brazen as handholding. Rather, the two sat bolt upright in silence, each masking acute awareness of the other's presence by a studied concentration on the movie, daring only stolen glances at the other's profile. The movie over, they thanked each other stiffly—the only words they had exchanged all evening—and left the same way they had come, separately.

What lies behind all of this chaperoned subterfuge is the unwritten rule against public pairing that still holds sway in the countryside. Youth may go to the commune movies, to the ice cream parlor (in Chinese, ice room), or for a walk with friends of the same sex, but not as a couple. Neither can young couples meet at home. For a young man to come calling is a serious matter, tantamount to a proposal of marriage, so that visits to a fiancée's family are usually reserved for the period following engagement. Since open courting is not sanctioned by local mores and there are no local activities open to young couples, they are left with no alternative to nocturnal trysts in secluded places.

After Ah Han had sat silently by Ah Ying's side through several movies, he gradually gained a measure of poise in her presence, and near the end of their fourth movie together he nervously asked if she would meet him alone the following night. She nodded without looking at him. From then on, they joined the numerous couples who seek out the privacy of rural roads for their after-dark assignations to avoid being seen together.

With the exception of winter nights too chilly to stay long outside, couples can be found perching on the shoulders of country roads and paths throughout the year. On one balmy night, I counted no fewer than twenty-one couples while driving along a half-mile stretch of road, each separated by regular territorial intervals of 50 meters or so. My headlights would catch only their hunched backs, for they self-consciously kept their heads turned away to avoid recognition. There was no kissing or petting on the road; at most the youth sat tightly together, shoulder to shoulder, knee to knee. But at later hours I sometimes spotted bikes parked at the edge of the road with their owners nowhere in sight. In the darkness of a deserted country road, youth have a choice of only two activities, conversation or coitus, and in Guangdong most couples wind up doing a little of both.

Surprising though it may seem, premarital sex is the one area of behavior in which rural Chinese youth may outdo their relatively liberated urban counterparts, who date more or less openly. The asceticism preached (but not practiced) by Party ideologues notwithstanding, sexual expression before wedlock is limited less by personal guilt than by more practical considerations, the most fundamental of which is opportunity. The passions of urban youth are frustrated by an almost total lack of privacy. Flats are crowded with parents and a set of siblings, parks are always swarming with people and frequently close at dusk, and movie theaters afford occasions for at most a little friendly groping. Not so in the countryside, where the coming of darkness provides privacy a few paces from the village.

Since sociological surveys are unknown in the People's Republic, it is impossible to know with precision the rate of youthful indulgence in premarital sex, but there is some suggestive evidence. One fortyish woman, whose outspokenness made her a good source of information, maintained that nine out of ten girls who have steady boyfriends experience sex before marriage. But courtships in the Guangdong delta are still, for the most part, short or absent entirely—enough so, I estimated, to lower the overall rate to around 35 percent. A local schoolteacher gave an even more conservative estimate, telling me that perhaps one-quarter of all young women went into marriage with prior coital experience. "This is just a guess," she cautioned. "No one knows for sure because these are not things that people talk about." But she agreed that almost all couples who go steady for any length of time experiment sexually. "It's inevitable," she concluded. "Parents no longer keep their daughters home at night since the land reform. Nature just takes its course."

These rates may raise eyebrows among Americans accustomed to thinking of the Chinese as a prudish people, but are hardly orgiastic given that almost all of this sexual activity occurs between partners who are over age 21 and will later marry. With the minimum age for marriage set at 25 for women and 26 for men, the only thing that keeps more women and men in their twenties from making their sexual debut before the sanction of a wedding ceremony is the difficulty that socially unskilled young adults have in initiating courtships in rural communities that frown on socializing between the sexes in public. The extremely high rates of premarital intercourse among those who have already paired off arises from the lack of a well-internalized code of sexual conduct. Young people are not told that sex is bad or harmful; they are told nothing at all.

"It is always the girl who is blamed for having sex before marriage," a middle-aged mother of two teenaged daughters complained to me. "But it is usually the boy who wants to, you know. The girl simply goes along. When my daughters have a boyfriend, I'll warn them that nine out of ten men will take whatever they can get [shi ge nanren, jiu ge tan]." She was unusual in her candor, however, because most women cannot bring themselves to say anything to their daughters. At most, a girl's mother will take her aside after she starts courting and tell her not to "make a mistake" (zou cuo), cryptic counsel whose meaning is likely to escape her unless (or until) she has already committed the "mistake" that she is being cautioned against. Since the young receive no sex education in the schools either, most enter into a relationship totally in the dark.

As might be expected with the subject of sex shrouded in taboo, premarital liaisons often result in pregnancy. A woman's work cadre recalled that pregnancy out of wedlock first became common in the early 1950s with the promulgation of a new marriage law, following which the parents of many young women no longer forbade them to go out at night. Since that time, the rate has remained more or less constant. The increasing availability of contraceptive devices, which came into general use during the 1960s and 1970s, has had little effect because unmarried youth, especially those in the countryside, find these difficult to obtain and embarrassing to use. In most villages I visited, cases of premarital pregnancy cropped up on the order of several times a year. Illegitimate births are unknown, however, since the situation is invariably remedied by either marriage or, more commonly, abortion.

Before the onset of the birth control campaign, premarital pregnancy was hastily followed by marriage, although the ceremony was cut down to a minimum and the woman and her family automatically forfeited anything more than a symbolic dowry and bride price. One family in Sandhead achieved local notoriety after three daughters in succession married in this fashion, picturesquely described as "boarding the bus before buying a ticket." "They had no face in the village," a neighbor of theirs recalled. "They gave away their daughters for nothing." The girl's family also loses face if there is talk, as there often is, that she used sex and pregnancy to entrap a reluctant male into marriage. When Zhang Wuming's daughter, still unmarried at the overripe age of 27, became pregnant by a man that she had only met a short time before, village gossip had it that this was the only way she could find a husband. Zhang Wuming was deeply shamed by the scandal, for which he blamed his daughter. Out of spite, he not only provided nothing in the way of a dowry, but went so far as to force her to leave all of her personal belongings behind when she shortly thereafter got married and went to live with her husband's family. Villagers talked for weeks about how she had gone to her new home barefoot because her father had refused to let her take even her shoes with her.

Entrapment can also work in reverse, although in this situation the blatant male bias of peasants often leads them to applaud rather than condemn a successful capture by the male sex. A young worker at the Southsand brick factory told me the story of an enterprising accountant who was tall, well built, good-looking—and still unmarried at 30. Despite his attractive combination of characteristics, he could not find a bride because his grandmother had suffered from, as his co-worker put it bluntly, "gummed-up wiring"—Cantonese for crazy. Each time a prospective bride's family found out about this skeleton in the family closet, they would hastily cancel the proposed match, fearing for the health of the future offspring. But this man proved resourceful enough (*you benshi*) to overcome his handicap on his own and make an enviable match with a woman he met at work and overcome her family's objections—by the simple expedient of making her pregnant.

In recent years, the marriage plans of a couple who have conceived a child out of wedlock have become moot: strict birth control laws mandate the termination of all illegitimate pregnancies as soon as they are discovered. The woman is scheduled for an abortion regardless of whether the couple consents to this procedure or not. Afterwards, she receives an I.U.D. and some rather belated instruction on contraception to prevent a repetition. Although compulsory abortion removes the primary spur to immediate matrimony, in almost all cases their families still announce the couple's immediate engagement if they haven't already. Shortly thereafter, the couple are united in a traditional wedding ceremony, after which they live separately, but not celibately, until they reach the age at which they can register their marriage with the authorities and take up residence together. The youngest of the several couples I came to know in this marital purgatory were a woman of 20 and a man of 23. They will be able to begin living together as man and wife in 1985.

If the typical couple is not so trouble-prone, this is because most move briskly from introduction to courtship, betrothal, and matrimony. Introductions are still universally employed to initiate relationships, for as one young man of 23, to date girlfriendless, put it, "A man has to be very 'thick-skinned' [not afraid of losing face] before he would make the first move himself." The use of go-betweens implies a social commitment even if the intermediaries are merely friends, as in the case of Ah Ling and Ah Han, and the couple are considered to be going steady from the start. If the introduction is performed by a relative, as many are, matters are more serious still, for the face of a family hinges on the nascent courtship's successful culmination in betrothal and marriage. This is likely to occur without undue delay, for a family usually helps its youthful members locate a mate only if they have already reached the "proper" age for marriage and are still without prospects. A 28-year-old truck driver whose 26-year-old bride had been introduced to him by his older sister-in-law only three months before told me that they had seen each other only six times before deciding to marry. "Why should we have waited?" he stated matter-of-factly. "We got along well together. We were both of marriage age. And our families approved of the match."

When recourse is made to one of the professional matchmakers still active in the countryside, events move even more swiftly. The phase of courtship is bypassed entirely, and the decision of the newly acquainted couple concerning whether or not to marry is often expected after a single meeting.

If all this sounds rather unromantic, it is because the Chinese do not expect to be "in love" with the person they marry. Chinese youth approach marriage unencumbered by the Western notion of romantic love, rather seeing wedlock in naked contractual terms as an arrangement for procreation, parenthood, and economic security. As a result, they are not led astray by fanciful expectations that have little to do with reality, and can clear-headedly evaluate potential mates from the standpoint of conscious calculations of self-interest. Unlike their grandparents, who often did not meet until their wedding day, the young now have the final say in selecting their spouse. It surprised me how often the generations find themselves in total agreement over the fitness of a prospective mate. Conflicts over this issue are less common than in the West, even though patrilocal residence means that much more is at stake, because level-headed Chinese youth marry as their parents would like them to marry, with an eye to the usefulness of their potential partner. The contemporary mainland Chinese equivalent of falling in love and getting married is a starkly utilitarian "making a marriage partner" (*gao hunyin duixiang*), surely an unsentimental appraisal of the task of getting hitched.

Even Party ideologists worry that youth will adopt the "standard of the exploiting class, which values money, station, and appearance above all else, in choosing a partner." As an ideological substitute for this youthful pragmatism, the Party plugs its own brand of romanticism, in which "a spouse is not merely a companion, but is also a comrade, a fellow soldier, together with whom you can plunge into the red-hot struggle for production."* The renewed stress on selecting ideologically committed partners may partly stem from the embarrassing decline of the value of Party membership on the marriage market revealed to me by one Young Communist League member. Before the Cultural Revolution, women wanted Communist Party members," he told me. "Now they avoid Communist Party members, preferring people with relatives overseas."

"Women are very picky, especially since the early seventies," a state employee turning 30, so far frustrated in his nuptial efforts, complained bitterly to me. "Women have become selfish and greedy. Nobody wants to marry a road maintenance worker like myself. The women all want factory workers, even though our salaries, as state workers, don't vary that much. They know that marrying a factory worker has other advantages. A worker in a factory making electric fans, for example, can bring home enough spare parts to make a fan for his own use, or he can trade the fan or the parts on the black market for other goods. What has a road worker got except gravel and dirt? What are those worth?"

Those state employees whose occupation does not give them access to scarce goods, such as road maintenance workers, garbagemen, ferrymen, and teachers, often have no choice but to take brides from the one group whose vocation is even less desirable than their own, the peasantry.

A promising occupation is only one of the many merits that women look for in a potential spouse. One Beijing woman in

* Guan Xin, "How Youth Should Treat Love," in *Love, Marriage, and Family* (Guangdong: Guangdong People's Press, 1979), p. 21.

her early twenties, who herself laughed at other young women for being what she called overly materialistic, could nevertheless tick off for me the ten attributes of an ideal mate: *yi biao rencai,* "first-rate talent"; *er lao gui xi,* "two elders who have already made the Western journey," that is, parents who are deceased; *san zhuan yi ti,* "the three things that go round and the one that you carry," namely, a bike, a sewing machine, a tape recorder, and a television set; *si shi ba jiao,* "forty-eight legs," a houseful of furniture the legs of which total forty-eight; *wuguan duanzheng,* "five features in proportion," that is, good looks; *liuqin buren,* "doesn't recognize the six kin," that is, he must be estranged from his relatives; *qishi kuai qian,* "70 rmb" a month; *bamian linglong,* "eight sides elegant," which means that he must be in with everybody; *yen jiu bu zhan,* "doesn't touch cigarettes or liquor"; and *shifen tinghua,* "ten parts obedient."

Finding such a perfect match is not easy, she went on saying that most women would be satisfied if their suitor's parents are deceased so they don't have to live cheek by jowl with them in an overcrowded apartment; that he is not close to his other relatives so that he has a minimum of responsibilities toward the rest of his family; and that he is personally easygoing, obedient, and a good provider. "I, too, would be happy with such a match," she asserted, dismissing looks, talent, and a bride price and dowry as being of secondary importance. The Western cult of the face (and body) that has unreasonably inflated the value of physical beauty does not exist in China, where a pleasant physiognomy is simply a little added extra. Also, talent is at a discount in China, where getting along with superiors is more critical for getting ahead. The largest bride prices are paid and the most impressive dowries underwritten by men who are deficient in other, more desirable qualities—by way of compensation.

Rural women set conditions which are generally similar, except that they tend to regard living with the older generation after marriage not only as inevitable, because of the strength of family ties, but as actually advantageous, because it means a mother-in-law at home to help with the housework. Another difference is that the custom of paying a bride price and providing a dowry is almost universal in the countryside, forgone only when the bridegroom is unusually endowed in some other respect, as when he is employed in an industrial job. Less favored suitors and their families must come up with a combination bride price and dowry that in the Pearl River Delta often approaches 1,000 *rmb*, a staggering sum several times what the average peasant makes in a year.

While articles in the official *People's Daily* continue to faithfully reflect long-standing Party policy by lashing out against "feudal customs" such as the payment of a bride price, the attitude of the low-ranking cadres actually charged with eradicating such seemingly mercenary practices and establishing in their place a new proletarian marriage-making style is often far from zealous. The sixtyish Party secretary of Almond Pavilion Brigade, who as a grass-roots activist, ardently supported the aims of the new marriage law when it first came out in 1950, regards it in hindsight as a perfect example of a policy that is "easy to talk about but hard to implement." He sounded almost cynical as he explained that, concerning such practices as bride price, dowry, and match-making, most cadres "speak harshly, but have soft hearts" (*kou ying xin ruan*). "Out of all the places I have visited, none has really implemented the Marriage Law," he continued. "Bride prices have not only not decreased over the past twenty years, in some areas they have actually increased. The dowry is carried through the streets as always, except now it comes from the man's family instead of the woman's [making it part of the bride price]. More than nine out of ten families demand a bride price. The only exceptions are those families where the couple involved are very close and agree to dispense with it, or where the man has a very good job or prospects."

Hadn't things been different when the marriage law was first announced thirty years ago, I asked him as he lit a cigarette. "Well, the propaganda was most intense in 1951–52 and some changes occurred at that time," he conceded. "But since then, there has been little pressure and no political campaigns. About the only thing has been occasional internal Party directives telling Party members to take the lead in establishing the new betrothal and wedding customs by not giving a bride price or dowry."

"And have they obeyed?" I interjected.

"Not if they want their sons to get married, they don't," he answered with a wry smile. "It is hard to attack these practices because they only affect the personal relationships of the families involved, so cadres just let people do as they please. What the marriage law really accomplished was to make marriage a matter of the two people most involved, the man and the woman, and stop interference by third parties. Otherwise, marriages here are still very traditional. There is really no way to stop the people from following customs that they want to follow."

8

Women: The Socialist Double Bind

Women hold up half of heaven.

Mao Zedong

Women do more work than men. They work harder than they did before the revolution and men work less.

Village woman, 1980

The most impressive woman cadre I met in China was Chen Xiaoying, who at 26 is the youngest of Sandhead Brigade's fifteen cadres. Although of only average height, she has the stocky build, muscular shoulders, and sun-browned skin of one accustomed to hard labor in the fields. "Xiaoying is not afraid to work," one peasant man whom I asked about her replied, his voice carrying grudging admiration. "Other cadres just look at your work when they come to inspect. When she comes, she works beside you."

She is memorable in other ways as well. Although she wears the long, thick braid of hair down her back that identifies her as an unmarried woman—still a girl according to the tenets of village custom—she has little of the shrinking uneasiness that so many young village women, even those who have been married for some years, display around men. And unlike the other female brigade and team cadres I met, whose responsibilities centered on the peripheral arena of working with women (which her unmar-

188

ried status would have made awkward in any event), Xiaoying was directly involved in the paramount task of the collective, agricultural production. She was one of the six senior cadres who were given charge of the six districts into which the brigade's thirty-three teams had been divided, and personally oversees a district consisting of seven production teams and 1,600 team members. Not only that, she is the leading cadre of the local chapter of the Communist Youth League, supervises the brigade's combined primary and lower middle school, serving as a sort of one-person school board, and heads the woman's work propaganda team. And during whatever spare time she has from these manifold duties, she engages in collective labor.

When I asked her if she had any difficulty in supervising her district, she replied modestly that there is much that she doesn't know about production. "I have never served as the head of a production team," she said, "and the other brigade cadres in charge of districts all have." But despite her occasional stumbles she has never felt that the other cadres looked down upon her because of her sex, she went on to say, and neither has she had any difficulty in dealing with the men in the teams. The cadres and team members I spoke with confirmed this, accepting her in the role she had been assigned by the brigade.

Yet Chen Xiaoying is less the forerunner of a new breed of capable, outspoken, and strong-willed rural women who will fill the ranks of rural cadres in years to come than the product of a unique personal history. Though born in Sandhead, she was sent by her parents at the age of 9 to live with an aunt in Guangzhou, where she finished primary school and lower middle school. Her population registration remained in Equality Commune throughout this time, and she was forced to return there to attend upper middle school. Following graduation in 1973 she was, like millions of Chinese middle school students during the GPCR, sent down to the countryside, which for her meant just a short forty-five-minute bike ride back to her natal village of Sandhead. She had worked hard during those tough first months in the fields, and she had attracted the attention of the brigade Party secretary, who offered her a job as a brigade cadre despite her tender age of 17. He had been influenced not only by her gutsy, tireless work performance, but also by the drive to develop more female career cadres unfolding at the time (a pet program of Jiang Qing's,

I was told by a commune Party secretary). He had settled upon Xiaoying as the best of the young women who had been sent down. He remains pleased to this day with his relatively well-educated, industrious, and self-confident protégée. Chen Xiaoying herself, while enjoying the responsibilities that she has been given, finds rural life limiting and nurses a private desire to return to the city and perhaps continue her schooling. But her household registration was changed from worker to peasant as the price of accepting the cadre post, and the brigade has refused to consider releasing her. "I have put in for transfer several times," she confessed ruefully, "but the Party secretary has always denied it. He says that it would be impossible to find a young woman here in Sandhead capable of replacing me."

The other woman cadre I came to know well was Sandhead Brigade's woman's work cadre, Chen Suzhen. Like Chen Xiaoying, she had made it in the man's world of collective farm management largely on her own initiative. More typical of female officials, she did only "woman's work"—promoting birth control, encouraging women to participate in collective labor, and representing the brigade at commune Women's Federation meetings.

Chen Suzhen was selected in 1969 to replace the previous woman's work cadre, who had been removed from her post and expelled from the Communist Party for having an affair. (Typically, the man received only an internal reprimand from the CCP for his indiscretion and continues to serve as a brigade cadre down to the present day.) Chen Suzhen is self-possessed for a village woman, and talks animatedly about her work and its challenges. Yet male cadres grumble that she occasionally misses brigade meetings, and I noticed that she often had her youngest child in tow when I saw her about the village. When I asked her if her husband helped out with the housework and babysitting, she replied with an embarrassed grimace. "My husband doesn't do anything at home," she admitted sheepishly. "I take care of our three children and the housework by myself."

Sandhead Brigade, with two female cadres out of a total of thirteen, is unusual. Most of the brigades I visited had only a single woman cadre. Neither does the situation improve moving up the Party and government hierarchy. Men dominate at all levels.

In the leadership circles of any factory, enterprise, or institute men outnumber women by ratios of five or more to one. Even in the silk mills and embroidery factories in the Pearl River Delta where the work force is upwards of 80 percent female and where fair promotion practices are all it would take to generate a leadership of the same sex, factory heads and their assistants are, with few exceptions, men.

This numerical inequality holds even at the highest levels. There women make their best showing in the National People's Congress, and 37 of the 235 members of the Presidium in 1981 were women, a higher proportion than the number serving in the parliaments of many Western countries. But while these latter bodies have real power, the National People's Congress is merely democratic window dressing, its members powerless mannequins who unanimously vote to support whatever program is put before them by the Party. It is those who sit on the high councils of the Communist Party who mind the store, and few women have made it into this rarefied elite.

The PRC, like America, has not followed the lead of such nations as Great Britain, India, Israel, Sri Lanka, and Argentina, where women have headed governments. Those women who have made it nearly to the top have done so not on their own, but by marrying well. The most famous example of spouse patronage is, of course, Jiang Qing, who used husband Mao as a springboard to vault into the powerful Politburo during the Cultural Revolution, only to be arrested and ejected after his death. The only woman serving on the twenty-seven-member Politburo in 1981 was Deng Yingchao, the aged widow of the late Premier Zhou Enlai. In all, only 14 women held seats on the 201-member Central Committee in 1980, a proportion similar to the number of women who sit in Congress.

In the government, the picture is even bleaker. The only female Vice Premier on the State Council in 1980 was Chen Muhua, a protégée of Zhou Enlai's, who attended cabinet meetings with 17 male Vice Premiers. Reagan's record of appointing women to high office (only 45 women to the 450 highest positions in government) may be worse than that of preceding U.S. administrations, but it still outshines the PRC, where out of 596 cabinet- and sub-cabinet-level positions in government only a niggardly 18 were held by women in 1980. The belated appointment of a woman to the U.S. Supreme Court may have marked an embarrassed first, but no women have served as justices on the PRC's Supreme People's Court, although the first Minister of Justice, Shi Liang, was female. While the U.S. may have had only a handful of women governors, no Chinese province or autonomous region has been led by a woman in the over three decades of Communist rule.

Those few women who do hold high office are often relegated to cameo roles and do not wield real power. Song Qingling, the wife of Sun Yatsen, held the highest figurehead position, serving until her death in 1981 as First Vice Chairman of the National People's Congress. Wang Guangmei, the wife of former Head of State Liu Shaoqi, was given a token post in the Chinese Academy of Social Sciences when her husband was posthumously rehabilitated. Other top women are shunted into work relating to women. Even Chen Muhua, the highest-ranking woman who appears to have achieved genuine responsibility as Minister of the Department of Economic Relations with Foreign Countries, was also inevitably assigned to head the Birth Control Small Group.

While those in positions of leadership are preponderantly men, at the same time no Party committee, government office, or factory organization is without its one or two female members. But like the women at the top either they are, in the words of one woman cadre, *you weizi meiyou danzi* (holding a position without responsibilities), or they do "woman's work." Both are forms of sexual tokenism, for to be invariably shunted into work with women's groups and female concerns regardless of one's abilities is no less a prejudicial consequence of male chauvinism than appointment to powerless posts of public prominence. And sex-typed work—taking a leading role in the birth control campaign, supervising nurseries, and encouraging women to participate in labor—is usually a dead-end, careerwise. Even in proportion to their limited numbers women do not share in power.

The Committee of Concerned Asian Scholars, an American group dedicated to taking Maoism at face value, a decade ago answered the question of why men still dominate leadership roles in the PRC by arguing that "women who have made it into leadership positions are almost always young enough to have entirely remolded their lives after 1949. Older women had already been so limited and deprived by the oppression they lived under that they could not shake it off completely." While this may still be part of the explanation (though it reads far less convincingly in the 1980s than it did in 1970), the continued failure of Chinese women to participate equally in political life seems to have more to do with deep-seated, inbred modes of male-female interaction which have survived down to the present and which relegate women to subordinate roles.

In the formal meetings of Sandhead Brigade cadres I observed, Chen Suzhen and Chen Xiaoying did not join the other cadres around the long plank table in the center of the meeting hall, but demurely retired to a separate bench along the wall. From this marginal niche they were content to listen to the men holding forth to each other, speaking up only when prompted by the Party secretary for their opinion. When I asked all fifteen brigade cadres to evaluate each other's work ability and performance, the two women were uniformly ranked lower than their male colleagues, not only by the men but by the women themselves. When questioned, several of the male cadres responded with masculine condescension that "women are simply less capable than men in many ways."

At higher levels in the administration such sentiments are considerably more muted, although still present. The highest-ranking woman in Equality Commune is a short, unimposing woman in her middle forties with a pageboy haircut and a hesistant smile. Although Lao Heying held a seat on the standing revolutionary committee that runs the commune as the only woman out of eight members, she had not been present at the welcoming banquet where I met the other commune leaders, and I made her acquaintance only the following month when she led me on a tour of the facilities of the commune's "Culture, Education, and Health Battle Line" that she was responsible for.

She seemed uncertain how to deal with me that morning and took refuge in a silence broken only by brief, uninformative comments as we visited the units that she was in charge of—the propaganda station, which broadcasts a combination of news, political slogans, and martial music that reaches every peasant home in the commune via loudspeakers; the so-called culture station, which runs the commune's movie theater and supervises a movie team consisting of five projectionists who show open-air movies in villages throughout the commune; the education small group,

in charge of the two dozen village primary schools; the health
small group, which operates the main commune health clinic and
six small outpatient clinics in the remote areas of the commune.
At each stop Lao Heying would introduce me to the cadre in
charge, in all cases a man, and then stand to one side saying
little as he briefed me on the work of his unit. I was struck by
Lao Heying's retiring behavior. It was only as we walked back
to her commune office that I was able to draw her out a little,
finding out that she had come with her husband to Equality Commune a decade ago when he had been sent here to serve as the
first Party secretary and commune head. "He became the first
Party secretary of Dragon's Course Commune to the north of
here two years ago," she shyly admitted, brushing her bangs back
from her face. "I have put in for transfer there."

"Lao Heying doesn't know how to use her authority," a young
male cadre in the propaganda station told me privately some time
later. "It was better when her husband was first Party secretary
here, because then he would help her. Now if we tell her we
have difficulties, she listens sympathetically, but nothing ever
comes of it. Recently we've started taking our problems directly
to the commune head." Lao Heying's career had been drawn
along in the powerful wake of her husband's, and was becalmed
in his absence. Though serving as a member of Equality Commune's revolutionary committee, she was excluded from the inner
core of power and responsibility, where decisions are made infor-
mally before they are taken up in formal meetings. Just as in
American corporations, it is these inner cliques, bound together
by male camaraderie and long association, that women have been
excluded from. Even today in the People's Republic the only culturally sanctioned behavior between unrelated men and women
is a distant reserve, and "comrades" of the opposite sex who
interact too easily and openly are presumed to be intimate. Especially in the countryside but in urban areas as well, informal networks of power remain closed to PRC cadres who happen to be
female.

However much the women who sit on Party, government,
and enterprise committees may lack genuine authority, their mere
presence represents progress, for there was a time when women

held no public positions at all. Traditional Chinese society was not just dominated by men, in a real sense it was man incarnate. The masculine principle was enshrined in a social structure in which male kinship not only was the focus of the family, but was extended outside the family in the form of clans. These great confraternities extended over hundreds of years and often encompassed thousands of members—all, from the hoary first ancestor down to neonate clanmates, of the male gender. Females were clan property, the chattels of first their fathers' and later their husbands' lineages, commodities exchanged in marriage to perform the necessary tasks of continuing the family line and keeping the household afloat and in trim. Even after her marriage a woman was no better than a slave, to be indentured or sold if necessity demanded, and necessity, in the form of drought, flood, earthquake, and pestilence, was never far removed.

Women were at the mercy of the masculine domain they were born into. The birth of a girl was cause not for celebration, as at the arrival of a manchild, but often for tragedy, for the lives of many female infants ended at birth.* Southern Chinese had a saying that daughters were *pei gian huo,* or "goods on which one loses," because one raised them to maturity only to have them marry into another family which reaped the benefits of one's investment. Ordinary peasant families minimized their loss by drafting daughters into the household labor pool as early as 7 or 8, an age at which their favored brothers still roamed about the village in ragtag play groups. Another strategy was to exchange a girl infant for another infant girl that the family would raise as a future bride for their son, a little daughter-in-law who could be early introduced to her role in life. More impoverished families had no choice but to sell their daughters as kitchen slaves or second wives to the wealthy. And for families who could not afford to raise a girl for the several years it would take for her to reach marketable age, there was always infanticide. Girls fortunate to be born into families that could afford the cost of their upbringing had their own cross. Their feet were bound in the excruciatingly painful process that deformed them into the dainty clubs that men of the Ming and Qing dynasties found attractive.

* The practice of female infanticide, long in abeyance in rural China, has recently reappeared in response to draconian state policies on population control. See Chapter 9.

A daughter was married at an age her parents considered appropriate to a young man that she had never set eyes on in a ceremony which required the young bride to make obeisance to her new family's ancestors and her parents-in-law. Her relationship with her husband was generally held to be less important than that with her new set of "elders." With her husband she was supposed to avoid the appearance of intimacy, while toward her father-in-law, by custom a distant and powerful patriarch, she was to be reserved and correct. The relationship of the new daughter-in-law with her mother-in-law was necessarily closer, for she came directly under the older woman's domestic control. As her own mother-in-law had done a generation earlier, this woman passed along to the younger the bulk of the domestic drudgery as the prerogative of her age and position. She also watched carefully to make sure that the daughter-in-law adhered to the *lijiao*, the "code of conduct" which prescribed, among other things, that she was not to venture alone across the threshold of her new home for three years after marriage.

A bride was required to serve her new elders, her father- and mother-in-law, by bringing them a basin of hot water in the morning to wash their faces and another in the evening to wash their feet, by folding up their bedding in the morning and laying it out at night, and by presenting them tea and inquiring after their health in a twice-daily demonstration of filiality. To be industrious and obedient was often not enough to win a mother-in-law's affection, however, for many of these older women anxiously viewed their young and attractive daughters-in-law as rivals for the affection of their sons, upon whom they relied as guarantors of their status and protectors of their old age. No amount of industry or obedience could completely quell the suspicions of many a mother-in-law that her daughter-in-law would weaken the bond that she had so carefully forged between herself and her son.

Bound as they were to the narrow circle of the family, expected to be totally submissive to parents, parents-in-law, and later husbands, women had drastically limited opportunities to develop their potential or involve themselves in the wider world of affairs. Few but the very wealthy bothered to educate their daughters, and women were forbidden to sit for the civil service examinations, much less serve as government officials. Women's inferiority was also underscored and reinforced by custom and belief. Women's clothes could not be hung on the second floor of houses, because at that height they would be over men's heads, reversing the natural order of things. A woman's person was regarded as ritually polluting because of the blood discharged during menstruation and childbirth. The tragic confirmation of the generally accursed state of womanhood in traditional China is that the majority of Chinese were male. Women, their numbers reduced by infanticide, childhood illness, suicide after marriage, death in childbirth, and physical exhaustion, simply didn't survive as long as men. The most disadvantaged minority in dynastic times was not the poor, but women.

Like any downtrodden minority they were caricatured by a pernicious stereotype, which held that women were weak-willed, dependent creatures lacking intelligence and initiative. In fact, the woman who successfully ran the beastly gauntlet that awaited them at birth were often tough, independent creatures as capable as any man. It was a back-handed compliment to able women that men who feared their wives were said to prosper (*pa laopo hui fada*). Even within their natal families, however, they were not deliberately mistreated. Many parents, though swayed by custom and straitened by poverty to put their sons first, did the best they could by their daughters. Their critical choice was deciding upon a marriage partner, and they would not deliberately marry their daughter off to a cur. Parents exerted themselves to make the best match possible, since marriage was freighted with consequences for their daughter's future. (They might in fact make a better match than their daughter would have made on her own, especially if she were confused by the onrush of her emotions.) But there were narrow limits to what women could achieve by strength of will and parental affection alone, however effective many older women may have been in dominating their home and those they had personal contact with. The larger society was weighted against them, and without culturally sanctioned and institutionally supported ways to develop their abilities even the brightest and most aggressive of them could not go far.

This grim picture had already been considerably modified by the middle of the twentieth century. Women in most areas of Guangdong had stopped binding the feet of their daughters

in the 1890s. The Empress Dowager issued an edict officially for-
bidding the practice in 1902, and I was told that the last old
women to totter about on "3-inch golden lilies," as their shrunken
feet were called, had died in the 1970s. "Blind marriages," where
the bride and groom did not meet until the wedding ceremony,
had become uncommon by the 1920s, and even village grandmothers I spoke with had seen their prospective husbands—and
had had the right to reject their parents' choice—before the match
was made. Opportunities for women to receive a formal education
began to increase, through the efforts first of missionaries and
later of the Kuomintang government, and it became respectable
for women, at least in urban areas, to work outside the home.
By the time the Communists bombastically intoned, "The People's
Republic abolishes the feudal institutions which hold women in
bondage," women were bound far less tightly by these flagging
institutions than their grandmothers had been. In many respects,
the advances made in China during the fifties and sixties appear
as natural continuations of trends that began in the Qing and
Republican periods.

The Communist Party, like the Kuomintang before it, passed
laws outlawing practices that subordinated women to men. The
first charter of the Communist regime, the "Common Program"
published in 1949, proclaimed that "in political, economic, cultural, educational, and social aspects of life women possess equal
rights and privileges with men." Each of the several subsequent
PRC state constitutions (four at latest count) has reaffirmed this
pledge, which American women's groups in the early 1980s were
still struggling to append to the American Constitution. In theory
Chinese women have achieved equality with their menfolk.

In practice it has proved much easier to liberate women on
paper than to liberate them in fact, especially in the countryside
where even today custom continues to triumph over legislation.
The exaction of money or gifts in connection with marriage is
officially forbidden, but young Chinese men must still give gifts
to their bride-to-be and pay a bride price to her parents if they
want to marry. The law states that a couple who register with
the local government shall be considered married, but in the eyes
of villagers the traditional marriage feast is still the only tie that
binds. The law reads that wives have the right to inherit their
husbands' property, but in actuality family property passes directly

to sons upon the death of the father. Daughters are formally guaranteed equal rights of inheritance, but in the countryside sons do not share their patrimony with their sisters.

Other changes in the status of women, trumpeted by the Communists and casual observers alike as advances, look different upon close scrutiny. Equal pay for equal work is established in principle, but rural women are paid 20 percent less than men for performing the same tasks. Nearly all Chinese women now work, but many are confined to menial, low-paying jobs even in the cities. Abortions are legal, and maternity leaves are standard practice, but many women would like to have more children than they are allowed under stringent family-planning regulations. A network of day care centers has been set up in urban areas, but in the countryside child care has been left in the hands of grandmothers and overworked mothers. Women have been liberated from the tyranny of recurring childbirth—even when they don't necessarily want to be—by a rigid program of birth control (a topic to which I will return in the next chapter). The declining number of children has eased somewhat the burden of domestic work in recent years, and should eventually result in every young couple's living with members of the older generation as these come to outnumber their offspring, but perhaps only half of all women today have a mother-in-law that they can turn to for help with the chores.

Nowhere have the advances been more striking or the shortcomings more apparent than in female education. The crust of ignorance which kept women illiterate and subservient has been broken, and girls today attend schools in large numbers. Enrollments of girls in primary schools have risen to nearly equal those of boys. But after primary school, especially in the countryside, educational opportunities gradually contract for young women as they come up against the hard economic realities of village life. By the senior primary grades, girls are already heavily burdened by such chores as taking care of younger siblings, doing the family laundry, cutting grass, and tending the family stove. Labeled as woman's work, these are sex-typed tasks that boys would not perform if they could, and often could not perform if they would. By contrast, by the time girls reach lower middle school most are already capable of the full range of household chores, from cooking the family meals to caring for the farm animals, and it is at that point that they begin to leave school in large numbers. In a household that has no grandmother, a girl will often be taken out of school by her parents after completing the five years of primary school and put to work at home. Even if there is a grandmother or older sister at home and the girl is allowed to continue in school, the chores she is responsible for mount rapidly as she enters her teens, and a cycle of poor attendance and poor grades is set in motion that leads to an early end to her formal education. In the rural eighth-grade class I briefly taught English to, there were only seven girls out of a total of thirty-three students, a skewed sex ratio typical of the countryside at that grade level. Although the sharp disparity in the numbers of boy and girl students in rural secondary schools is partially compensated for by urban schools with more balanced sex ratios, men outnumber women overall in middle schools and universities. Although statistics are hard to come by, one rare report revealed that a mere 28 percent of the PRC's college population is female. Another estimated that women accounted for only 30 percent of the country's scientific and technical personnel who had graduated from middle-level and higher schools, but made up fully 70 percent of the country's illiterates.*

But women's problems normally receive little play in the official press, which is more concerned with haranguing women to make self-sacrificing contributions to the Four Modernizations than with continuing sex discrimination. Neither are women permitted to take any kind of grass-roots group action to improve their position vis-à-vis men. There is virtually no women's liberation movement in the PRC, and no organizations exist to raise women's consciousness of inequality or to bring public pressure to bear on the government. The only extant group is the Women's Federation. Despite its feminist-sounding title, it is not an organization through which women struggle for equality, but through which they are mobilized by the Communist Party. It is in fact an extension of the Party, led by top Party women, whose institutional priorities are a mirror of the current Party line. "The realization of the Four Modernizations is current policy," the 1980 Women's Day announcement of the Women's Federation predictably instructed women. "Achieving the Four Modernizations will be

* The statistics on higher education appeared in an article in the *Beijing Review*, no. 1, 1980, p. 18, those on illiteracy in the *People's Daily* of March 20, 1980.

advantageous to our nation and to our peoples, and is the necessary road to follow for the complete liberation of females."* In this formulation, which is repeated with only minor variations year after year, the larger aspirations of women are to be satisfied only after politics, the national interest, and the interest of the people as a whole (that is, men) are taken into account. The organization is also charged with promoting better hygiene, improving pediatric care, and implementing birth control, but except for the last area, which is currently the focus of a massive effort in the countryside, its approach is passive. When asked what activities the Women's Federation organized for local women, one woman's work cadre, herself the head of a brigade branch of the Women's Federation, replied succinctly, "Participating in collective labor."

As the Women's Federation cadre's answer suggests, the biggest change in the lives of Chinese women under the Communist regime is that most of them now work outside the home. Except for the women of the Hakka—China's hill folk—women did not work regularly in agriculture before the revolution. Rural women were first of all homemakers, a reserve work force that helped in the fields only at the critical times of planting and harvest. But in Yanan and the other Communist base areas during the civil war, army drafts created a need for manpower that could only be filled by women. The necessarily self-sufficient economies of these blockaded areas came to depend heavily upon women for both agricultural and handicraft production, as they, like self-sufficient widows in China for centuries, mastered the economic roles vacated by their conscripted husbands. Later, tens of millions of women were turned out of the household and into the economy nationwide during the Great Leap Forward, when all able-bodied men and women were mobilized to labor on the newly organized communes, on giant construction projects, and in urban street factories. In the Pearl River Delta, many villages were emptied of men in their twenties and thirties as these were sent to distant coal mines and large-scale labor projects. The rule in the communal kitchens of the time was "no work, no eat," and the wives of these corvée laborers had no choice but to troop into the fields.

* Shanghai's *Wenhuibao*, February 1, 1980.

Even after the Great Leap went awry, government propaganda and economic pressure kept most women on the job. By the late seventies they held down perhaps one-third of the roughly 100 million nonagricultural positions in the Chinese economy, or on the order of 35 million jobs. Women make an even larger contribution in the countryside, where virtually all women between the ages of 16 and 50 work regularly in collective labor and constitute approximately half of the rural work force. In my experience, many communes now have more women working as field laborers than men, the men having gone preferentially into cadre positions or rural factories.

Communists have seen employment for women outside the home as the key to woman's liberation ever since Engels wrote in 1884 that "to emancipate woman and make her the equal of man is and remains an impossibility so long as the woman is shut out from social productive labor and restricted to private domestic labor."* Though the Chinese Communists offer similar rationalizations, one suspects that the Party was motivated as much by the potential value of women as a labor resource as it was by the desire to liberate women. The fate of feminists like Ding Ling, who like women's libbers in the U.S. demanded immediate social action to improve the status of women, is telling. Silenced as a rightist in 1957, she was accused of neglecting woman's economic role.**

The sizable dimensions of that role have contributed to the growth of the Chinese economy. Although the productive impact of women has been lessened by the surfeit of labor in populous China, women workers have been an inexpensive way of pumping up the economy without expensive capital investment. Recruiting domestically employed women didn't place additional demands on the urban infrastructure. It required no new housing, schools, water supply, or sewage disposal. The only institutional support required was day care centers, the expense for which was borne by individual factories and government offices. By preventing peasants from moving to the cities and by sending urban youth down to the countryside, the Communists minimized the need for urban renewal and construction during the sixties and seven-

---

* Frederick Engels, *The Origin of the Family, Private Property, and the State*, Eleanor B. Leacock, ed. (New York: International Publishing Company, 1972), p. 137.
** Ding Ling was finally rehabilitated in 1979.

ties, while at the same time building up the labor force by employing large numbers of urban women. Rural production increased as women entered the work teams and nearly doubled the number of laborers on the land. The net effect was to raise the ratio of producers to consumers. Young women who would have worked at home now work on farms and in factories; older women who would have supervised their daughters-in-law's domestic labors must now perform half of those labors on their own; and even older men, who still do little beyond drink and kibbitz, can occasionally be conned into child care and a household chore or two that they formerly would have spurned. The PRC, like the Soviet Union, owes part of its economic growth over the past quarter century to a rapidly increasing labor force as women were put to work.

If Beijing wants to keep women working because of their indispensable contribution to the national economy, women see work as a personal necessity, for few families can stay financially afloat on the earnings of the father alone. Wages in the People's Republic do not rise as rapidly with seniority as they do in America, and an unmarried youth of 25 making 30 *rmb* ($20) a month and doing nicely is only making 40 *rmb* ($27) a month ten years later—not enough to support the wife and young child that he probably has by that time. Only if the wife works will the family be economically viable. This is not, as in the U.S., an attempt to gain some breathing space in the family budget or to save up for luxuries. Wages have risen so slowly over the past twenty years (perhaps primarily because of the large increase in the labor force as women came into the job market) that two salaries are essential to meet basic expenses for food, shelter, and clothing.*

Fostered by necessity, women have come to accept employment outside the home as a normal, if not totally desirable, part of life. When country girls reach the age of 16, they go as a matter of course and register as a laborer with their local production team. Young women finishing lower and upper middle school in the city await their work assignments anxiously, knowing that such jobs generally carry a life tenure. One girl expressed surprise when I asked her if she would give up her job when she married.

* The wages of urban residents were largely frozen from 1958 to 1977. Across-the-board raises came in 1978–80, but these have been largely negated by inflation.

"Maybe if I marry the son of a *gaogan* [high-ranking cadre]," she said, laughing at the thought. "Otherwise I will just have to keep working."

Despite the fact that women work alongside men performing largely the same tasks in the fields and factories, they do not receive equal pay. In rural Guangdong women earn from 8 to 10 work points (the currency of the collective) per day, while all but the oldest and most enfeebled men make eleven or twelve. Although women I spoke to were not up in arms about this wage disparity, many viewed it as unfair. "We women can do anything that men can do," a sturdy, large-boned peasant woman from Sandhead Brigade told me flatly. "We can spade earth, harvest sugarcane, carry mud buckets, and weed the fields. Men say that women can't dig up mud [for fertilizer] from the bottom of the fish ponds, but it is just that we have never been allowed to try. Of course, it really is difficult work. Men also say that we can't net the fish at the end of the year. They say that the water is too cold for women because you have to wade up to your chest for several hours. But this is not as hard as men make it out to be. They really won't let us do it because"—here she hesitated, momentarily embarrassed—"they think that we are unclean [*bu ganjing*]. They think it will have a bad effect on the fish."

Although most delta men I spoke with did point to these two "difficult" tasks of mud-scrapping and fish-netting as justifying their higher wages, the team heads—all men—who actually assign work tasks and supervise their progress offered more realistic assessments, admitting that women often work harder than men. "The men like to go out and grunt and groan for an hour or two and then return home to rest," one long-time team head told me, offering a tortoise-hare version of the work patterns of the sexes. "Women work much more steadily for longer periods of time and in the end get more done." He also admitted that it was easier to supervise women because they were more reliable than men, who tended to shirk when given the chance. In his view women are unfairly discriminated against by the fixed daily work-point system, and most of them should earn 11 to 12 points a day just like the men on the basis of actual work accomplished, an opinion seconded by other team heads.

One irony is that the very industriousness of rural women has worked to keep them on the low end of the work-point scale.

Many women, in addition to the six-to-seven-hour collective work day, put in time in the morning and evening picking mulberry leaves and cutting grass, for which they are paid by piece rates. The extra work points earned in this way help close the 20 to 30 percent gap between their daily wages and those of men, and the annual work-point totals of some of the most energetic women actually exceed those of many men. For peasant men who unconsciously assume male superiority, this is an unfathomable and unnatural situation, which they correct by inflating their own wages while keeping those of women depressed. Again it was a male team head who confirmed this, illustrating his point by telling me how his team for two years during the "Destroy the Four Olds" phase of the Cultural Revolution had allowed the best women workers to earn 11 work points a day, a level formerly reserved for men only. "The women were able to do the work," he recalled, "but we finally had to move them back to 10 points a day anyway. The male team members were upset that women were earning as much as they themselves were."

The Cultural Revolution emphasis on time rates, designed as an "affirmative action" measure to hold wage differentials in check, thus had the unintended side effect of penalizing women. Conversely, women are among the unplanned beneficiaries of Deng's stress on increasing farm output by means of individual wage incentives. Under piece rates women—and men—are paid on the basis of what they produce, and a measure of equity has been restored to the relative earnings of men and women. Not surprisingly, some rural men resisted the move to piece rates, afraid that women would outearn men, and that they would lose income and, more importantly, face.

In the cities, although there is no direct wage discrimination against women, they tend to be concentrated at the lower end of the wage scale in low-status jobs. The labor force of small, neighborhood enterprises, which offer low pay and almost no benefits, is predominantly female. In the state-run heavy industry sector, where the pay, benefits, and prestige are highest, men predominate. Even within factories women are often sidetracked into more menial jobs. In a province-run bicycle parts factory I toured, the machine shops were mostly manned by men engaged in manufacturing gears and sprockets, while the workers in the packing sheds, who assembled and packed these parts, were without exception women. Even though the same eight-grade pay scale obtained for all workers in the factory, the machinery workers, because of their higher skill level, moved up the pay scale more rapidly than the women, who as a result averaged one-third less take-home pay than the men.

Women comprise the new lumpen proletariat of the People's Republic, a low-paid, unskilled, and expendable labor force that does the dirty work that men will not do. In China it is work gangs of women who sweep the streets and collect the garbage, carry heavy hods of bricks and mortar at construction sites (where the bricklayers are all men), and cart away rubble, who are bent over by stacks of firewood bound upon their backs that make them look like moving thickets, and who balance two buckets of gloppy mud slung from a yoke-like carrying pole. And who can forget the corvée labor scenes of the Great Leap Forward, with vast numbers of blue-clad—and on local projects mostly female—laborers swarming over the landscape like a human earth-moving machine carving out canals and throwing up dams. These are strength-sapping tasks that few of the house-bound mothers of the postrevolutionary generation had to perform.

Ironically, in view of the official ideology that working outside the home is a liberating experience, many women I spoke with felt that their lot had worsened since the revolution. Several middle-aged women expressed a nostalgia for the past, when women of their age could while away their afternoons on their front step chatting with neighbors. This was a pleasure that their mothers-in-law had enjoyed but that was denied to them by the new system, which obliged their daughters-in-law to work outside the home and subjected them to the incessant demands of household labor. Neither were younger rural women enthusiastic about their new "liberated" status as field laborers, especially since their collective travail had scarcely eased their domestic burden. Though they accepted work as an economic necessity, slaving at what one woman called "coolie" labor hardly serves as a respected or sought-after career. Even if fieldwork were an alternative to domestic labor rather than an additional burden, most rural Chinese women would choose to stay in the home, where work in their eyes provides more direct satisfaction because it is done to meet the immediate needs of their family at their own initiative and speed.

The final comment on fieldwork versus domestic work came from the mother of six who served as my cook and housekeeper, when I asked her which period of her life she had enjoyed the most. "This year, working at home," she instantly replied. "I can stay home and take care of my children and household and not have to go out and work in the fields every day." Though she had a mother-in-law to help out at home, she was glad to be freed from field labor. And this was not merely a question of increased leisure, for even at home she was always busy with one task or another in the household.

Of course, most Chinese women don't have the choice of giving up one of the twin yokes of field and domestic work to which they are shackled, but must remain in harness, and in some ways their double burden has grown even more onerous in recent years. Men are gradually leaving the labor pool of rural collectives to work in rural factories and enterprises, while women remain on the land. As a result, in many areas there are now more women than men working as field hands, and numerous laborious and heavy tasks that were in the past performed by men have fallen to women. At the same time, domestic labors still remain largely the province of women. An unusual letter published in the *People's Daily* in 1980, written by a female reporter from the New China News Agency, reported an investigation done by the Women's Federation of the Guangxi Zhuang Autonomous Region in Wutang Commune of Yongxing County, which revealed that in that region 75 percent of the field labor was done by women. During the busy season, the report noted, these women went to work at 6 or 7 a.m., and did not return home until the same time in the evening, and still had the housework to do before they could turn in. "Some women," the writer noted, "because they have been overworked for long periods of time, have gradually come down with various illnesses and 'women's disorders.'

"The reasons for this situation are numerous, but one important cause is the low level of knowledge among women, a lack of understanding of science and culture, which renders them incapable of serving in positions which require technical knowledge of one sort or another. When the nation recruits cadres and workers, when communes and brigades allot workers to their factories and enterprises, it is for the most part men who are selected. Left behind to carry out simple, burdensome, and tiresome tasks are the women. . . . Now that a certain amount of modernization is occurring in the countryside, this problem is becoming increasingly serious."

It would be a tragic irony indeed if peasant women, having risen from beasts of burden to second-class citizens, were to fall back to their earlier status as the initial payoffs of the slow process of rural modernization continued to go mainly to men.

The endless treadmill of domestic tasks and outside work that Chinese women face is beyond the ken of American women, even those caught themselves between the twin horns of home and work. Women in the PRC have no supermarkets to ease the burden of shopping, no frozen foods to take the pain out of cooking, and only primitive versions, if any, of the labor-saving devices that reduce the rigors of housekeeping. A daunting daily round of chores must somehow be performed around a full day of work—not the clean, physically undemanding clerical or service-sector employment that the majority of working American women perform, but grubby farm work or arduous factory labor.

The reality of life as a "liberated" working woman in the PRC was brought home to me by the labors of Gin Sau, "sister-in-law Gin" as she was known in the village, the 32-year-old mother of three I lived next door to for nearly a year. Though I often went over to Gin Sau's to talk to her, her husband, or her mother-in-law, I never found her sitting idle savoring a cup of tea as was her husband's habit in the evening, or taking a mid-afternoon nap as was her mother-in-law's wont. She was always up and about, busying herself with this or that task, but was still never able to do all that needed to be done or get ahead of her housework. She was, she described herself, as busy as a "headless fly," flying frantically in erratic circles here and there with never a moment's rest. The only time all year I saw her sitting still and simply chatting with callers was at the Chinese New Year, and even then she was constantly bouncing up and down fetching hot water and tea leaves, replenishing the *jian dui* pastries and ladling out bowls of rich New Year's gruel for the guests. And she paid in advance for what rest she did manage on that day with a penance of several consecutive days of food preparation and house cleaning at an even more grueling pace

than usual. Then, the day after New Year's, Gin Sau's life reverted
to its usual pattern of harried industry, beginning before daylight
and ending only at 10 or 11 p.m. at night.

From long habit Gin Sau awakens each morning in the hour
before dawn. Because their children are still young, she and her
husband still sleep together in the big wooden bed with the carved
canopy that came as part of her dowry nine years before, he next
to the wall and she away from it, so that she can rise early without
disturbing him. He sleeps an hour or so later each morning than
she, rising only when breakfast is ready. She reaches out through
the mosquito net and plucks her clothes off the peg halfway up
the bedpost where she hangs them each night, and begins to
dress in bed. This is a simple process, for she has no nightgown
to change out of. She sleeps in a pair of square-cut boxer shorts
and undershirt which are indistinguishable from her husband's.
Like all of their clothes, she made them herself. Over these she
draws on her long, baggy trousers of dark blue cotton muslin,
knotting the cord that serves as a belt tightly around her waist,
and pulls on her black top, fastening one by one the frogs that
angle up the side of the blouse diagonally. Like the other married
women in the village, she still dresses in *tang zhuang,* or Chinese-
style clothing, even though the younger unmarried women have
taken to wearing shirts that button up the front like city women.

She rises quietly from bed and runs the family comb through
her hair—her only concession to her appearance. Her hair is cut
into short blunt flaps around her ears, a no-nonsense style that
takes only a second to comb, does not blow into tangles in the
wind, and dries quickly after her late-night bath so she can go
soon to bed. She allows her daughters' hair to grow longer than
her own strictly utilitarian style—not as long as before the revolution, when young girls left their hair uncut and it grew down to
their knees by the time they married, but long enough to tie
into short pigtails.

Though the sickly gray of predawn is just beginning to signal
morning, women are already gathering around the well to draw
water for breakfast. Gin Sau takes the two buckets and carrying
pole out of their corner in the kitchen and hurries out to join
them. The clear water that had accumulated in the well overnight
will soon be drawn off, leaving but a few pails of muddy seepage,
and Gin Sau quickly lets her bucket down in the well with the

others. Some of the village women are less particular, and many of the women who live along the bank of the village canal use its murky water for cooking, giving their steamed rice a gray shade and a gritty flavor, but Gin Sau knows this to be unsanitary and is more careful. She smoothly hauls back home the two pails of clear water, walking with the slinking gait of the carrying-pole user under a back-wrenching load that would stagger men unused to it.

Back in her kitchen, she pours the water into the large crockery pot by the doorway and then sets about preparing the morning meal. Swiftly scooping out one and a half cups of rice grains into the battered and blackened rice pot, she adds several cups of water and washes the rice. The rinse water, now milky with rice polish, is poured into a large wok used for pig mash, new water is added to the rice pot, and it is hoisted onto the stove to steam. Adding several measures of rice bran (milled rice husks) to the large wok, she hefts it also onto the stove, setting it on the large far burner to simmer. There Gin Sau's mother-in-law will keep an eye on it throughout the morning, and will feed it to the family pigs after it has boiled into mash. If there were no grandmother in the house, this is a task that she would have to perform herself in the evenings.

Cooking for Gin Sau is both more and less work than Americans might imagine. It is more because everything is cooked from scratch. Not only are there no ready-to-cook meals, but even rice comes in the husk, and must be milled before it can be steamed. All food preparation starts from a gastronomic ground zero. The only way to reduce rice to flour for festival pastries, for example, is by turning ancient stone mills by hand, consuming one hour of labor for each cupful of fine rice flour produced. Cooking is done on a "wind" stove, a large, rectangular box of bricks with a flat, tiled surface that is broken by two or more circular openings for woks. The stove, fueled in the delta by dried sugarcane stalks, requires constant attention. The stalks and dried leaves burn through quickly and must be constantly replenished through a small port in the front of the stove to keep the fire from going out, but added carefully so that the fire does not flare up and incinerate the wok's contents. The preparation of the cakes, pastries, and other dishes of a festival may take a day or more.

For all this, cooking in normal times is not overly taxing,

for in between feast days stretches the Sahara of ordinary fare, a diet not merely plain but rigorously spartan. Gin Sau, like her neighbors, cooks only a plain rice porridge for breakfast, and for lunch and dinner serves steamed rice and finely diced salted turnips, occasionally supplemented with some greens from the family garden or, even more rarely, a few small pond fish or slices of fried pork fat. It is a diet dictated by poverty, not by her harried existence.

When there is hot water for tea and the rice has been boiled into a glutinous porridge, Gin Sau calls her husband and mother-in-law. Without waiting for them, she hastily spoons down a bowl herself and turns her attention to the laundry. The strain of doing an entire household's laundry by hand is outside the experience of the current generation of American women. But washers are unknown in China, and the wash is universally done by hand, a backbreaking task that takes perhaps an hour a day for most women. Although some women prefer to do their laundry squatting on the concrete steps at the edge of the canal where they can kibbitz in company with their friends, Gin Sau, like most of the village women, does hers in her own courtyard in an old wooden tub filled with well water. Detergent is nonexistent in the countryside, its place being taken by a hard, all-purpose soap that is, at 10 *fen* (7 cents) a bar, used very sparingly. Fuel is too scarce to use to heat water for washing. Clothes are cleaned primarily by scrubbing and pounding, though Gin Sau herself has a ribbed wooden washboard, a village luxury that reduces the amount of muscular flailing required. After rinsing and wringing out the clothes, she carries them up to her second-floor balcony where she strings them along bamboo poles which she then props up with sticks. Gin Sau is normally able to get the laundry done in the early morning hours, important because the thick cotton cloth of which the clothes are made does not dry easily in the high humidity of South China. But sometimes this task spills over into the noon recess, as when she washes the mosquito nets that hang over the beds, or rips apart the cotton quilts after a winter of use and washes, dries, and repairs wadding and lining.

It is nearly 7 a.m., and Gin Sau hurries to the team headquarters to pick up her work assignment for the day, check out the farm implement required, and take her place in the fields alongside the men and other women. The collective work regimen of hauling, spreading, spading, planting, watering, weeding, hoeing, cutting, chopping, and cropping that Gin Sau faces is a familiar one to farmers everywhere, but in China these are tasks that must still be done by men and women hefting buckets, wielding hoes, and swinging scythes. The collective work day is not long, and before eleven Gin Sau is home again preparing the noonday meal, and the family eats at noon.

As her husband and mother-in-law lie down for their noonday naps, Gin Sau goes off with two large baskets of plaited bamboo to forage for fuel. Each family in Sandhead is alloted an acre or so of a nearby sugarcane patch to pull off dead leaves and uproot dead stalks for fuel. But such kindling is often not enough, and Gin Sau must go as far as the hills that rise behind the fields, a twenty-minute walk away to glean dried grass and twigs. Returning home, she piles the dried growth in the corner of the kitchen farthest from the stove, scatters a handful of grain for the chickens, and awakens her husband for their afternoon stint of collective labor, which runs from 1:30 to 5 p.m.

In the late afternoon several times a week, Gin Sau takes her bamboo baskets and 8-year-old daughter to the mulberry fields, where the two of them pick together the mulberry leaves that will be chopped and fed to the silkworms. This is piece work, paid by the catty, and Gin Sau's fingers move quickly over the shrub-like trees, pinching the mature leaves off neatly at the stem to avoid damaging the twigs or wasting foliage, rapidly stripping it of all but its new growth. A good hour of work can sometimes net her a half day's pay, especially if it is drizzling out and the leaves weigh wet and heavy on the scales. On the way home she stops by the family's small garden and rapidly picks half a catty of string beans for the evening meal while her daughter plays along the edge of the nearby pond.

After the evening round of cooking, eating, and dishwashing Gin Sau takes up other chores. She sits down before her battered sewing machine, a pedal-operated Singer model dating from the 1920s that is a family heirloom, to sew a pair of trousers for her 4-year-old boy and mend her husband's trousers. There is a tailor in the village, but women who have a sewing machine, perhaps twenty women in all, or those who can borrow one prefer to make clothes themselves to save the 50 cents it costs to hire him to sew a pair of pants or a shirt. Still later in the evening there are poultry to be fed, floors to be swept, laundry to be taken in, bath water to be hauled and heated, and children to be bathed and put to bed.

Meanwhile her husband, who went wandering off after dinner to the team headquarters or a crony's house for several hours of desultory chatter, returns a little after nine to bathe and, if the evening is not too hot and muggy to get to sleep, go to bed. Only then, after the other family members have retired, does Gin Sau take what remains of the hot water and wash herself down. She makes a final round of the house, throwing the heavy wooden bolt to secure the outer gate, covering up the cooped chickens so that mosquitos will not put out their eyes, and checking that her children are snug in their beds. Finally, she climbs exhausted into bed herself, knowing that she will have to be up again before dawn the following day.

As hectic as Gin Sau's days were, she was better off than some of her neighbors, who had no live-in grandmother or whose husbands expected them to help with the private plot or the marketing. Gin Sau's mother-in-law cared for her three children during the day and tended the family's two pigs, cooking their mash and carrying it to their pens for their daily feeding, scrubbing them down with a long-handled brush, and flushing out their pens with pond water. Gin Sau's husband took care of the private plot, even doing the early morning watering which many men left to their wives, and marketed its produce.

I recall one of the poorer families along the alley I lived, in which the wife had four daughters in quick succession hoping for a boy child that had not yet arrived. There was no grandmother, and though the husband was known as one of the better workers in the team, the household burden remained hers alone. It was clearly too much for her. Their brick house was scarcely more than a hut, and their meager possessions consisted of a bed, a table and chairs, and a handful of wooden crates piled in one corner of the room, but it seemed in perpetual disorder and in need of a good house cleaning. Her children were always dressed in dirty and tattered clothes, hands and feet poking out of tattered sleeves and collars black with grime from the earthen floor. She herself dressed in clothes that were hardly cleaner than those of her children, and had a disheveled, defeated look about her. Her oldest daughter had already been pressed into domestic service to tend the fire, watch her baby sisters, and do other light household chores, but at 7 she was still too young to significantly ease her mother's burden. Gin Sau seemed a brilliant success as a working housewife and mother beside this strapped woman.

In some respects Gin Sau's domestic tasks were lighter than those her mother-in-law had faced when she had come as a new bride to Sandhead village thirty-five years before. An electric-powered mill had been installed in the village where a week's worth of rice could be husked in a few minutes. Thermos bottles made it unnecessary to kindle a fire to boil water for tea each time a neighbor stopped by. And those who were fortunate enough to have a mother-in-law could now expect her aid at home on a regular basis. But these gains are modest compared to the trial of daily field labor. Gin Sau used a traditional folk saying to sum up the current position of women: "Women are kept down at the eighteenth level of hell."

After listening to and observing village women over the course of a year, I am convinced that Gin Sau's evaluation of their collective fate is not overstated. Women are condemned to an endless domestic purgatory for the misfortune of having been born female. One sign of the special burden borne by rural women is the rapidity with which they age, even by comparison with their sun-blackened and weather-beaten men. "Women don't wear as well as men," one woman, whom I thought to be in her mid-fifties but who in fact had just turned 40, told me. And she was right. A young woman quickly loses her youthful blush, will be worn and faded by her late twenties, and by the time she reaches 50 will be wrinkled and haggish. Everywhere I went in the evenings I found men yawning over their teacups while their women scurried about performing this or that thankless task. When I commented on what was to me the glaring unfairness of this, most peasant men stared at me with as little comprehension as a lion might have shown when reproached for taking his proverbial share of his mate's kill. If he was goaded into a response, it was likely to take the form of the classic throw-away line of the reactionary. "Women have always done the housework," more than one man grunted to me.

Compared with the grim life of women in the countryside the life-style of urban women seemed, if not attractive, at least clearly endurable. While urban women are similarly mortgaged to both work and home, their dual burden is less physically demanding. Instead of hard field labor, most urban women work in factories, enterprises, and institutes, and urban life offers some amenities that make housework less burdensome, though it is still unrelenting. The smaller families of urban women—most young women now have only one child—and the general provision of day care centers have reduced child care to a part-time job. Most women in the big cities now take their cloth rations to a tailor and occasionally even purchase clothes readymade, saving the labor of sewing the clothes themselves. But shopping remains a nightmare of waiting in long lines for rationed goods and then trying to get home on the bus with an armload of purchases. Most urban apartment buildings, even those dating from before the revolution, have tap water, but hot running water remains a rarity, and women still do their laundry by hand in a tub of cold water. Cooking is done with coal instead of kindling, or sometimes even with natural gas, but there is no home delivery; the sacks of coal or heavy containers of gas must be picked up at the distribution point and lugged home. Housing is customarily assigned by the husband's unit, which usually puts him just a walk or ride (often on a special employee bus) away from work, while his spouse often finds herself facing twice-daily commutes of an hour or more across town on inefficient and overcrowded public transportation systems.

But urban husbands are conscientious helpmates compared with rural men, and are often willing to take a turn at domestic tasks, washing the dishes, helping to care for the child, doing some occasional shopping. Most men know how to cook, a skill many picked up during time spent with a political work team in the villages or while laboring on farms run by their units during the Cultural Revolution, and I have often seen men helping to prepare the family meals. Another stimulus to domestic partnerships in the cities is that wages are too low for most men to support families on their own. Women pick up their own paychecks in the cities, and their earnings make a critical contribution to the financial viability of the family.

Some urban women went so far as to claim that the domestic tables had been completely turned in a sizable number of households, and that among younger couples the wife is often the effective head of the household. A fine-boned, delicate-looking girl in her early twenties told me in no uncertain terms that she wanted to be in charge. Said she, "I want a husband who will listen to me and do what I tell him to do." Other young urban women I spoke with had equally nontraditional ideas about marriage, viewing it as an open partnership with all terms negotiable in advance. The traditional female role model of the "virtuous wife and good mother" (*xian qi liang mu*) holds little appeal for many young women who took to the city streets a decade ago in the Cultural Revolution marching, shouting, cursing, struggling, and doing battle shoulder to shoulder with their "brothers," and many favor a radically restructured family life.

Such women may be too optimistic about their ability to achieve a marital liberation of their own making. Too often, under the pressure of marital life, couples revert to the traditional pattern of the wife in a domestic, subservient role. None of the urban couples I became personally acquainted with had anything as innovative as a househusband, or even a fair and equitable sharing of the tasks of homemaking. Nevertheless, it is a liberation of sorts that in the cities such ideas can even find expression.

———————◆———————

In the countryside nontraditional ideas about woman's place in life are unheard of. Rural men portray their women as "empty-headed" creatures fit only for fieldwork and child bearing. I recall asking the Sandhead cadre in charge of the brigade's medical program why nearly all the barefoot doctors in the commune were male. "Women are dull-witted, incapable of learning as fast as men," he replied in a voice heavy with masculine condescension. "Aside from the midwives, who have to be women, we select bright young men for medical training." There may regretfully be some truth to what might seem to Westerners to be the baseless prejudice of a middle-aged male cadre: A little girl is not the pride of her parents that her brother is, and her education is often not taken seriously. She spends less time in school and doing homework, more time at household chores, and leaves school at an earlier age than her male sibling. As a group women are considerably less well educated than men, strengthening the conviction of male villagers that women are naturally less intelligent and able.

But a relative lack of educational opportunity is only one

of the disadvantages that rural women continue to labor under. Evidence of their supposed inferiority is also frozen into the cultural amber of customs, which often relegate women to a passive, subordinate role. A bride's family shuts the family gate quickly and securely behind her as she leaves for her husband's house to emphasize that she is no longer of her natal house. At feast times the women first serve the men before sitting down themselves to dine at separate tables. The women in a Guangdong funeral procession to this day turn back at the outskirts of the village, forbidden to go on to the graveyard because they are ritually unclean.

All this is both cause and consequence of an inbred attitude toward women as the second sex, a pernicious stereotype that is accepted by nearly all men and a surprisingly large percentage of women. Although Chinese women could with reason complain of being kept barefoot and pregnant, they more often echo the sentiments of their men and willingly admit to an inherited inferiority. More than any other single cause, it is probably these deep-seated and widely held prejudices that are responsible for the continuing low status of women. Certainly the employment of women outside the home, which is the Communist criterion for women's liberation, has produced consequences for women which are far less than emancipating.

Men continue to dominate formal positions of leadership at all levels down to and including the mundane rural production team. In central Guangdong it is men who manage the communal fields and fish ponds, and even the silkworm huts, within which only women work, are supervised by men. The immediate cause of this male domination is that only family heads are allowed to vote during the annual December meetings when the team members select their management council for the coming year. Since the overwhelming majority of family heads are men, women as a group have little formal voice in team affairs. The women who hold the post of woman's work cadre, which was established in part to ensure that women were represented in team council deliberations, often do not even attend the biweekly meetings of the council, and have thus largely failed to perform their appointed function.

Their lack of political suffrage carries over into the economic sphere, not only because women's wages are kept low, but because these wages are often not paid directly to them. Although work points are recorded daily for each individual in the team, in most teams I visited the accountant totaled the work points by family for the monthly reports. When the time came for distributions of cash, grain, and other crops, these allotments were made directly to the family head. The earnings of rural women are thus in most cases paid to their husbands or fathers-in-law, hardly a prescription for economic independence.

When meetings of all team laborers are called to discuss major planting and management decisions, many women do attend, but merely as spectators. The meetings I witnessed were sex-segregated. The men clustered in a tight inner circle in the center of the team office, while the women ranged themselves in an outer semicircle several feet from the nearest men. The men presented a solemn demeanor, squatting stilly on their haunches and listening to the comments of the other men on the proposals before the group. The women sat with their children playing at their feet or cradled in their laps and chatted among themselves, seemingly only half aware of the men's deliberations. Not once did I hear a woman, even one of the handful of widowed or divorced family heads, address the group. The closest they came to this were occasional ejaculations, such as the time when one team head announced that the over-quota portion of the year's sugarcane crop—some 6,000 catties of sugar—would be divided among the team's fifty-four households. "That much!" naively chirped one young mother, and the other meeting participants broke up with laughter. Most women, unaccustomed to speaking before a group that includes men and afraid of ridicule, avoid making even exclamations. "It is useless for a woman to speak out anyway," one woman said to me. "Women's speech has no effect; men's does. One sentence from a man is worth more than ten from a woman. Men don't pay any attention to what women say. Even if the woman is right, they say that she is wrong."

Although inhibited at meetings, many women, especially older ones, were not afraid to make their opinions known in less formal settings. They would snipe from a distance at passing cadres while working in the fields or would mutter criticisms when they encountered team leaders alone. Occasionally a woman will take matters even further, as happened one morning at the village well adjacent to my house. The well was a busy place in the hours around dawn as a steady stream of people crowded around its opening and filled the air with the bustling clatter of buckets and their noisy chatter. Normally, only women and children came to draw water, but on this morning the head of No. 3 Team, a robust, square-jawed man in his late thirties, came swinging up the path to the well, empty buckets in hand. As soon as the women noticed his approach, one of their number, a grandmotherly-looking woman in her late fifties who no longer worked as a field laborer and was represented in team meetings by her son, lit into him.

"Why is this year's work-point value so low?" she railed loudly. "What kind of team head are you? Last year we made 70 *fen* [47 cents] a day. This year we make maybe only 60 *fen.*"

The team head made no reply to the old woman, keeping his head down as if he were the struggle object at a political meeting, letting each bucket down in the well and drawing it up again in one swift motion. ("He would lose face if he publicly argued with a woman," a neighbor woman told me later.) His silence evidently further infuriated the old woman, who by now seemed more termagant than grandmother, and her public tongue-lashing grew more fierce.

"Aiiyah!" she shrieked. "We're all going to starve to death. Idiot. You're stealing our money. Crazy man. You give all the easy work to your family and friends. You dead demon. You're dead. You're dead."

Her tirade continued as he walked back up the village path, back slightly bent by the weight he was carrying. As he passed under my balcony, I heard him mutter in a venom-filled voice "dead person," but the imprecation was spoken too softly for it to carry back to the old woman beside the well, who was still busily hurtling curses at his retreating back.

Although such episodes underscore the sterility of the rural stereotype of women as dependent, helpless creatures, they scarcely compensate for the absence of proportional representation on the committees that control life in China. One articulate team-level woman's work cadre, Li Yuting, who tried to put the dearth of female cadres in her brigade in the best possible light because her brother-in-law was the brigade Party secretary, told me that one reason there are so few women cadres is that most women reject opportunities to serve as cadres. "It is their own fault," she claimed. "Women who have been recommended for posts often refuse to serve despite the enthusiasm and encouragement of other team members. They are afraid to take on more responsibility. Women are mostly concerned with their own families, not with other families, and want to mind their own business. They turn down positions by saying that their educational level is not sufficient for them to do well in such important work. But the real reason is that they already are weighed down with household tasks and work and are afraid to take on any more." Her argument that women are not willing to serve in team posts because they are family-centered, less confident in public roles, and already overwhelmed by domestic chores has some validity. Much team business, for example, is transacted in the hours before and after the collective working day, a time when women are tied up with domestic tasks.

Nevertheless, at root here is not female reticence, but male prejudices. Contrary to Cadre Li's claim, very few women are nominated for anything except woman's work posts. Gin Sau, more outspoken than most village women, put it in the following way: "People, especially men, think that women don't have a head for collective affairs, and so don't want them on the team committee. Some women do have ability, but their opinions are ignored. A woman on the team committee would be ineffective because no one would listen to her." She concluded by making the same point that Cadre Li had made to me earlier, but drew from it quite different conclusions. "It is true that women are busier than men," she said. "They don't have time to sit around the team office and solve the problems that occasionally arise. Of course, if women were on the committee, they wouldn't waste so much time just sitting around as men do because they are more active. People would have to work harder with women in charge." But she hastened to add, "Of course, women won't be put in charge."

Although in the villages it is the woman who keeps house and cares for the children, the man is the unquestioned head of the household. It is the man who represents the family in meetings of the collective, formal dealings with other families, and at weddings, births, and funerals. Within the family it is most often the man who manages the family finances, taking the cash allotments that come to him from the collective and doling them out to his wife as necessary to meet daily expenses.

In my experience, the long Chinese revolution has done less to rectify the inequitable position of women vis-à-vis men than it has to iron out inequalities within the ranks of rural women themselves. No longer are peasant women divided into misses, who avoided physical labor, and maids, who served them. Mothers-in-law have become less tyrannical toward and more cooperative with their daughters-in-law, dutifully sharing the burden of keeping the household afloat and in order while the younger woman is away working in the fields. The whittling away of differences among women based on status and age is progress of a sort, but has left a more fundamental inequality, that between males and females, largely untouched. Old women bemoan their loss of leisure, young women complain about the double burden of work at home and fieldwork, and all serve as the handmaidens of their men, waiting on them, fetching for them, and deferring to them.

Most rural women I spoke with claimed that they had been happier before wedlock than after, which I had initially attributed to the wrenching readjustment of leaving their natal family and home village to move in with a family of strangers in a community foreign to them that they had faced at marriage. But it turned out that there was more to the matter than just adapting to a new social environment and homesickness for the old. A female team custodian offered in further explanation the folk saying that married women are subject to *jiapo jian, ernü jian, laugong jian,* which means "husband supervision, mother-in-law supervision, and offspring supervision." "After you marry you are controlled from all sides," she clarified. "You are not free to go where you like or do what you want. Of course, mothers-in-law always complain about and criticize their daughters-in-law. That's just the way they are. The main thing is that many women are not treated well by their husbands. Here we say 'Bad mothers-in-law are like chickens clucking, but bad husbands cut off all hope.' This was especially true in the old days, when a husband could beat his wife to death and nothing would be done. Now we have the village security defense committee and wives are given some protection against their husbands, but many husbands still beat their wives."

I already had considerable evidence that in the countryside a marriage license was considered to be a hitting license by the time I had been in China for three months, but my last doubts that the continued subordination of women to men and their families rested ultimately on physical force were dispelled by a public beating I witnessed at about that time.

The voices of the Liang family can frequently be heard shrilly raised in anger by the other residents of Shifa Alley where they live. The family consists of a grandmother, who is the nominal head of the family, her son, a daughter-in-law, and the couple's four children, aged 5 to 11. Since marrying into the family thirteen years ago, the daughter-in-law has been waging a protracted, often heated struggle with her mother-in-law for dominance of the domestic scene. Although the other women said she did her share of collective labor, they condemned her as "not a good daughter-in-law" because she didn't do more around the house. One evening she refused to wash the dinner dishes, saying that she had worked hard in the fields that day and was too tired. Her mother-in-law told her that she wasn't tired, just lazy, and the fight was on. The younger woman, quick-tongued, quick-tempered, and equipped with a voice that could shout its way through half a dozen brick walls, quickly got the upper hand in the argument. The mother-in-law soon retreated from the house into the alleyway, closely pursued by her daughter-in-law, who continued without pause to revile the old woman with insults and curse her family's forebears back to the first ancestor. The mother-in-law shortly broke down completely and, giving up the effort to trade insults, began saying between sobs that she should never have sought a wife for her son, that she had been miserable since the day *that* woman came to live with them, and that she was soon going to end her ill-fated and unbearable life.

This was too much for her son (as perhaps it was intended to be), who up to this point had not intervened. He came out of the house and ordered his wife to stop cursing his mother. This attempt at firmness accomplished little more than the replacement of his mother's name with his own in her invective-loaded sentences. He told her again to shut up, threatening her with his raised hand, but she continued to taunt and curse him. The man stood motionless for a few seconds and then suddenly struck her in the face with his clenched fist. She crumpled down into a crouch, huddling with her hands over her head, but otherwise made no attempt to escape his blows. The man struck her slowly and with great force, a measured and painful drumming on her back. The first punch had cut off her curses, leaving only the hollow thump of each blow echoing up the alley, clearly audible to me where I was standing 30 feet away. I wished I were somewhere else. After perhaps twenty blows she finally broke her silence and began crying in great, jagged sobs. The man, evidently taking this as a sign of her surrender, left off his beating. Breathing heavily from his exertion, he turned away from the woman without saying a word and went back into the house with his mother, leaving the woman huddled in the alleyway.

The most surprising part of the episode to me was the reaction of the crowd of neighbors and relatives that had gathered. Not only did no one move to interfere when the husband began to physically punish his wife, several had in fact been urging him on to such measures as soon as he appeared, and as the beating was administered, the crowd appeared to watch with a certain grim satisfaction. When it was over, not a single person moved to console the woman for the rough handling she had received. She was left sobbing alone as they murmured approval of the man's action. One older woman, echoed by many others, said that it was a good thing, "Now she will be good for awhile." In the countryside, beating remains the final resort of husbands against recalcitrant wives.

9

Birth Control: A Grim Game of Numbers

Birth control is a way of slaughtering the Chinese people without drawing blood.

People's Daily editorial, 1952

Socialism should make it possible to regulate the reproduction of human beings.

Vice Premier Chen Muhua, 1979

The Chinese government, it turns out, is deadly serious about birth control. That is not what you would think from the sheer mass of the Chinese population, numbering over 1 billion, or one-fifth of the world's population, at last count. And that is not the way it seems when you enter the main gate of the Yuexiu Park in the northern section of Guangzhou City on any day of the week to be confronted with a 1-million-square-meter carpet of people of all ages. Nor is that the impression left by walking through the narrow alleyways of a Chinese village and encountering band after band of little urchins playing in front of their high-walled brick homes. But it is what I found when I attended a family-planning meeting at Equality Commune.

Family-planning meetings, which all women who were pregnant with their third or later child were required to attend, or who had had their first child within the last four years, had already been in progress for four days in each of the commune's twenty

224

brigades, and over 300 women had agreed to terminate their pregnancies under urging from local cadres. An equal number of village women had not acceded to the cadres' demand, however, and the commune revolutionary committee had decided to move the meetings to the commune headquarters, where their progress could be more carefully monitored and senior cadres placed in charge. The sessions continued to be segregated by brigade and led by high-ranking cadres, usually the Party secretary or assistant Party secretary of the brigade in question, but now a member of the commune revolutionary committee was present as well. Their goal was to implement the directive issued by the Guangdong provincial revolutionary committee restricting couples to no more than two children, thus holding down the rate of population increase in the commune to the prescribed 1.0 percent.

From Sandhead Brigade there were eighteen women, all from five to nine months pregnant, and many red-eyed from lack of sleep and crying. They sat listlessly on short plank benches arranged in a semicircle about the front of the room, where He Kaifeng, a commune cadre and Communist Party member of many years' standing, explained the purpose of the meeting in no uncertain terms. "You are here because you have yet to 'think clear' about birth control, and you will remain here until you do." He spoke to the women with an ease that bespoke many years of experience in mass meetings, but his message to the women was anything but reassuring. "China must develop, and we will gradually develop China into a strong socialist state," he continued, "But whether or not we develop depends on controlling our population."

Then he began to reason with the women about their concerns. "We know that you want a son in order to be secure in your old age. But remember that you are still young. As the country develops, it will create welfare programs. By the time you are old, you will not have to worry about who is going to support you. The government will support you." Speaking directly to the several women present who had brought along their girl children, he said, "You must remember that some girls can be as filial as boys. And you can always call in a son-in-law. I know one in Sandhead Brigade who treats his mother- and father-in-law as if they were his own parents. I hope that everyone will think more clearly about this problem, discuss this problem with relatives, and agree to an abortion."

Up to this point he had spoken in a persuasive, not unfriendly fashion, but then he heard one of the women mutter something about the Communist Party to her neighbor, and his voice became loud and hard. "Don't say anything against the Communist Party," he warned sternly. "It is very concerned about you. The Party is not saying that you are not allowed to have children, just that two children are enough, and that it is best to have just one child."

The sudden edge in his voice surprised me. He Kaifeng was of medium height, with close-cropped gray hair and a benevolent, grandfatherly expression. He kept his Mao jacket open at the neck, and he wore sandals, unlike most of the other ranking commune cadres, who wore leather shoes. He had originally been a peasant, and still had something of the folksy, downhome manner of the villager. But at the meeting he was official and distant, all propaganda and Party line.

I was even more taken aback by his next remark. Looking coldly around the room, he said slowly and deliberately, "None of you has any choice in this matter. You must realize that your pregnancy affects everyone in the commune, and indeed affects everyone in the country." Then, visually calculating how far along the women in the room were, he went on to add, "The two of you who are eight or nine months pregnant will have a caesarean; the rest of you will have a shot which will cause you to abort." Several of the women were crying by this point, and Comrade He Kaifeng apparently decided that his words had had the proper impact, for he went back to the table at the end of the room and took his seat with the other cadres.

There matters were left for a half an hour or so, in order, He Kaifeng told me afterwards, to allow the women time to think about what he had said. "They must be made to realize the seriousness of this matter before they will think clear about abortion," he explained. At the end of this intermission, Chen Shunkui, the assistant Party secretary of Sandhead Brigade, strode to the center of the room and began to talk to the women. In contrast to He Kaifeng, who had been stern and authoritarian, even threatening the women, Chen Shunkui was relaxed and easygoing, and joked with the women at several points. He was a slender man of medium

Blind and lame, this old man makes his living as a village storyteller

Second graders taking an exam

A village primary school housed in an ancestral hall built circa 1920

Village elders

A village grandmother making "spirit money" to burn in honor of the family ancestors

Netting fish for sale to the state

The state fish collection station: shipping fish to Hong Kong

A peasant girl caring for her baby brother

A young girl tending silkworms

At the state slaughterhouse: peasants who raise the pigs must share half the pork with the state

A bride and groom at a village wedding

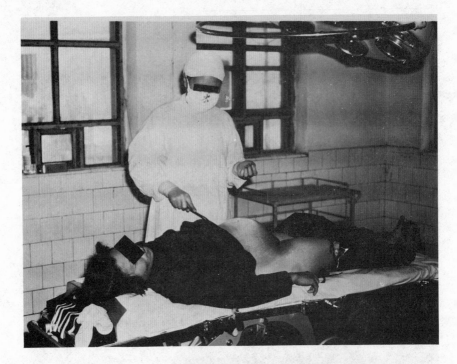

Above: In the abortion clinic operating room: a woman seven and a half months pregnant being prepared for an abortion by Caesarean. Right: A tubal ligation in progress

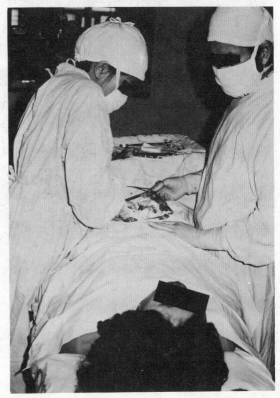

height, with a sort of awkward pleasantness about him. Although a cadre, he was called by his first name by his fellow villagers, and he was even more informal with them, often using their nicknames.

"We aren't forcing you to abort," he said, taking the edge off of He Kaifeng's concluding remark. "The decision to undergo an abortion has to be made by you yourselves. But in making this decision, you have to consider not only yourselves but the country and the collective as well. Obviously the country needs to control its population for the sake of the Four Modernizations. The collective, as well, needs to limit its population."

This was, as I knew, perfectly correct. At the time of the 1952 land reform Sandhead Brigade had had only 3,480 residents all told. The 1979 annual census registered a total of 8,010 brigade members, for an increase of 130 percent in twenty-seven years. Like most other collectives, Sandhead had already brought all available land under cultivation, and further population expansion would only lower per capita resources to even more marginal levels.

"There is already only one-sixth of an acre for each person in the village," he continued. "Having more children is only going to make it more difficult for all of us to make a living."

Chen Shunkui spoke in a light and rather matter-of-fact fashion, befitting the fact that he was talking with friends and neighbors. "The commune Party committee is quite concerned about you. They have even"—here his tone brightened even further—"arranged to have cars pick you up and take you to the commune clinic for the operation and back to the village when it is over." Several of the women laughed out loud at the outrageous thought of riding in a car, a Cinderella-like fantasy for peasant women, some of whom have never even ridden on a bus. The laughter broke the ice, and one woman, voicing a concern of many, called out, "What about safety?" Chen Shunkui had a ready answer. "The commune has arranged for two doctors from the Red Wind People's Liberation Army Hospital in Guangzhou to take charge of the operations. The abortions will be done properly. You will be safe and secure. The doctors are experts." Chen Shunkui paused momentarily to gain the women's full attention before continuing with his next line. "Mosquito nets have even been brought over from the commune reception center [a kind of hotel used by visiting cadres] for your use while you are in the clinic."

This the women found amusing as well, but their bemused chatter stopped as Chen Shunkui brought the meeting back to its main point with a question. His query, "Who would like to undergo an abortion?" was greeted with silence. After a pause, a woman flanked by two young daughters raised a question that was on all of their minds. "Will we be allowed to go home tonight? If not, then we have to go home to fetch our blankets." The women had been told during the earlier round of brigade meetings that once the commune meetings began, they would have to stay in a commune dormitory until they agreed to an abortion. Hoping to have an excuse to go home at least briefly on the evening of the first day, they had agreed among themselves not to bring bedding. The atmosphere grew tense as the women waited for Chen's answer.

"Well, we aren't going to make everyone stay here," he began in conciliatory fashion, but he quickly went on to make clear what the price of going home was going to be. "We will allow you to go home, but only to convince your husbands, mothers-in-law, or fathers-in-law, or others at home that it is best that you have an abortion. You must first tell me that you agree to an abortion and are going home to convince others. If not, then you must stay here tonight." He ended on this note, stepping back to the table and taking a seat. Again the women were left to mull over his remarks among themselves.

Except for a break for lunch, the meeting continued in this fashion throughout the day, with Comrade He Kaifeng, Chen Shunkui, and Sandhead Brigade's woman's work cadre taking the floor in turn. The commune cadre would usually take a hard line, while the two brigade cadres just as often took a more amiable approach. Although the atmosphere of the meeting was less tense when the brigade cadres were speaking—they were, after all, fellow villagers—the gist of their argument was identical to that of the commune cadre: the women must agree to an abortion. After each cadre spoke, there would follow a half-hour break to allow the women to consider what had been said.

Finally, late in the afternoon, Chen Shunkui strode again to the center of the semicircle of benches and announced that it was time for the women to decide whether to stay overnight at the commune or go home. Taking out a small notebook, he began to read out the names of the women one by one.

"Lin Xinlan," he called out. Everyone in the room swung around to regard the woman flanked by two small daughters who had earlier raised the question about going home. Her face remained expressionless. "Do you want to go home?" Chen Shunkui pressed, deliberately avoiding the use of the word "abortion." The woman's control suddenly broke, and she cried out that she would "never abort."

Ignoring her outburst, Chen Shunkui smoothly read out the next name on his list. "Su Shaobing." A very young and very pregnant woman replied in a small, hesitant voice that she wanted to go home. "Good," the cadre said quickly. "Go home and convince your parents-in-law that you should have an abortion. Remember that you have already agreed."

Chen Shunkui continued down the list, reading one name after another, noting each woman's reply to the question "Do you want to go home?" Although one other woman, whose only child, a lad of two and a half, was severely retarded, shouted out that she was going to bear her child regardless of the consequences, the rest of the women responded quietly and fatalistically. Of the twenty-four women whose names were read out, three agreed to abortions, all of which were scheduled for the following day, five agreed to go home to convince their families that they should abort, and ten refused an abortion. Six of the twenty-four who had been instructed to attend that day were not present, and would each have 2 *rmb* deducted from their family's income, a fine that would continue to be levied each day they did not attend.

Overall, that first meeting brought jarringly home to me certain realities of China's effort to control its population growth. Although the program is officially described as planning births, it might more appropriately be entitled "restricting births," for its goal is to limit births to the lowest number possible. The technique of reeducation in public meetings adopted to achieve this goal is similar to that used in China's numerous earlier sociopolitical movements. Alternately threatening and cajoling, persuading and reasoning, the cadres explain over and over why it is necessary to follow the Party line, applying a steady psychological pressure that deadens reason and gradually erodes the will to resist. Experience has taught the Chinese that arguing back at authority will only make matters worse, and so they listen passively and finally come to agree to whatever is being demanded of them. The whole process is reminiscent of the Chinese proverb "Water drops can pierce a rock."

But a more appropriate metaphor for the birth control meeting that I attended would be "like a hot knife through butter." The easily cowed, inarticulate young village women, whose sex, age, and social position combined to place them at the opposite end of the rural hierarchy of status and power from the senior male cadres who ran the meeting, were particularly easy for these cadres to convert to the proper way of thinking, even though the issue was something as near and dear to them as their bodies and their babies. What I observed that day was nothing more—or less—than a mild but still very effective form of the process that has become known in the West as brainwashing.

If China is applying an irresistible force to the solution of its population problem, then that population itself, if not quite an immovable object, has in its massiveness a vast, lead-like inertia accreted over millennia. China's population was already 60 million at the time of the birth of Christ and reached ever-greater peaks during later dynasties—80 million in the ninth-century Tang Dynasty, 110 million in the twelfth-century Sung, 200 million in the sixteenth-century Ming, and 425 million in the nineteenth-century Ching. In the century preceding the Communist conquest of the mainland, however, the Malthusian checks of war, famine, and disease kept the death rate hovering near the birth rate, and the population remained under 500 million. With the end of the civil war in 1949, China's population took off on an upward trajectory that added nearly 20 million new citizens every year for the next decade to the newly founded People's Republic, a number equal to the total population of East Germany or California.

As self-evident as the need to control China's population growth already seemed to many in the early years of the PRC, Chairman Mao did not see it that way. Rather he took the standard Marxist position on overpopulation, diagnosing it as just one more symptom of the disease of capitalism. Once disorganized capitalist society has been replaced by a smoothly regimented socialist one, in which wealth is distributed equally and all are engaged in productive work, the doctrine went, then the nightmare of overpopulation will simply disappear in the dawn of the socialist millennium. Not only did he overrule Malthus's dismal theorem, which held that population constantly tended to exceed the food supply, he went so far as to take the opposite position. He regarded a large and growing population as an asset, an important element of national power, vital for economic progress. Mao argued, with typical exuberance of language, that "every stomach comes with two hands attached," by which epigram he meant to emphasize man's role as a producer of wealth over his role as a consumer. Not only was family planning unnecessary, it was a positive evil, a sort of genocide. In 1952 the *People's Daily* condemned birth control as "a way of slaughtering the Chinese people without drawing blood. . . . [The people are] the most precious of all categories of capital."

The census of 1953, which revealed a population near 600 million, apparently shocked certain members of the ruling circle into reconsidering the issue, and public discussion on the advantages and disadvantages of family planning was allowed. Professor Ma Yinchu, president of Beijing University, Professor Chen Ta, a well-known economist, and others wrote articles warning of the dangers of uncontrolled population growth. As a result, some efforts were made in 1956–57 to promote birth control in urban areas, although little was done in the countryside, where energies were directed at making collectivization work. With the coming of the Great Leap Forward, however, those who had come out in favor of birth control were denounced as rightists who were carrying out political intrigues in the name of the population problem. The purge that followed ended all discussion of birth control for several years.

But it was perhaps just the catastrophe called the Great Leap Forward and its aftermath, "the three difficult years," that finally roused Mao from his dogmatic complacency about overpopulation. During the three years from 1959 to 1961 China's population overtook its resources. A combination of bureaucratic mismanagement and natural disasters caused tens of millions of deaths from disease and famine. Properly chastised by reality for ignoring it, Mao went through a reluctant conversion on the issue of birth control from a doctrinaire Marxism to a more pragmatic policy of population planning. Beginning in the early sixties and continuing to the present day, China has pursued a consistent and ever more stringent policy of birth control.

The gathering momentum of the program has nevertheless been twice deflected by political movements, the first time during the Cultural Revolution from 1966 to 1968 and more recently during the period following the overthrow of the Gang of Four. During both periods the local powers that be were preoccupied simply staying afloat in the sometimes violent political currents of the times, and birth rates bounded. The reverses of the period following the downfall of the Gang were described to me by the woman's work cadre of a brigade located down the West River from Guangzhou. "We performed 168 tubal ligations in our brigade during 1976," this woman said. "Then late that year the Gang of Four was overthrown. Throughout 1977 all of our meetings at the brigade and commune level and all of the directives from the county and the province concerned criticizing the Gang of Four and rooting out their influence. For over a year we held no birth control 'high tides' [short, intense campaigns] because we had no instructions to do so. Only twelve women had tubal ligations performed in 1977 and only two in 1978." Left to themselves, the villagers let nature take its course, and nine months later the birth rate began an upward swing that took it from 1.69 percent in 1977 to 2.17 percent in 1978 and 2.61 percent in 1979, a ten-year high.

These two stutter steps aside, the campaign continued to move forward throughout the sixties and seventies and scored early successes in China's cities, where conditions encouraged smaller families. Shanghai, the largest of China's cities, has consistently reported rates of population growth under 1 percent a year for the last decade, and other cities are not far behind. One of the axioms of modern demography is that urban areas have significantly lower birth rates than rural, and this is especially true in China, where couples live in cramped quarters and most women hold down full-time jobs, making it difficult to manage more than one child. And these pressures have grown more intense over time. In the 1950s each Chinese had an average of 5.4 square yards of housing. But the building of apartment houses has not been given high priority in the program of socialist construction, and a gradually expanding urban population has mostly been crowded into thirty-year-old flats. By 1977 there were only 4.3 square yards of living space per person. In the early 1950s only a minority of women were employed outside of the home. For the last two decades nearly all women have worked. Another factor is that many couples, especially those in which the husband and wife are college or technical school graduates, have been given work assignments which keep them apart for all but a few weeks out of the year. This makes it difficult for such working "single" mothers to take care of even one child, and it is sometimes difficult to conceive that child as well in a marriage that consists of a series of relatively brief conjugal liaisons each followed by a long period of separation.

Financial considerations tend to inhibit large families as well. Many urban couples simply cannot afford to have more than one or two children. At the senior middle school of Rongqi Town in southeastern Guangdong, Guo Fangxu, a tall, handsome teacher with a university degree in Chinese literature, told me how he and his wife, a doctor stationed in a commune clinic 25 miles away from Rongqi, were just able to support themselves and their two children, a boy of 9 and a girl of 6, on their combined salary of 99 *rmb* [$66] a month. "My income of 54 *rmb* is only sufficient to provide for my boy and myself," he complained. "I pay 10 *rmb* a month for my apartment and over 30 *rmb* a month for food. The rest goes for miscellaneous expenses like cloth, shoes, electricity, and so on. My wife is a little better off, because she lives in a free commune dormitory, and because the commune day care center that our daughter attends is only 3 *rmb* a month. We would be totally unable to make ends meet if we had a third child, though."

Yet it is not just Chinese urban life-styles, with their lack of space, time, and money, that have reduced the size of urban families; it also is the enforcement of strict birth quotas from the early seventies onward. Each year all urban residence committees and production units are given quotas of children that their residents and workers will be allowed to bear. Pressure is applied on headstrong couples from three directions at once—through their neighborhood residence committee, through the husband's work unit, and through the wife's work unit. Chen Taitai, the stout, middle-aged head of a local residence committee in the

Yuexiu District of Guangzhou, explained how the system was enforced in her ward of 2,100 people. "Every woman who has yet to have a tubal ligation is given a gynecological examination once every three months by the clinic at her place of work, and any woman who is discovered to be pregnant is ordered to attend birth control meetings. Her husband's work unit and the residence committee where the couple lives will also be notified so that they can help with the 'thought work.' The heaviest responsibility for averting over-quota births belongs to the woman's work cadre at the pregnant woman's place of work, but she will be assisted by the residence committee of the woman's neighborhood, who will visit the woman at home in the evenings. The husband will be approached at his place of work and encouraged to put pressure on his wife to agree to an abortion. The system is quite effective. Last year only fifteen babies were born in my ward, only one over the quota of fourteen."*

Thought work is not just a matter of appealing to pregnant women to terminate their pregnancies for the sake of China's future, much stronger arguments are available. Entering the birth of an over-quota baby in the household registers maintained by the local police station can take a year or more, during which time the infant is not eligible for rice, cloth, or other rations, all of which his parents have to purchase at high prices on the black market. If a child is to be a couple's third, 10 percent is deducted from their wages beginning from the fourth month of pregnancy as an inducement to abortion and to cover increased community costs after birth. But the ultimate recourse of the work unit against an intractable mother-to-be is dismissal. This is a break with Marxist orthodoxy, for job security is one of the ten commandments of socialism, and work assignments in China have customarily been for life. Women fired from positions in the industrial and service sectors, which offer relatively high salaries and generous retirement benefits, have no choice but to seek low-paying jobs in neighborhood cooperatives or as short-term laborers. Staying unemployed is almost always out of the question, for few families could afford to live on only one salary, especially with another mouth to feed.

* Beginning in 1981, this same quota system was implemented in the Guangdong countryside.

China can win the battle against births on the urban front and still lose the war in the vastness of her countryside, where over 80 percent of the population live. Certainly the birth control program made little headway in the early sixties, when free contraceptive devices were first made available in rural collectives and the advantages of having fewer children were suggested to skeptical peasants. These early efforts had little effect on the number of births in the villages, in part because many couples had lost children during the "three difficult years"; women continued to have four or more children each.

But the infant and child mortality rate declined steadily after that time as rural health care improved, and peasant women came to realize that it was no longer necessary to bear three or four sons in order to have an odds-on chance of raising two to maturity. Moreover, female participation in field labor was mandated after the formation of the communes, tying up rural women in the same work-home double bind that urban women were in. As a result of such pressures, the rural birth rate started downward, dropping from 3.8 percent in 1963 to 2.9 percent in 1970 in one prosperous Guangdong county that I visited. Later, in the early seventies, the first monetary incentives were introduced. In one Pearl River commune women were paid a cash reward of $4 (roughly equal to a week's wages), and $3 worth of pork and fish ration coupons if they agreed to a tubal ligation. This smallish inducement led most women who had already borne two or more sons to accept sterilization, and the birth rate may have been levered downward slightly as a consequence, but it was too modest a measure to persuade those women who did not yet have as many sons as they desired to begin contraception.

Since 1974 the principal method of encouraging smaller families has been to hold annual or biannual family planning "high tides." At meetings and during home visits, women are barraged with all kinds of propaganda, from the reading of family-planning regulations and directives about rewards and sanctions for those who accept and reject birth control, to arguments advanced by cadres against having large families and against simply letting nature take its course.

Women are not paid their regular work points for the days that they are in meetings. This amounts to an enforced idling of, in most cases, one-half of the family work force and acts as a strong prod toward the alacritous acceptance of family planning. "It seems harsh," a local brigade cadre admitted to me, referring to the meetings-without-pay principle, "but the collective had no choice. If we were to continue to give them work points for not working, they would never 'think clear' about contraception." What keeps the women in the meetings and out of the fields is that women who miss meetings are fined 2 *rmb* a day for each day they are absent, an amount equivalent to more than a day's wages.

Chinese peasant women have never been given to vague, romantic statements about fulfillment through motherhood and the like. They were led during the course of family-planning "high tides" to rethink their reasons for wanting children in an even more hardheaded way, and the younger women that I spoke with no longer gave the continuation of the family line as the primary reason for having children. Mencius may have believed that "there is no behavior more unfilial than to have no male descendants," but young rural Chinese women are no longer so sure. "Though my mother-in-law says that you have to have a son to carry on the family name and lineage, I really don't think that this is a very good reason," one young woman, pregnant with her third child, told me. "I have already agreed to have a tubal ligation performed immediately following delivery, regardless of the sex of the child." She paused momentarily and then added with a wan smile, "I hope it is a boy."

Many women now say that they would be satisfied with two children, that this would be their ideal number of children, but only if both turned out to be boys. Otherwise they would continue to bear children until they reached this number of sons, even if it meant having a string of girls in the process. "Many sons mean a happy and prosperous household" and "Boys are precious, girls worthless." are among the traditional proverbs that rural women for hard, practical reasons, still quote when cadres are not around. Jwang Yaguan, the secure mother of two teenaged boys, told me that "a woman needs a manchild because without one she will be poor and picked on in her old age. Families with only girls have little voice in village affairs. Everyone knows that the girls will sooner or later marry out. A son will stay by your side until you pass away."

Sons are the only social security system known to peasant parents, for the vast majority of rural collectives are too poor to provide for the welfare of the elderly. Neither can daughters render long-term assistance, for in the countryside custom decrees that they take up residence with their husband's family upon marriage and sever all economic ties with their natal family. Only sons continue to live at home after marriage, the sole support of aging parents.

Unlike Americans, who see old age as a grim and dreary finale to life, Chinese look forward to it as a relaxed time of leisure and high status. The "entering the ancestral hall" ceremony at age 60 celebrates a man's release from the backbreaking slog of field labor. Thereafter he spends his days in the courtyards of the village ancestral halls, smoking and chatting with the other old men of the village. But whether he actually retires at this point depends on having one son, or better yet two, to slog in his place. I remember seeing a grizzled old peasant at work on a private plot some distance from the village on a dreary winter's day, his hoe rising and falling in a slow, tired rhythm. In his tattered black cotton trousers and coat of coarse burlap, shoeless despite the cold, he made a pathetic figure alone in the fields. I judged him to be nearly 70, and asked my companion in surprise what such an elderly man was doing in the fields. "That's Old Man Wang," he replied. "His wife died several years ago, and his daughters have all married out. He lives alone." Then, after we had gone a few steps farther, he grimly observed, "You see, that is what happens when you have no sons." Wang, dirt-poor and pitied by his neighbors, has no choice but to continue toiling in the fields until he dies. For the Chinese villager there remains no greater misfortune in life than to have no sons to "inherit the ancestral estate and pass along the generations." To his government this is feudal nonsense which hinders the program to bring reproduction under state control, and thus threatens the success of the all-important modernization program.

To counter the argument that only one's sons can provide support in old age, the cadres advocate "the boy's going to live with the girl's family." The problem is that brides have traditionally resided with their husbands' families after marriage, and in contemporary rural China this custom continues. The claim that one can call in a good son-in-law as easily as a daughter-in-law runs counter to local experience. He Kaifeng's claim that he knows a son-in-law in Sandhead Brigade who treats his parents-in-law very well was scoffed at by the women. "Why shouldn't he treat his parents-in-law well? They practically support him," one young woman who had attended the meeting said to me privately afterwards. "He is a lazy good-for-nothing," she continued, "and he is the only son-in-law in the entire village who lives with his wife's family." As she spoke, she grew more impassioned. "Listen to me. People are having fewer children nowadays. If everybody has only one boy and I have two girls, who is going to give me their son? I'll tell you who: Nobody! Sons are becoming more and more valuable." She also rejected the argument that she could go and live with her daughter after she married into another family. "My son-in-law will have parents of his own to support," she countered. "He certainly won't welcome me. I would be worse off than if I stayed in my own village, where at least I have friends and other relatives."

The village women I spoke with were more receptive of the idea of a pension program, though many doubted that their own brigades would be able to afford one anytime in the near future. Cheng Binglan, one of the holdouts against abortion in Sandhead Brigade, echoed the appeal of the brigade's plans to eventually establish a pension for the elderly. "As things stand now," she said, "a person without a son has nothing to lean on in old age, but I would agree to a tubal ligation if the brigade would guarantee my support when I can no longer work."

Despite these reservations on the part of village women, much progress has been made in recent years. Consider, for example, the extent of contraceptive use in Sandhead Brigade at the end of 1979. Of the 892 women in the child-bearing years, defined as all married women 36 and under, 699 were contracepting. The most common method of contraception was female sterilization, with 417 brigade women having undergone tubal ligations by September 1979. The next most common method was I.U.D. implantation, used by 234 women, most of whom had only borne one child to date and were waiting four years to have a second. Other methods in use were birth control pills (fifteen women), prophylactics (sixteen couples), and vasectomies (seventeen men).

Of the 193 then not practicing contraception, 129 had yet to bear their first child, or had born their first child more than four years ago, and under the 1979 regulations were free to reproduce.

Nationwide, over 170 million birth control operations were carried out from 1971 to 1978. This figure represents the total number of abortions, tubal ligations, and vasectomies—euphemistically referred to in the Chinese press as the "three operations"— carried out during this period, and is truly a staggering number. Although vasectomies are easier to perform surgically that tubal ligations, the procedure remains uncommon in the Chinese countryside, where most men equate the operation with castration. And though tubal ligations were once more common than abortions with the intensification of the program in the mid- to late seventies the reverse became true. Even if just half of the above total represented abortions, it would mean that nationwide an average of over 10 million abortions were performed annually throughout most of the seventies. Though this figure is impossible to confirm, I did obtain accurate figures for smaller rural units. On a visit to one prosperous Guangdong commune of 60,000 people in the spring of 1980, I was informed by the cadre responsible that 743 of the "three operations" had been performed there in the first quarter of that year alone. "We have been performing about two abortions for every sterilization," she told me. "We have performed 247 sterilizations, all but sixteen on women, and 496 abortions."

As a result of such overwhelming efforts, the rate at which China's population has been increasing has come down considerably in the last fifteen years. As late as 1971 it stood at 2.3 percent, a rate that would double the population, and impoverish the countryside, in just thirty-one years. By 1979 it had fallen to 1.2 percent, a rate at which the population would take a much more leisurely fifty-nine years to double, and one coming close to the 1 percent former Chairman Hua Guofeng set as the target for 1980.

In contrast with many underdeveloped countries, China's birth rate seems hardly catastrophic. The population of Bangladesh, for example, continues to expand at a rate of nearly 3 percent, and many regions are burgeoning at even greater rates. Yet Beijing has ample reason for concern. The population of China has more than doubled in the thirty years since the revolution, and was disclosed to have exceeded 1 billion in 1981. With such a large base, even birth rates that are low by the standards of the Third World produce a bumper crop of babies. At the modest 1.2 percent rate reported for 1979, the population still increased by 12 million, a number equal to the entire population of Australia. Not all Western experts are convinced that China has accurate census information; some estimate that the birth and death rates reported may represent underenumerations of 10 percent and 15 percent, respectively. Another reason for concern is that China's baby-boom generation of the fifties is coming of marriageable age, and Beijing's birth planners expect them to produce a baby boom of their own in the early eighties. All this will hinder the achievement of the next stage in China's struggle against overpopulation, a reduction of the rate of natural increase to 0.5 percent by 1985.

Whether this ambitious goal, or the even more far-out one of zero population growth by the year 2000, will be met depends in part on how the local population responds to the system of rewards and punishments designed by national, provincial, and local governments to force down the birth rate. A new national family-planning law came into effect in late 1980, after being circulated in draft form for nearly a year, and most of China's twenty-seven provinces, self-governing cities, and "autonomous regions" have added additional provisions depending on the severity of the local population problem. And at least in Guangdong, the new and extensive provincial regulations have been further supplemented by county and commune planned-birth "procedures."

For most rural families the national measure with the most bite is the deduction of 10 percent of a family's salary for each child after the second. Over the past thirty years, significant gains have been made in rural health care, education, and welfare, in programs paid for out of community coffers. As a result, parents have been partly insulated from the rising costs of raising children. The income deduction will change all this, effectively shifting the burden of community costs to the consumer. For added effect the deductions will begin from the fourth month of pregnancy, presumably because there is still then time for the family to reconsider its finances and terminate the pregnancy.

Another Beijing provision designed to put an economic

crunch on overproducing families concerns private plots. These carefully tended gardens, which produce approximately 25 percent of household income in Sandhead, will not grow along with the family as they did formerly. Instead, collectives have been instructed to allocate plots on the basis of a two-child family. A couple with three children will have to provide vegetables for the family dinner table from the same-sized parcel that a family with only one child will till. Such a couple will also be forced to purchase oil, cloth, and other rationed goods, even grain in areas which grow primarily commercial crops, since ration tickets will be denied the extra mouths. It is this sanction that will cost parents the most, since current free-market food prices run from 50 to 200 percent higher than those charged under the government subsidy program. Together, the above measures will more than double the cost of raising a child in rural China, from birth to age 16, from $900 to over $2,000.

Beijing is also encouraging rural collectives to establish social security programs. By providing the elderly an economic alternative to total dependence on their offspring, such programs will have a certain, though not immediate, effect on fertility. A problem is that many communes in the hinterlands remain too poor to fund an adequate program. Even in one relatively prosperous commune I visited, only one of twenty brigades has been able to institute pensions, though cadres from other brigades say they are definitely interested, not least because the brigade which pioneered the program also happens to have the lowest birth rate in the commune.

The national program also decrees rewards for having only one child. In addition to receiving an extra share of private plot land, rural families will receive from 300 to 400 extra work points a year, providing approximately 10 percent in extra income. Despite such inducements, peasants in many areas remain unresponsive.

The economic value of children to their parents remains high in rural China. By their middle teens they already produce more than they consume, and they still constitute the only social security system known to peasant parents. To bring its birth rate down and hold it down over the long run, Beijing is banking on making children too expensive for rural Chinese to afford more than one or two. The main obstacle to the success of the program is that the best investment and, in China's socialist economy, the only investment that many Chinese ever make is their children. The government understands this, and has been emphasizing the need for lower-level units to take even more drastic steps to curb births when necessary.

"In order to control population increase, achieve the planning of births, and thoroughly implement the policy of 'few births, late marriages, and late births,' " and more specifically to aid the success of the March 1980 family-planning "high tide," one rural commune in Guangdong rewarded cooperating couples in three ways. First, all women who underwent an abortion during the "high tide" received 10 or 20 *rmb*, 10 *rmb* if the abortion could be accomplished by the scraping technique and 20 *rmb* if the pregnancy was in its later stages and a caesarean was necessary. Second, for each year after marriage that couples postponed conceiving their first child they were to receive 10 *rmb*. Revealing the commune cadres' lack of faith in the long-term efficacy of this bonus, the directive went on to add that if no conception had occurred by the fourth year of marriage, then the couple were to present themselves to the commune clinic for a medical examination. If one of them was discovered to be infertile, the bonus would stop.

The third local provision, as well as its fate, was even more symptomatic of the problems that plague the birth control program. It declared that those couples who agreed to sterilization after the birth of their first child were to be awarded 500 *rmb*. Unlike the rewards for undergoing an abortion or postponing starting a family, which were too stingy to have any real impact on fertility behavior, the one-child bonus gave peasants pause, for 500 *rmb* was more than double the local annual income for a field hand. In the six months following its announcement, this sum proved sufficient to induce two dozen couples to pledge that their first child would also be their last. But the program proved too much of a strain on commune resources to be continued indefinitely. By September 1980 12,000 *rmb* had been paid out to contracepting couples from the rapidly diminishing general welfare fund, and the bonus paid to one-child families was abruptly dropped to 100 *rmb*. Not surprisingly, peasant applicants dropped to zero.

The commune authorities found themselves in a typical Chinese predicament: they could not afford politically to let the peasants have as many children as they wanted, nor could they afford to pay them enough to bring them into line. As in past movements, they proceeded instead to what one of the local brigade Party secretaries termed "a too easy recourse to force." On the surface, the pressure came in the form of economic sanctions. The three rewards above led off the commune directive but were followed by no less than twelve different sanctions to be levied on those who violated the principle of "few births, late marriages, and late births," all in addition to those in force nationwide. The most trenchant of these provisions, designed to "eliminate" all third births, stated that couples were to be subject to a one-time fine of 300 *rmb* upon the birth of their third child, were to pay a 20-*rmb*-a-month fine from the fourth month of pregnancy until the child was 14 years of age, and were to pay double the normal amount to participate in their brigade's collective medical program. These same fines were also levied on couples who did not wait at least four years from the birth of their first child to have a second and couples who had a child before receiving official permission to marry, although they ceased when these requirements were satisfied. Even in the rich Pearl River Delta, where average annual per capita income from the collective is double that of the national average of 83 *rmb*, these are hefty fines.

In an unusually frank conversation a brigade cadre, a short, powerfully built man in his thirties, revealed the inside assessment of these regulations. "There is no doubt that they will prove impossible to implement," he stated flatly. "They will sooner or later have to be revised." He paused and took a drag on his cigarette, then continued. "In fact the process of revision has already started. The 'procedures' state that all third babies must be delivered in the commune clinic."

"The commune regulations go on to add ominously that the clinic will not be held responsible for any mishaps that occur during the births of these 'excess' babies," I interjected. Cadre Huang looked significantly at me before continuing.

"Originally, the commune announced that a fine of 30 *rmb* would be levied against any midwife who delivered such a child at home, thinking that this would force women to go to the clinic," he said, adding in reference to my comment, "even though they are afraid to. Only afterwards did it occur to the commune revolu-

tionary committee members," he said with deliberate irony, "that
there may be problems with their policy. Labor often comes suddenly, and there may not be time for the woman to be taken to
the commune clinic. What if it is a difficult birth such as a breech
birth? Is the brigade midwife still not to help? What if a woman
dies during delivery? Who is responsible? Because of such considerations the 30-*rmb* penalty has just been revoked only two weeks
after it was announced. And this is only one example. The real
problem with the new procedures is that the fines are too severe.
They don't leave a family with enough money for food."

Putting out his cigarette, he took my pen and notebook in
hand to illustrate what he meant. "Take a family in which there
are two laborers, a husband and a wife, who make a total of 800
work points a month. After the 10 percent deduction of work
points required by national policy, they would have 720 work
points left," he said, writing down the figures as he spoke. "Now
in our brigade a work point is worth an average of only 0.05
rmb, so that their 720 work points translates into a total of 36
rmb per month. From this subtract the 20 *rmb*-a-month penalty
assessed by the commune and the extra 3 *rmb* a month in collective
medicine fees. The family has only 13 *rmb* left." He circled the
net income of 13 *rmb* for emphasis, adding, "And this is it. The
private plot of land of the family will not increase with the birth
of the third child, and the family may not have enough vegetables
for their own table as their children get older. A farm family
that has to buy vegetables is in a sorry state. Even if they manage
to grow enough for themselves, they won't have any left over
to sell in the free market, cutting off this source of income. Nor
will they have any extra grain to raise pigs or even chickens. They
also cannot work in brigade enterprises where they could earn
more, for the procedures have forbidden the employment of 'vio-
lators.' Unless they have help from other relatives, this 13 *rmb*
is it," he said, pointing to the bottom line, "and it is not enough.
A family of five needs to eat at least 100 catties of rice a month.
Even if they could purchase rice at the rationed price of 14 *rmb*
a month, they would still be in trouble. The revolutionary committee has gone even further, however, saying that not only the third
child but its parents as well will have to purchase rice at the
market price, which is currently 27 *rmb* per 100 catties. It will
be impossible for them to stay alive," he concluded forcefully.

"When people starve, they won't go to the commune with their complaints, but will come to us at the brigade for help."

"How could the commune cadres even consider implementing regulations of such severity?" I asked. "Surely they understand the economics of peasant families."

"In part it is because there is an activist in charge of our prefecture of thirteen counties, who has told the leading cadres here to take a hard line against 'excess births,' " he answered. "The procedures were drawn up by the commune's birth-planning group following suggestions made by county-level family-planning cadres. When the procedures were presented to the commune revolutionary committee, they met with no enthusiasm but also with no serious objections. Everyone knew that this was what the county and prefecture wanted, and so discussion was very limited. They were passed quickly."

"Didn't anyone object?" I pressed.

"I understand that one brigade Party secretary did," my informant said with a grin. "He told the commune Party secretary that he couldn't participate in the 'high tide' that was to begin in a few days—all brigade Party secretaries had just been instructed to attend—because he had"—here my informant paused to milk what was obviously a punch line—*"qi guan yen."* In the delta Cantonese that I knew, *qi guan yen* meant throat infection. This seemed a strange excuse to use for not participating in an event still a week hence, strange but hardly humorous. Seeing my perplexity, Huang explained that the term was also a homophone (these abound in Chinese) for "controlling too strictly," and that the sense given by the juxtaposition of meanings was that the whole plan, procedures, meetings, and all, "stuck in his throat." "You see," he concluded, "he was telling the leader of the commune to his face that he didn't agree with the plan."

"Economic sanctions in themselves are not objectionable," I said, "as long as they are reasonable. But the commune regulations don't seem designed to be implemented at all. One pregnant woman from your brigade said to me, 'The regulations are just used to scare us into accepting abortions.' "

He nodded immediately, in full agreement with the point. "The regulations really worry the women," he said. "Except for a few who have regular remittances from Hong Kong or Singapore, the women know that their families will 'eat bitterness' if they don't agree to an abortion. So they agree. The procedures are nothing more than a plan to force the women to abort."

It would be wrong to leave the impression that women throughout China are being brutally pressured into abortions and sterilizations that they are opposed to. I don't know this to be the case. There are areas which have done considerably better than Guangdong, most notably the western province of Sichuan, whose 100-million-strong population was reported to have increased by only 0.6 percent in 1978; but it is not clear by what means this has been achieved. It is certainly true that most areas of China are too poor to be able to reward peasants into giving up their second and later born, and there is not enough time given the current blistering pace of birth control to allow reasonable economic sanctions to take effect. At least in Guangdong and perhaps elsewhere, the real work of birth control in the villages is accomplished at nonstop "Think clear" meetings held during spring and fall abortion campaigns. Here the objective is not just to familiarize women with the penalties they will face if they have a second or third child, but to use "100 strategies and 1,000 tactics," the Chinese equivalent of "by hook or by crook," to convince already pregnant women that they have no alernative to abortion and sterilization.

Such hard-nosed, callous efforts at the local level are a coarsened but still recognizable version of the uncompromising resolve at the national level on the issue of population control. Vice Premier Chen Muhua, the female head of China's Family Planning Board, put it bluntly. "Socialism should make it possible to regulate the reproduction of human beings so that population growth keeps in step with the growth of material production," she said in 1979.

It is no accident that her statement reads more like an order than an argument. Thus far the identifying characteristic of China's demographic transition from high to low birth rates has been the fact that it was created and is maintained through the liberal use of political power. This makes it historically unique. With the exception of India's ill-fated sterilization campaigns of the early 1970s, one looks in vain for parallels. The decline of birth rates in the West, recognized only after it was well underway, was a passive response to the forces of modernization, industrialization, and urbanization. Governments remained largely indifferent. And the current programs of other Third World nations, which make do with persuasion, posters, and part-time workers, have had little or no demonstrable effect. Beijing, not content with half measures, is determined to lower its birth rate in advance of, and to facilitate, modernization.

Clearly implied in Vice Premier Chen's statement was that the state was going to assume regulatory power over reproduction, formerly an unquestioned human right. This puts the program beyond the pale, not only of conventional morality but also of demographic theory, the first of which assumes that a husband and wife should be, and the second that they in fact are, free to have children. If they desire more children for reasons of love, custom, or money, or if they want fewer children because they have other interests, concerns, or responsibilities, they are free to act on their preferences.

This assumption is no longer totally valid for China. The peasants are no longer independent actors in the endless drama of procreation and birth, but are increasingly acting under the duress and direction of bureaucratic forces. This came out clearly when I asked women how many children they wanted. "What does it matter?" one woman echoed by others responded. "The government has said that we can have only two." Chinese peasants are nothing if not realistic. What does it matter, indeed, how many children you would like to have in the face of a government decree specifying how many children you or your collective will be permitted to have, a decree enforced by the impressive organizational skills and human resources of the Chinese Communist Party and the government bureaucracy?

China brings a powerful troika of human and bureaucratic strengths to bear on the regulation of the reproduction of human beings. With a rural administration extending down to the grass roots, mass organizations with cells in every hamlet throughout the country, and a cadre of rural officials trained in social control, it is in a formidable position to press forward with birth control.

With the establishment of collective agriculture in the mid-fifties, rural China was swept into the tight embrace of the expanding Chinese bureaucracy. Townships became communes, villages production brigades, and hamlets production teams, and these newly forged administrative units were the lower rungs in a ladder of command and control that reached upward to Beijing. Rural dwellers became susceptible in an unprecedented way to the direct influence and control of the Chinese state. This three-tiered system of rural collectivization and administration—the communes, brigades, and teams—has proved invaluable in implementing birth planning. It is through this system that the household registers are maintained and annual population reports are compiled. And it is this organization that allows the efficient organization and execution of the "high tides" and the ready enforcement of the new birth control regulations.

Reinforcing this omnipresent administration is the Women's Federation. Established to subordinate women to the Party's social, economic, and political line, in recent years it has been entirely coopted for the purpose of implementing the birth control program. Like all organizations in China, the Women's Federation is organized hierarchically and is headed by Beijing officials, who direct the activities of over 5 million local federation officials, one in each of the country's million production brigades and teams. These cadres are responsible for the legwork of the program at the team and brigade level. They educate peasant women about population policy and maintain records on contraception use and fertility. They are further charged with detecting pregnancies and accompanying women to the health clinic for abortions and sterilizations.

Finally, Beijing can rely on a vast phalanx of rural cadres, Communist Party members, and activists to advocate and advance the official line in the countryside. Especially cadres at the brigade and commune level, who occupy important positions in the rural administrative structure, possess redoubtable persuasive power, honed to a scintillating sharpness in the dozens of political movements of the Mao decades. With their authority and communications skills, they are especially effective in group settings. Alternately threatening and persuading, cajoling and reasoning, they are more than a match for the inarticulate young village women, who are further inhibited by their fear of giving offense. They are only too aware that it is invariably those peasants who bend to the cadre's wishes who are allowed to go to work in brigade or commune factories, who are given much-prized home sites, or who receive smaller but still important favors such as the loan of 1,000 bricks for the construction of a pig sty or a travel permit to journey outside the county limits or to stay overnight outside the brigade.

The specific organizations responsible for Beijing's past success in birth control—the collectives, the cadres, and the Women's Federation—are in one sense merely different facets of China's bureaucratic totalitarian form of government. With a centralized bureaucracy, a totalitarian political apparatus, a largely state-run economy, and close supervision of all social groups, Beijing is able to carry out programs that would topple less firmly seated governments with little fear of popular unrest. Few countries so thoroughly enmesh their people in a web of economic, political, and social controls, and fewer still presume a right to dictate not only behavioral norms but also personal values. The Chinese success in reducing the birth rate, as in controlling dissent and preventing immigration to urban areas, is the direct result of this power to subordinate individual preferences to state goals. Beijing's birth control program will be exportable only to countries whose citizens do not have inalienable rights vis-à-vis their government.

One manifestation of the government's power—the primary precondition of the program's success—is its ability to pass costs along to the producer rather than pay for them from central government funds. The cost of sending all women who threaten to exceed their fertility quotas to meetings for months on end would be prohibitive if the costs were borne by anyone except the peasants themselves. In one brigade of 4,000 members the income lost by the involuntary peasant participants in the 1979 spring and fall "high tides" totaled approximately $6,000, no mean sum in a collective where a year's labor only earns a peasant between $100 and $200. With semiannual family-planning campaigns occurring nationwide, China probably "spent" over a billion dollars of peasant and cadre labor in 1979 alone. Meeting participants receive no compensation for the time lost during meetings, and agricultural production may have suffered slightly as part of the work force was kept out of the fields in meetings. Another burden on the rural collective is that Women's Federation cadres at both the team and brigade level, as well as other brigade cadres who became involved in the movement, continue to draw their regular salaries from collective funds during the course of the meetings.

The state does pay the salaries of commune and higher-level cadres engaged in birth control work, but these expenditures account for but a fraction of the true economic cost of the program.

The second precondition of China's success on the population front is program stability. There can be little doubt of the government's current commitment to setting and adhering to strict birth quotas. Recently promulgated documents have directed cadres to "with one hand grasp production, and with the other birth control," placing birth control on a par with the perennial problem of feeding China's masses. Birth quotas have been given to counties and communes, and demotion and dismissal await cadres whose units exceed their alloted number of babies. (It is not surprising that cadres whose careers are threatened in this way commit excesses in the name of population control.) Birth control is written into China's 1978 Constitution, and a new set of birth control regulations came into effect in 1980.

But will Beijing continue to be unsparing in its demand for the regulation of the reproduction of the fifth of humanity that it controls? Past pendulum shifts in policy as party factions vied for power would seem to call into question Beijing's ability to sustain a program over the long course. The lesson from the Guangdong countryside is that by the mid-seventies leftists and rightists seemed to have reached a consensus on the necessity for birth control. Though the leftists formerly opposed family planning, rationalizing uncontrolled population growth with such short-sighted slogans as "Every stomach comes with two hands attached," during the last years of their tenure in power (1973–76) mass sterilizations were vigorously pushed, and regular family-planning "high tides" were held. Should the leftists recover their former preeminence, there is no reason to expect birth control to go aground on the shoals of shifting policy. On the contrary, they seem certain to keep the program on the same basic course. At worst, birth control would be becalmed during the period of political transition, as it was for the two years following the fall of the Gang. Future leftists would probably continue to rationalize their policy somewhat differently from the so-called pragmatists, stressing the social and familial benefits of family planning to be gained, rather than the purely economic advantages.

This apparent consensus of the right and left is critical, for the population program will indeed have to be continued over the long run. China's population increase rate was lowered from 2.3 percent in 1971 to 1.2 percent in 1978 by direct, consciously applied pressure from Beijing, not by serendipitous social and economic change. Should the program be discontinued tomorrow, there would be a baby boom in the Chinese countryside that would make America's postwar boom seem in retrospect more like a whimper. For left to themselves, as they were during 1977 and much of 1978, the peasants would have as many children as necessary to reach their two-boy ideal. Population increase rates would return to levels last seen a decade ago, reaching 2.5 percent a year or more. To curb its population, China's birth control program will have to remain in force for decades; to reduce it will require restrictions on fertility for generations to come. The consensus that has emerged is a guarantee of the stability and continuity vital to the program's ultimate success.

With the revolutionary vision that has become their trade-mark, China's leaders have not been loath to look ahead. Beijing has targeted 2000 as the year by which the plateau of zero population growth should have been reached. Even more distant goals are emerging: the merits of gradually reducing China's population to levels more in concert with natural resources have been debated in newspaper articles. How such awesome social engineering is to be accomplished is already apparent: couples are to have just one child. In June 1979 Hua Guofeng told delegates to the Fifth People's Congress that families which limit themselves to one child should be suitably rewarded. Within a few months the line had hardened appreciably. The major conclusion of a national conference on the population problem held in Sichuan Province in December 1979 was that the primary task of birth control work is to universalize the one-child family. At the beginning of 1980 all of China's major newspapers simultaneously published a report on a series of population projections based on varying assumptions regarding average number of children per family made by researchers of the Chinese Academy of Social Sciences. Only if, they reported, all couples have only one child after 1985 will zero population growth be possible around the turn of the century. According to their estimates, China's population would then peak in the year 2004 at 1.054 billion, thereafter gradually decreasing to 960 million in 2028, 613 million in 2060, and a mere 370 million in 2080.

In the spring of 1980 the assistant mayor of Shanghai, Yang

Kai, described his city's birth control goal for that year in terms of the universalization of the one-child family. "We must exert ourselves to the utmost to raise the percentage on only children, which should reach 90 percent in the urban area and approximately 75 percent in the suburban area," he said. "We must severely limit second births, and absolutely halt third births, in order to restrict population growth to 0.6 percent or less." By the end of 1980, the same phrases had percolated down to rural communes in Guangdong and Guangxi, indicating that the drive for *yi-hai-hua*, or "single-infant-ization," was on nationwide. In Guangdong it was announced in 1981 that all state employees, over whom the government exercises an obvious leverage, would henceforth be permitted only one child; 70 percent of the residents of cities and towns were to follow suit, as were 50 percent of the peasants. The plan is to continuously push up the percentage of single-child families in the towns and villages, with the goal of reaching 100 percent by 1985.

How this will be accomplished is diabolically simple. "The licensing of first births" was how one birth control worker privately described it to me. "Every brigade will be given an annual quota of babies," she explained. "Newlyweds who wish to have a child must apply to the commune family-planning office for a birth permit. To receive this, they must meet two conditions: they must fall within their brigade's yearly quota, and they must agree to have only one child. If they go ahead and have the child without a permit, they will be violating the birth control regulations. Their baby will be a 'black market person,' no grain, oil, cloth, or other ration coupons will be issued, and the parents will have to pay a monthly fine of 20 *rmb*." Couples who conceive a child without first obtaining a birth permit will be ordered to attend birth control meetings, at which they will be pressured to accept the one-child limit and sterilization. "After all, sterilization is better than abortion," the cadre concluded.*

---

* Sonless peasants do not always agree. On my frequent trips to Hong Kong, after leaving China, I began to hear reports of female infanticide from Chinese friends who had made trips back to Pearl River Delta Commune. That the "one child per family" policy is responsible for this brutal practice there can be no doubt. Sandhead residents had earlier heatedly denied to me that girl babies had ever been put to death in the village, even during Qing times. "Ours is a 'land of fish and rice,' " one wrinkled old midwife told me. "Everyone has always been able to raise their daughters."

Population is no longer taken as a given in the Chinese jigsaw puzzle of prosperity, but is being shaped by the state for the good of the greater collective. It somehow seems a logical, even inevitable extension of the Chinese state's already formidable powers that it should arrogate to itself control over the reproduction of its citizens. After the fashion of bureaucratic socialist states, Beijing ministries already closely control the output, distribution, and consumption of material goods and foodstuffs. Children, too, have long been regarded as the property of the state, which oversees their education and later assigns them work. Controlling the production of what might be called raw humanity further facilitates the rational, socialist planning of China's command economy. Looked at from this perspective, Beijing's move is a natural step, completing its cradle-to-grave embrace of the Chinese people.

Surprising though it may seem, given the enormity of the problem to be contended with, controlling China's population may turn out to be one of the simpler tasks of the modernization program. Instead of relying on costly imported technology or difficult-to-master business management techniques, it draws upon skills of directed social change and control through mass movements long in use in revolutionary China. This social calculus is a home-grown specialty, developed by Mao to a high, if Machiavellian, art during the four decades of his rule. The cadres, organizations, and administrative infrastructure required for the successful implementation of the birth control program are already in place and operating in the Chinese countryside. Birth rates, already reduced to impressively low levels for a developing country, continue to be eroded away by wave after wave of "high tides." Though the timing may require some adjustment, it is not premature to predict that China will achieve its goal of zero population growth.

China hands of an earlier generation were fond of remarking that the teeming masses of China could never pass entirely through an archway, for they would multiply faster than they could advance. Beijing has set out to prove them false. The fifth of humanity that it commands has been organized, regimented, and given its marching orders. By dint of will and organization, it appears that the Chinese people, four abreast and in lockstep, will ultimately be marched through to the last man, woman, and child. One can only hope that the drive does not turn into a stampede.

———————◆———————

The birth control plan is quintessential Chinese socialism: the state setting forth a far-reaching blueprint to reengineer society. The people are expected to fall uncomplainingly into line despite the shortcomings of the state plan. The plan in operation exacts from the population a heavy toll to which the state remains largely oblivious.

Though I had gained glimpses of the human cost of birth planning Chinese Communist style while attending meetings and interviewing cadres, I only apprehended the full dimensions of the sacrifice being demanded of Chinese women during a visit to a commune clinic during the 1980 "high tide." I found that this facility had been transformed into an abortion clinic for the duration of the campaign, an impression confirmed by Dr. Chen Buozhen, one of four clinic codirectors (and the only one of the four with any medical training). "At this early stage in the high tide we have been giving priority to abortions over sterilizations," he explained as we sipped tea in the clinic office. "Our seventy beds are currently all occupied with women undergoing abortions, our surgical staff has been organized into special abortion teams, and our two operating theaters are in use throughout the day performing caesarean sections and induced abortions. We have even called up four barefoot doctor midwives from the brigades to help with the patient load."

Despite the concentration of all available medical resources, the clinic had averaged only a dozen abortions a day the first four days of the "high tide," and the waiting list of 170 women was growing longer with each day of meetings. One reason for the slow pace was a lack of space: as a concession to the women's fears, they were accompanied by family or cadres during their three-to-four-day stay in the hospital. But the main reason, Director Chen confided, was that the commune cadres, worried lest premature births spoil their drive for 100 percent compliance, had directed that all pregnancies of seven or more months be terminated first. "On a woman seven or eight months pregnant, performing an abortion is a complex and time-consuming procedure," Chen pointed out. "We begin by injecting Rivalor, an abor-

tifacient, into the uterus to destroy the fetus and cause birth contractions to begin. The fetus usually expires within twenty-four
hours, and is expelled on the second day. In the cases where
expulsion does not follow within forty hours, we have no choice
but to perform a caesarean." "And if the fetus has not yet ex-
pired?" I asked, wondering what the clinic staff would do when
faced with the awkward problem of how to dispose of a live baby
delivered by caesarean. "We always wait until the fetus expires,"
he answered firmly.* While passing quickly for the harried clinic
staff, this death watch can seem interminable to the women themselves, I found out later that day when I visited the patient wards.

Alongside the entrance to each of the small wards a slip of
red paper with the characters *yinchan sushe* (literally, abortion dormitory) had been posted. This was, I realized, an imitation of
the traditional Chinese lunar New Year practice of festooning
homes, especially doorframes, with slips of red paper on which
have been brushed happy and auspicious sayings. Under the present circumstances, however, which were as unhappy as they were
inauspicious, the slips of red paper seemed a grotesque touch.
None of the wards had doors, so I simply selected one at random
and stepped inside. The room was a 10-by-10-foot square of raw
concrete slab crowded with three plank beds placed against the
walls so that the head of one was against the foot of another.
Two of the beds were occupied by young women who lay covered
by thick cotton comforters. On the third, alongside a neatly folded
stack of bedding, a fiftyish woman sat erectly. I advanced and
introduced myself to her.

As I had sensed from her age and some subtle nuance of
authority, she was a woman's work cadre. She explained that she
and her young roommates were all from the No. 8 Production
Team of Southhead Brigade, and that it was her responsibility
to stay with them during their confinement. The young women
were here, the cadre went on, because they did not have permission to give birth. "She is seven months pregnant with her second
baby," she said, pointing with her chin the way the Chinese do
at the woman in the far bed. "But it came too soon, only two

---

* But I did uncover cases in which women very close to term were given injections
only after their labor pains had already begun naturally, a method used by
officials to overcome the women's fear of a caesarean. In such cases the baby
either is born dead or dies shortly after birth.

years after her first. She won't have a quota [*renwu*] for two more years." Nodding at the nearer bed, she added, "Ah Hui here doesn't have a quota because she is only 22 and is not yet officially married." The girl in the middle bed the cadre had called Ah Hui had levered herself up into a half-sitting position as we were talking and now interjected, "My husband and I had a wedding feast in the village last November"—apparently after she discovered herself to be pregnant—"but the commune wouldn't let us register our marriage because I was not yet 23. In three months I will turn 23, so I was hoping that I could keep this baby, but the cadres told me that I will not be allowed to have a baby until nine months after registration." She lay back down, and her voice became more subdued as she told me that she had agreed to an abortion the day before because, after a week of holding out, she was sick of day after day of endless meetings. Besides, she added with rather more spirit, she was young and would have another opportunity to give birth, perhaps next year.

This plucky young woman, already looking beyond a present in which she had been given an injection of what she called "poison" (the peasants, not interested in the niceties of names, called the abortifacient what it in fact was, poison, and the injection a *du zhen*, or "poison shot"), seemed under the circumstances to be bearing up amazingly well. The woman in the far bed was clearly in much worse shape. Her swollen and blood-flecked eyes had regarded me briefly when I entered the room, but soon moved listlessly away. Thereafter she took no notice of my presence, lying inert under the mantle of her blanket, seemingly unaware of her surroundings. I had thought at first that she was under medication for pain, but the woman's work cadre informed me that, aside from the "poison shot," she had received no medicine. (According to Dr. Chen, none of the women received pain pills, tranquilizers, or sleeping pills.) Nevertheless, the cadre hastened to add, the woman was not in any pain.

Not in any *physical* pain perhaps, I mentally corrected her as I moved over to the woman's side, intending to ask her how she felt. But before I could get the question out, she turned away from me to face the wall and pulled her heavy quilt up over her head as a further shield. I could see her body compact itself under the quilt as she curled up in a ball around her dead fetus. I heard the cadre say from behind me that she was scheduled for an abortion later that afternoon. The final step for this woman and the others in the abortion dormitory was a trip to the operating room, and it was there that I concluded my visit to the clinic.

The operating room was constructed of the same gray concrete as the rest of the hospital but was better lit, with large windows in each wall. The low operating table in the center of the room was already occupied by a short, stocky peasant woman in her late twenties. She lay midriff unclothed on her back as a nurse busily painted her exposed, swollen stomach with a yellow antiseptic solution. An occasional curious face appeared surreally at the windows, only to be quickly driven away each time by the shouts of the nurse. When she had completed her work, a doctor swiftly made a series of injections of local anesthetic in the woman's abdomen. As he waited for the shots to take effect, he explained to me that the woman had been given an injection of Rivalor early the previous day, that it had been determined this morning that the fetus had died, but there was still no sign of uterine contractions. Now, he went on, oblivious to the woman lying underneath his gesticulating gloved hands, the fetus would have to be removed, thus and thus. The woman for her part stared fixedly at the ceiling throughout his verbal dissection, her body immobile. Only her laboring, calloused hands, clenching tightly at the edge of the operating table, gave a hint as to her state of mind. I left the operating room unbidden as the doctor made the first incision.

I came away from that clinic visit appalled at the physical and mental anguish of the women I had seen, but even more puzzled by the absence of opposition to it, not only from the women themselves, but from any segment of Chinese society. In contrast to America, the question of abortion, even when involuntary and performed late in term, has not flared into a public issue in China. In part this may be because the state-controlled media impose an almost total blackout on any kind of criticism of current government policy. But even through the rural grapevine I heard no reports of fiery confrontations between placard-carrying marchers and the authorities, of "pro-life" crusaders staging sit-ins at clinics and hospitals protesting the late abortions, of "pro-choice" advocates crashing the birth control meetings to demand that women be free to make individual decisions on abortion privately and without pressure. Little or none of the explosive moral and political drama that has surrounded this issue in the U.S. has disrupted PRC efforts at population control.

One reason for the damping of this issue is that in China there are not many who would risk confrontation with the establishment over abstract questions of human rights raised by birth control excesses. Then, too, while the worst excesses of the birth control campaign are occurring in the countryside, China's few dissidents are concentrated in the cities, where their attention is held by other issues. Moral outrage is limited as well by the sometimes "nasty, brutish, and short" character of life in overpopulated, famine-prone China, and by a lack of a religious tradition grounded in the sanctity of human life. Man is not made in god's image in China. Confucious never said, "Thou shalt not kill."

What moral indignation there is over the program in the Chinese countryside is kept in close check by the juggernaut of state power, the implicit threat of which so cows most people that they attend closely to the state's desires and behave accordingly. Not that the PRC is above making open threats when necessary, as in the 1978 fertility-planning regulations of Guangdong Province, whose section on rewards and punishments contains a chilling warning to those who, for whatever reason, oppose the provincial government's will: "Those who attempt to defeat the fertility plan by engaging in rumormongering, distorting the truth, attacking and harming fertility-planning workers and activists, and generally breaking the law and running amuck must be dealt with severely. If they have actually obstructed the implementation of the fertility plan, then they must be brought before the law for punishment. Those enemies of the people who attempt to defeat the fertility plan must be exposed immediately and resolutely attacked."*

In view of the state's uncompromising attitude, those among the cadres inducing the women to abort and the doctors actually carrying out the abortions who are conscientiously opposed to the program dare not make any public expression of disapproval or opposition. The only instance I came across where the program was openly challenged by those who were charged with its enforcement involved the Party secretary of a brigade in Hetang Com-

* Guangdong Provincial Revolutionary Committee, *Implementation Regulations Governing Certain Problems in the Area of Guangdong Provincial Fertility Planning Work* (Guangdong: Fertility Planning Office of the Guangdong Provincial Revolutionary Committee, December, 1978), section 8, article 26, last paragraph.

mune, Xinhui County, Guangdong, who, supported by several of his fellow brigade cadres, refused to implement the birth control procedures handed down by the county in the spring 1980 campaign. The reaction of the commune revolutionary committee to this insubordination was immediate and devastating. With the approval of the county, a work team was sent to the brigade to organize mass criticism meetings against the offending cadres, the predictable outcome of which was the removal of the mutinous Party secretary and his supporters from office. The work team then stayed on to ensure the full compliance of the brigade members during the remainder of the "high tide."

Most cadres are too canny and cautious to openly buck the system, and keep their complaints about this issue very muted and private. One brigade cadre, who was distressed by what he saw as excessive pressure on women to abort, burst out to me, "If Liu Shaoqi"—the moderate former Chairman of the People's Republic who perished during the Cultural Revolution—"had stayed in power, we would never have seen this day. The problem of population growth would have been taken care of by gradualism." A doctor told me that many of his colleagues were very upset about the abortions on seven- or eight-months-pregnant women, but that no one had considered protesting publicly by refusing to perform such operations. "The consequences would be very serious. There would be criticism, transfer, demotion, struggle, perhaps even labor reform," he told me. "No doctor that I know is prepared to take that risk."

Although it is the peasants whose security, privacy, and family continuity are most threatened by the program, they are for the most part politically inarticulate and naive about matters beyond their own rice bowl. Even the young peasant women themselves, who stand to lose the most, mount only individual and passive resistance to the program. They keep their pregnancies secret, telling only their families, and avoid prenatal physicals, knowing the brigade midwife will report their condition to the authorities. They continue to work in the fields as usual, binding up their abdomens under their baggy pants and blouses from the fourth month on so that they will not show. Many in this way avoid detection until they are only two or three months from term, thinking that they have a shorter gauntlet of meetings to run. Those who can afford to pay the fines go away to the hills or to the home of a relative, coming back only after their infant is born. Those women who attended the meetings I witnessed were largely silent, less defiant than resigned, less rebellious than fatalistic, each enduring on her own. On the one occasion when a woman unexpectedly railed bitterly against the cadres, I saw the other women self-consciously look away, distancing themselves from the protester. They seemed as helplessly isolated as their unborn babies, incapable of uniting in even verbal opposition to a policy that each one of them privately opposed. Neither did their husbands or other family members back in the village work to undermine or circumvent the program, or even go so far as to criticize it publicly. To be sure, men grumbled and cursed that the program was taking away their sons and grandsons, but only within their family gates and only to family members and trusted friends.

Yet I did witness several spontaneous outbursts by individuals against the policy, the most striking of which came during the course of a birth control meeting. One of the young mothers present, who had two girls but no boys, had started talking during an interlude about how she had managed to keep her pregnancy a secret until just a few days previous when "they" became suspicious and ordered her to undergo a physical. "They are so strict now," she continued, tears welling up. "I just want to have this one more baby, and then I'll be glad to have a tubal ligation. In the village there is no way to survive when you are old if you don't have a son. Sons are like heavy cotton quilts in the winter; if you don't have one, you will freeze to death."

She was sobbing heavily by this time, and, thinking it best to end the conversation, I stood up to go.

"They won't let me have my baby," she burst out. "I will agree to anything they want if they only let me have my baby."

I was anxious to shut off her torrent of words, but was carried along by her intensity.

"If I talk to you like this, is it illegal?" she asked suddenly, eyeing the two cadres present who had sat with faces averted during our conversation.

"No, it isn't," I answered with an assuredness that I definitely did not feel.

"I don't care if it is," she went on without really listening to my reply. "Vice Premier Deng says that we are to 'tell it like it is.' All I am doing is telling you the truth."

I nodded, noting apprehensively that the cadres were casting glowering sidelong glances at the woman.

But she was not to be cowed. Looking directly at the two cadres, she cried, "They are forcing us to have abortions!"

Occasionally, protest has gone beyond the merely vocal and become violent as well, as happened in a village in the Pearl River Delta where the birth control campaign was pushed with special vigor by a young, ambitious brigade Party secretary. Finally all but one of the village women pregnant with an over-quota child had reluctantly gone to the commune clinic for an abortion. The lone holdout was a woman whose husband, himself an only son, was desperate for a son to continue the family line. They held out against the cadre's harassment and veiled threats for several weeks more before finally caving in. When the woman's seven-month pregnancy was aborted, she was found to have been carrying twin boys. In the eyes of rural Chinese, who prize sons above all else, this was a monstrous tragedy, and word of it quickly spread beyond hospital walls to the woman's horrified husband. This man went into a black fury and, shreiking that his two sons had been murdered, tore wildly to the Party secretary's home. Seizing the man's two sons, aged 8 and 10, he heaved them into the courtyard well and then leaped in himself. All three drowned.

This household-shattering double murder and suicide, as tragically poignant as it was, touched me less deeply than a quiet ritual I observed, which better exemplified the passive Chinese acceptance of acts of gods, fate, and the state. During the early April *Qing Ming Jie,* the "bright and clear" festival on which Chinese remember their ancestors, I visited a neighbor woman who had gone through a late abortion a month earlier and found her just completing the domestic portion of the memorial ritual. Eight sticks of incense were smoldering on the high mantle before the family's ancestral tablet, clothing, money, and ingots made of paper were being transsubstantiated by fire into the nether world for the use of the ancestors, and she was chanting prayers for the peace and prosperity of the household members, both living and departed. But instead of ending the rite at that point as customary, she lit a final length of incense in a corner of the room and briefly stood crooning before it. It was, she explained to me afterwards, for "the unborn one."

10

Political Campaigns: The Human Costs of Social Engineering

Three years of suffering leading to a thousand years of happiness.
Great Leap Forward slogan

From a distance of a kilometer or so, the huge people's hall in the Nanshan County seat of Dali is an impressive structure. Three stories high, it is the national Great Hall of the People at one-half scale, fronted by the same massive columns and broad, stately stairway. But it has a different impact up close. There the steps can be seen to be uneven and crumbling, the columns' outer layer of concrete to be scaling off in large patches exposing the naked brick below, and the entire massive front to be mere façade for a dark, dank, and cavernous auditorium. Because no provision was made for electricity, running water, or sanitation during the building's hasty construction, it was only as an afterthought that bare electric wires were run helter skelter along the interior walls to lighting fixtures, a series of wells were dug to provide a supply of potable water, and a platoon of latrines were erected in the back. Though completed in 1959, the hall looks decades older.

When I first laid eyes on the Sandhead primary school, I thought I was looking at the village school described in the local gazetteer of the sixteenth year of the Republic (1927), if not at a relic of dynastic times. The weathered brick walls were pock-marked and crumbling, the floors were of uneven packed earth, and the traditional beam roof had begun to sag dangerously under its weight of heavy tile, so much so that several classrooms had already been condemned for fear they might suddenly collapse on the heads of the schoolchildren below. The elementary school's ravaged appearance made a sorry contrast with the local junior high school, housed in a sturdily constructed ancestral hall with a handsome open timber roof, still magnificent despite the defacing of its ancestral icons and religious bas-reliefs by the Red Guards. The disparity was paradoxical: the ancestral hall dated from the early part of this century, while the primary school had been built in 1958, only twenty-two years before. Like the Dali people's hall, it is a product of the Great Leap Forward.

The Chinese countryside is littered with similar structures, dreary hulks of brick and concrete thrown up by small armies of unskilled laborers in a month or two and almost as soon dilapidated. Although I was soon able to place these period pieces at a glance, they continued to draw my attention. Like the Great Wall, these mute reminders of the Great Leap have too many bones buried under them to be taken for granted. Until recently, just how many Chinese lost their lives at that time remained a matter for guesswork, often ideologically motivated, that put the numbers on the low side.* More objective assessments of the Great Leap Forward had to await a critical reappraisal of its chief instigator, Mao Zedong, and it was only two decades after the event that the outlines of the tragedy were finally emerging. Mainland economist Sun Zhifang admitted in a 1981 article published in the official journal, *Economic Management,* that as a result of the economic dislocations caused by the Greap Leap's "blind methods and [its] emphasis on the importance of will" and exacer-

---

* For example, one long-term resident of Beijing, Anna Louise Strong, wrote of the Great Leap Forward, "Nobody used the word 'famine'; no people were fleeing their homes; no corpses lay by the roadside; no bloated children wailed for food at railway stations as they did in the pre-liberation past. Friends like Rewi Alley and Dr. George Hatem (Ma Hai-teh) with decades of experience in China, told me that in 'the old society' such natural calamities would have meant famine with at least ten million dead. But now, people were saying: 'Nobody must die of hunger.' . . . On the whole . . . the Chinese slogans were carried out." Cited in *China: Yesterday and Today,* ed. by Molly Joel Coye and Jon Livingston, 2nd ed. (New York: Bantam Books, 1979), p. 383. Like the peasants, who were ordered not to leave their villages, Ms. Strong apparently spent the Great Leap Forward at home, at her typewriter.

bated by natural calamities, the population actually declined by 11 million during 1960. Since China's population had been burgeoning at a rate of approximately 20 million a year during the 1950s, this means that the number of deaths in 1960 alone as a result of the Greap Leap was somewhere between 11 million and 30 million. Nearly all of those who lost their lives were peasants.

The Great Leap Forward began in early 1958 with the establishment of rural communes, an effort to pull the countryside up by its own bootstraps by uniting smaller cooperatives into a larger unit that would have sufficient manpower and resources to provide education and health facilities, open new land to cultivation, build dams and irrigation networks, and start small-scale rural industries. But the rational pursuit of these laudable goals soon gave way to a frenzied chase after an instant utopia. The official press gleefully led the way, crowing triumphantly that "the Greek mythology of ancient times was only a tale, a dream, an ideal. Today, in the era of Mao Zedong, heaven is here on earth. . . . Once the Party calls, tens of millions of the masses leap into action."* To ensure that they would not hold back, Chinese were told that the journey to the Maoist promised land, though arduous, would soon be behind them. "Three years of suffering leading to a thousand years of happiness" was the game plan given by one contemporary slogan. At least until the food ran out, people did work hard, but even so they could not keep up with the ever-expanding expectations of their leaders.

With reports coming in from throughout the country of the economic miracles achieved by the communes in 1958, targets for 1959 were raised and raised again. Coal production was to go from 30 million tons to 270 million tons, grain from 185 million tons to an impossible 525 million tons, and so on throughout the economy. Lest they suffer by comparison with the inflated claims of others, local cadres grew ever more frantic to demonstrate that they too could conjure up socialist production with nothing more than will and human flesh. The bigger and more conspicuous a project was, the more it served their real purpose— constructing vanity monuments to impress Party superiors with their ability to mobilize the masses using the thought of Chairman

* *People's Daily*, Beijing, October 1, 1958.

Mao. It was no coincidence that the Dali people's hall stood on a small knoll squarely facing the road coming from the provincial capital of Guangzhou, or that the Sandhead school was situated squarely behind the two huge magnolia trees that marked the entrance to the village.

Of the crash programs of that period, none is better known than the campaign to surpass Britain in the production of iron and steel by encouraging the construction of "backyard furnaces." (At the time Britain was producing 40 million tons of iron and steel a year, the PRC 5 million. No more need be said about the fantastic nature of this economic flier.) Over 600,000 coke-and-coal-burning furnaces were hastily constructed before the campaign exhausted itself four months later. The nearest thing to an official explanation for the program's embarrassingly rapid demise that was given out was the low quality of the pig iron and steel produced by these teapot-sized smelters, much of which was so low-grade that it had to be resmelted before it could be used, but peasants clued me in that the real problem lay elsewhere—in the supply of raw materials.

In the highly charged atmosphere of the Great Leap Forward, it was often only after a furnace had been built that cadres belatedly began casting about for iron ore and the fuel to fire it. In areas that had no ready supply of coal, which is to say most of China, cadres turned to felling local trees, quickly denuding their villages of the belts of greenery that had been one of their most attractive features. In Sandhead only the huge, gnarled magnolias that had guarded the village entranceway for generations survived the axe. In fact, these two trees had been ordered cut down along with the rest by the local Party secretary, but the villagers had refused, grumbling that this would undo Sandhead's *fengshui*, that special geomantic relationship with the physical environment that kept the community populous and prosperous. In any event, the village was soon out of firewood to stoke its furnaces.

Iron ore was equally difficult to come by. Sandhead, located along a channel of the Pearl River, exercised an option not open to areas without water transport by bringing in ore by cargo launch from a small open-pit mine 80 kilometers away. Even so, shipping costs proved prohibitive. After ritually firing up their furnaces a few times and smelting ore in amounts more or less symbolic, local cadres shut them down permanently. Then, still under heavy pressure from their superiors to somehow produce iron and steel in respectable amounts, they went on a scavenger hunt. Anything ferrous became grist for the cadres' mill. In scenes repeated all over China, cadres wrenched out the iron gratings from the windows of homes and left the peasants to replace them with bamboo. They "borrowed" Old Wang's small store of scrap iron, leaving a promissory note that proved uncollectible. They even made kitchen calls insisting that women donate their cooking utensils—wok, pot, and barrel—to the commune, glibly explaining that these were no longer needed "now that we are all eating together in the commune mess hall." The scrap metal thus collected was handed over to county authorities along with self-congratulatory covering reports describing blast furnaces built and tons of iron and steel turned out. The reason why most of the 10 million tons of iron and steel that the backyard furnace campaign netted had to be resmelted at regular state refineries was that it consisted largely of unusable iron scrap.

The entire chaotic period was rife with imbecilic undertakings, but nothing I heard about topped for sheer witlessness a project entered upon by Equality Commune. Inspired by the fact that the commune lies in an area of the Guangdong delta crisscrossed with channels, the newly appointed commune leaders decided to raise a series of dikes across the channel that ran past the commune to the south, imagining that they could convert this 7-mile-long, 100-yard-wide conduit into a string of gargantuan ponds and, presto, raise fish production. Throughout the winter months of 1958, a thousand women and adolescents (the younger men had for the most part been dispatched to coal mines in neighboring counties) labored with hod and carrying pole bringing in the tens of thousands of cubic meters of earth needed to build two dams across the channel. Its modest winter flow was diverted back to the main course of the West River at low water and the branch channel successfully blocked off. But with the coming of high water, despite desperate last-minute shoring efforts, the earthen dam at the channel entrance burst. Seven peasants drowned as the water swept down the channel to the downstream dam, which was carried away as well. In well under an hour a winter's work, an investment amounting to hundreds of man-years, had been washed away by the roiling waters. "It was crazy," a middle-aged peasant woman who had been one of the dam conscripts concluded acidly. "Everyone knew it. But no one dared to speak up. If you did, they would say that you were a counterrevolutionary."

As this illiterate peasant woman understood instinctively, to voice criticism of this or other Great Leap Forward ventures was to commit a dangerous political heresy. That these schemes were often rash and impractical was beside the point, which was rather to confess, in as tangible, collective, and public a way as possible, faith in the Maoist shortcut to modernization. The projects of this period reminded me of nothing so much as a Maoist mutation of a New Guinea cargo cult whose devotees carve landing strips out of the jungle in the fervent hope that this will prompt planes laden with the products of industrial civilization to land. It was as if the smelters, the schools, and the great, middling, and minor halls of the people that the Great Leap spawned might by a similar alchemy conjure up the industrialized, educated, and democratic society of the Communist millennium.

The Great Leap Forward is but one of the more spectacular examples of the kind of crash campaign that is perhaps the single most salient characteristic of the Chinese Communist system. While only a few of the more protracted and far-reaching of these movements—the Hundred Flowers, the Great Leap Forward, the Cultural Revolution, and the Four Modernizations—have attracted more than passing attention outside of China, in fact there have been dozens. Far from being temporary aberrations from the mainstream of Chinese life, campaigns—single-minded efforts at directed social change—are as much a part of the tempo of life in the People's Republic as the wheel of the sun or the cycling of the seasons. From the "Three-Anti" (*sanfan*) campaign of 1951–52, in which "corruption, waste, and bureaucratism" were attacked in the person of offending cadres, to the 1982 revival of the Cultural Revolution slogan "Learn from Daqing," holding up China's largest oil-producing and -refining complex as an economic model, rare is the year that has not seen a campaign of some kind or another set in motion. Be it intended to purge cadre ranks or remold public values, adjust management practices or totally transform the collective economy, a campaign bursts upon the social landscape with the killing suddenness and destructive

force of a late summer typhoon, engulfing the Chinese in a mael-
strom of radical politics.

Despite their wide divergence in purpose, all campaigns gy-
rate through a roughly similar cycle. The cycle begins after a
period of political quiescence with the top leaders' chafing at the
lack of evident progress, even backsliding, that has occurred since
the last campaign and deciding that some set of values, behaviors,
institutions, or policies requires radical modification. Although
the official term for what ensues is *qunzhong yundong*, or mass
movement, in actuality the campaign, at least in its inception, is
a carefully orchestrated bit of mass manipulation. Unlike true social movements, the Chinese campaign arises not from the concerns of ordinary people, but from the calculations of the political
elite. Participation is not voluntary, but required.

The opening chord is customarily struck by the *People's Daily*,
the official organ of the CCP, in a series of editorials which criticize
certain beliefs or practices and suggest, with the force of an order,
alternative cultural patterns to be followed. Because each article
appears simultaneously, or nearly so, in all of the major newspapers in the country, its signal importance is unmistakable, and
the rest of the government-controlled media quickly begin to hype
the emerging campaign. State-run publishing companies churn
out propaganda by the bale, all in slavish imitation of the tone
and content of the initial editorials. At the same time internal
directives alert the Party apparatus of the impending drive, and
meetings stressing its importance begin to ripple down the hierarchy.

Soon the whole country is caught up in this socialist call to
arms. Meetings are organized by factory, office, and commune
cadres for the members of their organizations, and propaganda
materials are distributed and explained. Corps of activists, those
who have a commitment to the campaign or designs to exploit
it for their own ends, are mobilized in each unit to aid in its
promotion by example and suasion. Those individuals who hold
back, especially if they come from ideologically suspect groups
like ex-landlords, former capitalists, and intellectuals, are publicly
and often physically abused for their backwardness.

Up to this point, all has proceeded more or less according
to plan. But now, exaggerated reports of "great victories on all
fronts" begin to flow up the chain of command and into the capital.

Certain that they are on the verge of achieving breakthrough success, leaders at all levels step up the pressure. The flurry of propaganda and directives thickens into a blizzard, eclipsing other concerns. The campaign goes into a Stakhanovite speed-up, taking on an all-consuming importance; to its pursuit ever more resources are diverted. Those who dare voice objections (along with many who don't) are trampled underfoot as incorrigible heretics by the zealous and the self-serving. The campaign is now out of Beijing's control, bound on its own peculiar trajectory through time, obeying only its own internal dynamics.

But an excess of *yang* leads inevitably to a resurgence of *yin*. Production flags in enterprises and areas marginal to the campaign. Endless rounds of propaganda meetings, numbing in their monotony, dampen enthusiasm among the population at large. Discipline becomes a problem, forcing cadres to rely increasingly upon fiat and coercion. The number of "counterrevolutionaries" identified, abased, and brutalized grows alarmingly. Beginning at the grass roots, disillusionment with the excesses of the program spreads, gradually working its way up cadre ranks, finally reaching the center, which calls a belated halt to the long-since counterproductive campaign. The country only gradually settles back to normalcy, only to be roused by the next campaign before it completely reaches that state.

When the Central Committee cranks up an all-out campaign for a specific goal—such as grain production or birth control—some gains are made, but always at tremendous cost. The negative consequences that followed one minor campaign, the "Put grain first" policy pushed especially hard during the Cultural Revolution, were laid out for me by a brigade Party secretary. This man, one of the most able and energetic local leaders I met while in China, had taken exception to the blanket application of this policy, and had planted other crops, namely bananas and turnips, on higher ground less suitable for rice production. The county Party committee had objected strenuously, saying that this would adversely affect grain production (on which their own performance was primarily judged). "I told them that they'd better get used to eating only rice, because no one is going to plant bananas for them to eat," he recalled with some satisfaction. "The leaders really fear running into me, for I turn over their arguments with a sentence." He admitted that he was unusually audacious, though, saying that most village cadres "speak to officials as officials, and to ghosts as ghosts," outwardly going along with, even praising, whatever program Party higher-ups are pushing at the moment. His brigade's heretofore excellent record in grain production also presumably bolstered his courage. In any case, his criticism of the "grain first" policy proved prophetic. The "grain first" policy did indeed come to approximate "grain only." The production of grains made modest gains, but peasant diets nevertheless deteriorated as vegetables and fruits either leaped in price or disappeared from the market altogether.

What puzzled me was why, given the enormous human and economic costs exacted by campaigns, they continue to be launched with such daunting frequency. I saw that campaigns originated in the same tension between Beijing and lower-level Party and government bureaucracies that kept them careening along the edge of chaos once unleashed. To the Western eye, the Central Committee wields a curious combination of political strength and managerial weakness. It can dictate that its directives be read by or to every Chinese in the land. But because its perception of events outside the capital is delayed, dimmed, and distorted by the intervening layers of bureaucracy, it can never be sure its orders are obeyed. The slack in the system means that Beijing is able to lead the country only in fits and starts, rather like a wheeled toy on an elastic string.

Although the People's Republic goes to great lengths to cover up its institutional deficiencies, a crippling lack of the sort of information necessary to govern effectively has come through clearly, if inadvertently, at times. In 1959, well after the Great Leap Forward had entered its crisis phase, Mao appeared critically underinformed when he dismissed the possibility of disaster lightly, even flippantly, by saying, "Just because for a time there were too few vegetables, too few hairpins, no soap, a lack of balance in the economy and tension in the market, everyone became tense."* Spoken at a time when hundreds of millions of his countrymen were understandably anxious because they were starving, this was either brutal callousness or a complete ignorance of what conditions were like at that point for the hoi polloi.

But if not immediately, then gradually over time Mao should

* Quoted in Dick Wilson, *Mao: The People's Emperor* (London: Hutchinson & Co., 1979), p. 350.

have awakened to the inefficiency, excesses, and waste that the campaigns, most of which were his handiwork, invariably spawned. A campaign was, to be sure, a means of reasserting at least a semblance of control over a continuously ossifying administrative structure by setting a clear priority and pursuing it relentlessly. Mao's distrust of conservative bureaucratic ways is well known. But ultimately, Mao's willingness to wage "continuous revolution," a phrase he began using late in his long career, must be attributed to his utter faith in his personal vision. Mao, like Lenin, was first a rebel and only later a Marxist. He found in Marxism a rationale for his radical bias, in the Leninist Communist Party an organizational tool with which to advance his revolutionary aims, and in Stalinism the will to ruthlessly implement his blueprint for the future. It is hard to escape the conclusion—one shared by many Chinese—that Mao believed his imagined utopia would be cheap at any price. In the tart words of one middle-aged cadre, a man who had been actively involved in nearly every campaign that had come down the pike, "Without the movements, how would Mao have known that he was building socialism?"

But the cycle did not cease with Mao's death. Although critical of the past reliance on campaigns, in early 1982 alone the Deng regime set in motion three minor campaigns of its own as industry was instructed to study the self-reliance of the Daqing oil complex, the Party apparatus was subject to yet another "rectification," and a number of Mao's less radical early essays were promoted in a push to "study theory." Campaigns seem certain to continue, the inevitable outcome of the tug-of-war between change-oriented leaders and a bureaucracy content with the status quo. Like his predecessor, Deng Xiaoping is a tireless proponent of a singular blueprint for China's future. For all that, the current leadership may be able to avoid a repetition of the costlier excesses of decades past in the push for modernization. Deng, far more than the late Mao, seems to take notice when his theories are bloodied on the hard rock of fact.

———

At no time did theory and reality collide more violently than during the Cultural Revolution, Mao's last and most aberrant campaign, one that ended only after his death. If the Great Leap Forward had been the economic equivalent of locking a crew of farm workers in a junkyard and ordering them to assemble a jumbo jet, then the Great Proletarian Cultural Revolution was the political equivalent of herding a group of nonbelievers into a Marxist temple to chant Maoist sutras until they, like it or not, achieved a state of Communist nirvana. Beginning in 1966, Mao set out to reeducate his entire people in a program whose avowed purpose was "not only to demolish all the old ideology and culture . . . but also to create and cultivate among the masses an entirely new, proletarian ideology and culture, and entirely new proletarian customs and habits."

The vehicles of this cultural metamorphosis were to be China's youth, those who were least tainted by traditional Chinese culture or sullied by prerevolutionary Western influences, and who, by virtue of their callowness, were easily incited by idealistic appeals. Mao called for them to eradicate the remnants of feudalism and capitalism. In their earnest idealism, they did not disappoint him. After taking control of the schools from their teachers and organizing themselves into Red Guard units, they began house-to-house searches for cultural contraband, that is, for anything that could be connected with the past or with the West. Western suits and traditional Chinese gowns, crosses and carved god images, Dickens novels and kungfu tales—all were flung alike onto bonfires that burned day and night in China's cities at this time.

But culture does not exist primarily as artifacts or in the abstract, but in people's heads. The Cultural Revolution became yet another witchhunt to root out all those suspected, in Chinese parlance, of "having problem thoughts," or whose behavior had somehow deviated from the proletarian straight and narrow—an old professor who had once studied abroad, a middle-aged man whose parents had formerly been wealthy, a young girl who had relatives overseas, a woman who told fortunes for a living, a professional who once spoke out against a government policy, a cadre who was seen to have been corrupted by power. These were the sorts of individuals who were forced to recant deviant opinions and renounce past acts, real or imagined.

The instrument used to reform their thinking was the "struggle," a political purification rite unique to the oriental version of communism practiced in the peoples' republics of China, Vietnam, and North Korea. More commonly known in the West as brainwashing, it was developed during the Communist years in the Chinese hinterland as a tool to lever dissidents into line with Party policy, for which purpose it is still in common use today. The central element in this process of thought reform is the "struggle meeting," a long session of criticism and humiliation at which the accused is made to stand with bowed head and humble demeanor before a hostile crowd of people, usually from his own unit but sometimes including outsiders, who denounce him for his supposed crimes and demand a full confession.

It is impossible for a Westerner to fully grasp the dread that these mass confrontations arouse in the one singled out as a "struggle object." Throughout the meeting, the atavistic "flight or fight" response to threat repeatedly injects charges of adrenalin into a body immobilized by the sure knowledge (and often also by guards) that the slightest show of resistance will suffice to spark the mob to scream threats and obscenities, if not to outright violence. Thus shackled by terror and further despondent over seeming betrayal by colleagues and friends, the struggle object usually makes a quick and total confession, whatever the charges in the case may be. Experience has taught the Chinese that a less than alacritous confession only serves to add the onus of "resisting the will of the people" to his or her other crimes. The point of the punishing regime of meetings is to break the will of the struggle object and obtain not only a confession but a proper display of penitence as well. One former brigade accountant, an incredibly strong-willed fellow who was falsely accused of embezzling village funds during the "four cleansings" movement immediately prior to the Cultural Revolution (a charge from which he was finally cleared only in 1979) vainly protested his innocence for forty-three consecutive days. He capitulated on the forty-fourth day, recalling ruefully that "they messed around with me until I had no opinions whatsoever. I just wanted to go home."

While the full horror of high Maoism is quite simply beyond the ken of Americans who have experienced nothing more politically traumatic than a peace march or a presidential election, the degree of torment necessary to twist even the most basic of human values into bizarre shapes can be imagined if not fully comprehended. An embassy friend of mine recounted how two recently rehabilitated professors from Beijing University, one of the ignition points of the Cultural Revolution and a place where it raged on for years out of control, were invited to a showing of "The Diary of Anne Frank." When the movie reached its tragic denouement, where Anne and her family were led away to the death camps by the Gestapo, one professor leaned close to the other and offered, "They didn't have it so bad. At least they had a place of their own until nearly the end." The second professor was reported to have nodded in agreement, adding, "And at least Anne died quickly and painlessly."

With the old and foreign ideas of one culture bearer after another being extinguished like candles in a draft, the burden of building a new and proletarian culture was taken up in earnest. Teachers were to play a crucial role. Long after the military had been called in to pacify the Red Guards, whose factional struggles by 1968 had escalated to armed clashes between rival groups outfitted with tanks and howitzers, teachers were still undergoing political indoctrination. Every winter and summer school recess from 1966 to 1978 they were ordered—total participation was strictly enforced—to attend ideological training sessions. In the countryside, the first day of each recess would see all of the teachers, backpacking their bedrolls and often with young children in tow, trekking from their village schools in to the local commune seat. There they would stay until the recess ended several weeks later, sleeping in commune dormitories, eating in commune mess halls, and studying in commune meeting rooms. The regimen used to reform their thought was simple. They spent their days in small groups, each led by a commune cadre, where they read and discussed political articles and essays taken from the *People's Daily*, the Party's theoretical journal *Red Flag*, and Mao's *Selected Works*. Few of these pieces had anything to do with education.

Each meeting followed a set formula. The day's study material would be read out loud by one member of the group while the others read along silently. Then the cadre in charge would summarize the article. Finally, he would call upon those present to express their "opinions." Chinese friends stressed that participation at this point was mandatory. "Everyone had to say something," one elderly teacher, whose polite, even genteel manner gave him a Confucian air, revealed to me. "For someone not to do so would have been considered uncooperative, and he would have been struggled," this man reported. "The only thing it was possible to say was that the article was totally correct, even if you really didn't agree with it at all." With assignments and promotions dependent upon one's political report card and the slightest hint of ideological nonconformity, even a slip of the tongue, sufficient cause for heavy and prolonged criticism, the atmosphere of the meetings was tense. Neither did it help that the politically more "advanced" cadres who chaired the meetings, and usually were far less educated than the teachers in their charge, often seemed to take a perverse pleasure in correcting, even humiliating, these "stinking intellectuals."

That even at these meetings psychological pressure could reach excruciating levels was driven home to me by the revelations of Wang Yalan, a well-educated, highly regarded primary school teacher with twenty-five years of experience in the classroom. During an afternoon spent discussing the twists and turns educational policy had taken since the revolution, I had found Yalan to be a delightful person—bright, warm, and good-humored. When at one point I asked what she had learned from her decade of obligatory political meetings, Yalan pointed at her head in the universal gesture of mental incompetence, said contritely that her thoughts were still very backward, and then belied it all with a broad grin. She was such a thoroughly healthy person, in all senses of that word, that I was hit doubly hard by what she told me in closing.

"I came very close to suicide," she revealed casually, as if talking about a small purchase she had almost made. "It was during the winter recess of 1972. Our small group was talking about Chairman Mao's instruction that 'teaching must wake up the mind, not simply inject ideas.' I said that, of course, this was a good idea, but that we weren't told how to put it into practice. The cadre shouted that I was criticizing our great leader Chairman Mao, and for several days after that I was singled out for criticism and struggle. Several friends of mine were in my discussion group, but no one dared say a good word about me. They all followed the lead of the cadre in criticizing me. I lost my appetite and couldn't sleep at night. I would lay awake and wonder what they would accuse me of the next day. Matters got worse and worse. By the fourth night I was so tired, weak, and depressed that I decided to end it all by drowning myself. The only thing that stopped me was the thought of my four boys, the youngest of whom was only 3 years old. I had brought the little one with me to the commune because he was too young to stay at home with his brothers. I picked him up and held him tightly the entire night as he slept. They stopped struggling me on the fifth day."

Yalan's experience was unusual only in that she was struggled for a relatively brief period. Many of the people I came to know in my year in the People's Republic had personally suffered through a similar but longer-lasting episode at some point during the Cultural Revolution. Even more recounted to me the tale of a less fortunate relative or friend who perished in the Red Guard fighting, succumbed while being struggled, or died by suicide after being forced to the breaking point. Although the exact number of Chinese who lost their lives during these eleven years may never be known, partial statistics released as part of the state's case against the Gang of Four set a base line for the slaughter. In Yunnan and Inner Mongolia, it was reported, 34,000 people died as a direct result of the Red Guard terror, while the figure given for Beijing was 12,000. If these figures may be taken as roughly representative, then they say that across the face of China's twenty-nine provinces and municipalities, half a million Chinese perished. But this figure, enormous though it is, would not include deaths from other causes—heart failure, suicide, and illness—brought on by the anarchy of those times and the lack of proper medical care for those incarcerated. Nor does it speak to the fact that for every fatality there were dozens, if not hundreds, of Chinese who were arrested, beaten, injured, struggled, confined, or attempted suicide. But the radius of this twelve-year reign of terror extended well beyond its tens of millions of immediate casualties to encompass the whole population. In a sense, virtually every adult in mainland China is a victim of the Cultural Revolution.

The terrible period of high Maoism, like the Stalinist brutalities of the Soviet thirties, has been slow to produce its own literature. Those accounts that have appeared to date, again as in the Soviet case, have come from refugees and resident foreigners and have been published outside of the People's Republic.*

* One of the earliest and best accounts of the violent phase of the Cultural Revolution from 1966 to 1968 is former Red Guard leader Ken Ling's *The Revenge of Heaven* (New York: Putnam, 1970). For the same period from a radically different perspective see Anthony Grey's *Hostage in Peking* (London: Michael

Within China, except for the two years from mid-1978 to mid-1980 when stories hinting at the atrocities of the prior decade were permitted in print, the vacuum pack of totalitarian censorship has remained tightly in place, suffocating all open discussion. Still, I had read enough accounts of this particular holocaust to partly cushion for me the shock of hearing first hand the tales of Yalan and others who had lived through it.

What I was totally unprepared for, however, was the permanent psychological devastation that the Cultural Revolution had left in its path. Not that everyone carried identical scars. Phlegmatic peasants submitted to struggle with the same fatalistic resignation with which they faced floods and famines, and seemed to have recovered quickly from their physical and emotional maulings. On the other hand, professionals and intellectuals were hardly capable of accepting struggle with the same physical resilience and reflexive equanimity. The intensity of feeling with which these people related tragic episodes that, though personal, had occurred as long as twelve years ago suggested to me that they had scarcely begun to come to terms with their past, perhaps inhibited by the political risks of releasing their burden of memories in an open expression of hurt, anger, or loss, perhaps because they were wounded too close to the core for complete regeneration to be possible in any case.

While I occasionally encountered people who shied away from any discussion of the Cultural Revolution, more common was the opposite reaction, where a single question on my part was enough to rouse Chinese to a long litany of personal agonies lasting through an afternoon or an evening. Even such individuals, though, often alternated between anger and anxiety as they recounted their ordeals. One commune cadre in his early thirties was telling me how he had joined the Red Guard group as a fervent Maoist in the opening stages of the Cultural Revolution but had soon become disillusioned at what he saw as the rampant factionalism, cynicism, and hypocrisy of local and national leaders alike and had ultimately been fiercely struggled for his change of heart. "Although Chairman Mao," he continued—and then

---

Joseph, 1970). Grey was the Reuters correspondent in Beijing in 1967 when he was taken as a hostage by the PRC regime and held for two years, during which time he was struggled by the Red Guards.

broke off in mid-sentence. Glancing about nervously even though we were alone on the second floor of my house, he asked for a piece of my notebook paper, scribbled something on it, and then handed it back to me. I glanced down at the message I held in my hand. Whatever it was that I had expected to see, this wasn't it. It read, "Although Chairman Mao made great contributions to the success of the revolution, he made a number of mistakes late in life." As Deng himself had already begun to criticize Mao in similar terms, this hardly seemed to me to be a daring deviation from the Party line, certainly not enough to warrant his furtive, almost paranoid manner. After I had taken in the note's contents, he took back the paper, carefully folded it up into a small square, and slipped it into his pocket. Before I could question him, he excused himself and left, leaving me alone to puzzle over his strange behavior.

For a while, I thought his action merely idiosyncratic, one of those mental tics that one frequently finds even in the most normal-seeming of individuals, but I soon came to know several other Chinese who were similarly clandestine in their private criticisms of the regime. A doctor who had been telling me about his family said that he and his wife were able to spend only two weekends a month together, and then nervously took to paper to explain: "The policies here don't favor the family. Husbands and wives are often assigned to positions some distance apart and get to see each other only rarely." A cadre at a lime factory who had been explaining his unit's sales procedures suddenly took out his pen to write, "Sometimes to sell lower-grade lime we have to give a red envelope [a bribe or kickback] to a purchasing agent." It was as if these people found it difficult to give voice to any sentiments that reflected unfavorably on the current regime.

But no one quite matched a commune barefoot doctor, a PRC rural paramedic, in the exercise of such calligraphic caution. With him I had entire "conversations" in which he scarcely uttered a word, until finally I too got into the habit of writing out my questions and we sat like two deaf-mutes passing scribbled notes back and forth in absolute silence. On one occasion, he walked into my house unannounced, nodded me a wordless greeting, and immediately wrote, "The policies of this government take the people for fools [nongchun renmin]."

"Why do some people write these things instead of speaking

them?" I wrote back, less interested in his message, which I had heard from others, than in the decidedly odd medium he had chosen for its transmission.

"Because they are afraid. And they are afraid because they have been beaten into fear [*da pa ren*]," he immediately penned under my note.

"But aren't things better now?" I parried.

In answer to this, he scrawled out a whole paragraph as I read over his shoulder. "Things are better now than during the Cultural Revolution. At that time, a sentence spoken from a different standpoint from the Party was enough to send you to a struggle meeting, labor camp, or even prison. Everyone has seen it happen. That period still has a strong effect on people's behavior. They have a lasting fear. Even today we have to be very careful about what we say. People dare to become angry, but they don't dare to speak. This is the way things are here."

"But," I countered, this time breaking our unspoken vow of silence, "isn't it more dangerous to write a criticism than to speak it? Writing leaves evidence that could be used against you."

He looked both helpless and sheepish as he wrote, "It's impossible for me to say these things out loud."

Inwardly battered, outwardly submissive, and, at least to outsiders, a little odd, this barefoot doctor and others like him were the working wounded of the Cultural Revolution, for despite their traumas, they continued to function in their state-assigned roles. There were others less dogged or resilient, however, who had simply declared themselves to be socially defunct.

One of these was Dr. Liu, a distinguished graduate of the School of Medicine of Guangzhou's Zhongshan University, formerly one of the university hospital's most accomplished resident surgeons, currently a self-employed basket weaver. Although he lived in one of Sandhead's satellite villages, it was only by accident that we met during my final weeks in the countryside. Passing by a modest but well-kept brick home in the little hamlet of Clamhead, a part of the brigade I did not often visit, I saw a man at work in the courtyard. He did not immediately notice me, for his attention was fully engaged by the basket that was taking shape before him, and for a moment I stood silently watching his skilled hands deftly interweaving bamboo strips. "That's Dr. Liu," my assistant whispered, clearly in awe of the man. I nodded, having already concluded from his slender build, thick spectacles, and a certain aura of what the Chinese call "brush and ink" that this was no ordinary peasant, and stepped into the courtyard to introduce myself.

Dr. Liu took my intrusion gracefully, saying that he had hoped for an opportunity to meet me, and invited me into his home for a cup of tea. After a few minutes of small talk, I asked the obvious question: how had he, a doctor, come to be here? "I was born in this house," Dr. Liu smilingly replied. "I was the oldest son of a doctor of Chinese medicine. My father taught me much about herbal medicines. But he wanted me to learn Western medicine, particularly surgery, so he sent me to the Medical School at Zhongshan University. My family was not wealthy, and my school expenses were a heavy burden. My father managed by selling off pieces of land. I graduated in 1950, right after the revolution, and stayed on at the university hospital."

At the time of the 1952 land reform, when everyone's class status was decided, Dr. Liu was classified as a student, which is what he had in fact been before 1949. His family, however, were classified as small landholders, only a little better in the Chinese Communist scheme of things than landlords, because they had rented out their modest amount of land and thus "exploited" others instead of working it themselves. It was a fateful determination. Fourteen years later, it was this bad family class background that led "Landlord Liu" to be one of the first doctors at the hospital to be struggled.

"I was interested only in medicine and had never paid much attention to politics," Dr. Liu recollected. "Maybe that's why at first I thought that I could reason with the Red Guards. I told them that I was a doctor. They said that class standpoint was more important than occupation. I said that my individual class status was student. They said that I was the corrupt product of a small-landholder household. I said that I had not lived with my family since going away to middle school in Guangzhou at the age of 14. They said I had grown up on landlord's milk. Whatever I said only made things worse. They said I was just trying to cover up my crimes. So I finally decided not to say anything. They shouted that I was not cooperating, that by refusing to confess, I was proving that I was reactionary to my bones."

"But the worst blow was my wife's death," he continued,

furrowing his forehead and fixing his glasses. "We didn't have any children and were very close, you understand. She was a doctor too. She committed suicide shortly after they began struggling her by hanging herself. After that, I didn't care much what happened to me. They went on struggling me for months. They finally decided that I was an 'active counterrevolutionary.' In all, I spent three years in confinement."

It is hard to drop out of one of the world's most regimented societies—it entails economic hardship and political risk—but this did not deter Dr. Liu. Released at long last, he returned immediately to Sandhead. This move violated the population registration law, which forbids unauthorized internal migration, and so made him ineligible for rice, cloth, and other ration coupons in his former home village. Instead, he passed a precarious existence outside the state economy as a small artisan, selling his wares and buying his necessities on the black market. As the son of a small landholder he could have been struggled again, but the villagers had been kind, largely out of respect for his profession, though they had kept their distance. I found out later that the university Party committee had indeed written the brigade requesting that Dr. Liu continue to be struggled, but that the local Party secretary, secretly in sympathy with the doctor's plight, had responded that Liu was not officially a member of the brigade and so did not come under its jurisdiction. A second letter, requesting that Dr. Liu be taken into custody and returned, was ignored.

"I have lived in Sandhead now for ten years," Dr. Liu continued in his relaxed manner. "It's very peaceful here. Once a week or so I take my baskets into the market to sell them and make a little cash. This last year I was finally able to register as a member of the brigade, and so now I have a garden plot and receive ration coupons. I make enough to get by. I still don't have much contact with the villagers. I prefer to keep to myself. Occasionally a doctor from the local clinic or a barefoot doctor here will ask my advice, and I give it, though I don't treat patients. The university hospital has repeatedly sent cadres to ask me to come back to my old position, but I have refused." Doctor Liu's voice, which had been calm and measured, now tightened perceptibly as he said, "I will never go back. I just want to be left alone. I don't want to be a doctor anymore."

As I thought about Dr. Liu's self-imposed professional exile—
not only what had sent him back to his birthplace but also what
had kept him there all these years, which seemed to me the greater
puzzle—his last words came back to me. "I would not survive
another movement," he had said firmly as we parted. This made
it all fit together. As privately apocalyptic as the Cultural Revolution had been for him, what underlay his continued preference
for a life-style befitting a Taoist hermit was less a haunting memory
of the past than a dark prescience of the future. Likewise, what
kept the wounds of the barefoot doctor and others who had been
traumatized in the Cultural Revolution from healing properly was
not just a suppurating bitterness toward the past but the unnerving
uncertainty of the future. Burned out in the past, they are kept
in that wasted state by the endless cycle of campaigns, which
continuously provoke them into a paralyzing insecurity.

The fluttering inconstancy of the present distresses not only
groups obviously victimized by past campaigns, such as professionals, the former rural gentry, or the intelligentsia, but nearly
all other segments of the population as well. With the exception
of a certain stratum of leading cadres, I found a mood of hopeless
anxiety to be pervasive among Chinese from all walks of life,
including the peasantry, so much so as to constitute virtually a
mass neurosis. For the 1 billion Chinese who live out their lives
in a baffling world capable of dissolving at any point into chaos,
it would be perversely heartening if the future were merely
opaque. As it is, the repeated arrival of unpredictable campaigns
has abraded away all certainty except the singularly unsettling
conviction that another is on the way. One of my most articulate
peasant friends fumed to me upon reading that the "four big
freedoms"* were soon to be abrogated, "Our policies are always
changing, depending on the whims of those in power. No one
knows when another political movement will explode forth, or
when they will be criticized or even struggled. This makes every-

* The "four big freedoms" were the freedom to put up big character posters
and to engage in "big debates, blooming, and contending," the last two being
a reference to the 1957 Hundred Flowers campaign slogan "Let a hundred
flowers bloom and a hundred schools of thought contend." Since many of the
current leadership, including Deng himself, were the butt of big-character-poster
attacks during the GPCR when they were "bloomed and contended" right out
of power, they were perhaps understandably leery of these Maoist "freedoms"
and abolished them in 1980.

one nervous. No one has any confidence that things will be better in the future. They expect the worst."

One consequence of this perpetual uneasiness about what lies beyond the bend in the river is a renewed interest in fathoming the world and divining the future by other means. Peasant fatalism and folk beliefs, far from being gradually eliminated by repeated campaigns against "feudal superstitions," have instead merely gone underground, where they have not only survived but flourished. I remember a young peasant of rugged build and hearty manner from a suburban commune just south of Guangzhou telling me earnestly that although things were good this year, they were sure to take a turn for the worse in the next. There had been a minor epidemic of fleas the preceding summer, he explained, which as everyone knew was a reliable portent of trouble to come two years hence—maybe a bad harvest, maybe a political campaign. Bemused by the thought of fleas as evil omens, Westerners may find his explanation merely ludicrous. This is to miss its significance. Lest reason become impotent, experience fail to make sense, and life itself approach absurdity, any explanation for the inexplicable, however unreal it may seem to the uninitiated, is better than none at all. Chinese peasants too unsophisticated to understand the true mechanics of disasters, natural and man-made, resort to hypotheses drawn from the circle of their own experience to interpret, and in interpreting come to terms with, not only the age-old cycle of natural calamities but also the political oscillations of modern times.

Underneath the continued adherence to traditional folk beliefs by many in China, there is a deeper problem of belief and nonbelief at issue here, one which is central to the continued legitimacy and survival of China's Communist system itself. Within the PRC, "scientific" Marxism-Leninism-Maoism is ceaselessly promoted, serving in effect as the secular substitute for religious belief, a way of channeling all ideological devotion to the service of the state. Any religion, even the equivocal case of communism, must provide a secure and stable world where the individual can operate with some assurance, largely by promoting a world-view that harmonizes with the way things in sheer actuality are held to be. But the state orthodoxy propagated by Beijing, except for a few vague pronouncements in the Maoist canon concerning the necessity of "continuing the revolution," has flagrantly failed to help Chinese to cope with the endless merry-go-round of high-pressure movements. Given their lack of alternatives, it is perhaps not all that surprising that Chinese peasants grasp at fleas to convince themselves that God is not mad.

11

Political Myths: Peasants, Progress, and the "New China"

Valued in the Chinese peasant's terms, the revolution has been a magnificent achievement, a victory not only for Mao Tse-tung, but for several hundreds of millions of the Chinese people.

John K. Fairbank*

Rumors had swept China for months that Deng Xiaoping, stripped of his posts as Vice Chairman, Vice Premier, and Chief of the General Staff in April 1976 and sent in disgrace back to his native province of Sichuan, would soon be returning to the seat of power. When the announcement finally came in late 1977 that Deng had been restored to all of his former positions, a genuine groundswell of relief surged through China. It was shared by Chinese of all classes, from out-of-favor cadres who saw in Deng's rehabilitation the promise of their own, to workers who anticipated the revival of wage bonuses and other incentives linking work performance to pay heretofore reviled as capitalist, to intellectuals and professionals who foresaw an end to the hysterical know-nothingism of the Cultural Revolution, to peasants who counted on a deemphasis of rigid collective farming to usher in more flexible—and profitable—individual and family farming arrangements. Above all, Chinese welcomed Deng back because

* *China Perceived* (New York: Random House, 1974), p. xvii.

285

of the promise of a more temperate, reasoned, and unheroic politics implicit in his own checkered political past and in the Franklinesque homily for which he was famous, "Black cat or white cat, a cat is a good cat if it catches mice." If I had harbored any doubts about the sincerity and spontaneity of the welcome extended Deng, these vanished when I heard from villagers that when word of the Vice Chairman's emergence from exile reached the Chinese people, state stores throughout the Pearl River Delta quickly sold out their substantial stocks of firecrackers. In ageless Chinese fashion, peasants celebrated Deng's return with the effervescing snap and crackle of strings of ladyfingers. Peasants and cadres alike swiftly shifted their attention to and fastened their hopes on the diminutive Deng, whose name dominated the dinner-table discussions that I heard. Though benevolently featured posters of the late Mao and the living Hua, who would not be deposed from his Party chairmanship until two years later, were still a fixture of rural homes when I was in China, they themselves seemed to have been relegated to the realm of the departed ancestors over whose altars they hung.

Once back in power, Deng set aside the radical social policies of his predecessors and dramatically reaffirmed the regime's commitment to honest economic growth along the lines laid out by the late Premier Zhou Enlai shortly before his death. China was to modernize, and this manifestly apolitical goal galvanized the nation behind it. After more than two decades of desultory economic progress, the Chinese people were electrified by the promise of a strong, modern China, an excitement compounded by equal measures of heartfelt relief at what they took to be the cessation of erratic political campaigns and burgeoning expectations for a better material life. Some Chinese also imagined Deng to be committed to a gradual political liberalization, a perception that reached its peak during an interview with the American columnist Robert Novak, when Deng bestowed his blessing on the Xidan Democracy Wall with an oracular "Xidan good."

It was springtime in Beijing. To the astonishment of long-time foreign residents, some young couples took to holding hands in public, residential back streets were cordoned off for impromptu evening dances, and in an alleyway off Wangfujing Street a low-life establishment called the Peace Cafe opened its doors, catering to an assorted crop of youthful deadbeats. Crowds at the Democracy Wall grew larger, small underground journals spread from Beijing to cities throughout China, and a self-declared candidate for a local people's congress proclaimed boldly that he did not believe in communism. In the villages of Guangdong ancestral tablets and god images that had been cached away during the Cultural Revolution began to reappear on long empty altars, resurgent Cantonese opera troupes took to the stage with their first productions in fourteen years, and rural collectives quietly abandoned the egalitarian wage rates that had disastrously lowered productivity during the Cultural Revolution and instead began paying members on the basis of work actually accomplished. However much the gray-faced guardians of the state order may have worried that the masses were slipping the noose of control, most of the Chinese were solidly ranked behind what they took to be Deng's policies.

The outside world seemed almost as relieved as the Chinese themselves that the People's Republic was finally going straight. After the economic mumbo-jumbo of the Great Leap and the mindless assault on culture of the ironically misnamed Cultural Revolution, here at last was a campaign that Westerners could understand, and they responded with enthusiastic applause to China's commitment to economic growth. Western well-wishers saw in Deng's much-acclaimed pragmatism the harbinger of sound economic policies, businessmen began to have heady visions of the profits to be racked up in a market of some 1 billion, and observers of the Chinese political scene such as Richard Nixon began to speculate that the PRC might gradually slough off its mantle of Communist totalitarianism and metamorphize into a nation that was merely socialist, a prediction somewhat oddly seconded by disappointed radical fringe groups who shrilly cried that China was "changing color."

Yet I had been in China for no more than a few months when I began to pick up the first stirrings of unease among the people, and by the time I left China in July 1980 the national mood had shifted dramatically. Gone was the initial euphoria that had greeted Deng's return and the announcement of the modernization program.

The spirits of some of my more thoughtful friends had been dampened by the Party's drive to crush dissent that began in March 1979 with the arrest of Wei Jingsheng and a number of other dissidents and accelerated in the months that followed with the closing of the Democracy Wall and increasingly harsh restrictions on free expression. With these moves, Deng in effect served notice on overinquisitive intellectuals that, except in circumscribed scientific and technical spheres where it could serve the modernization program, their cognition was still excess baggage on the lumbering Marxist train of thought. A well-educated young cadre in the Dragon River Commune administration, bitter over what he saw as Deng's betrayal, spit out a diatribe about the impossibility of true democratization. "Whenever people are encouraged to speak out, it is always because the Party has some political need," he said acidly. "The Democracy Wall and all that was because of the need to purge the Gang of Four. After that, the wall was used to attack Deng's enemies. But it is really a political trap. As soon as the Party has finished using those who speak out, they will be called to account so as to frighten the people into silence again."

Events after I left China certainly bore out his apprehensions. The campaign to crush the remnants of the Democracy movement peaked in 1981 with the banning of underground journals, the arrest of editors and other activists who persisted in publishing and distributing them, and scathing attacks in the official press on writers and artists whose works overstepped the narrow bounds of ideological orthodoxy. Compared with the indiscriminate repression of the not so distant past, the campaign was carried out with surgical precision. The results were, however, the same: by 1982 the voices of dissidence had been effectively stilled, and the People's Republic had reverted once again to being a culturally two-dimensional society, a flatland of the mind.

This repression, disturbing though it was for the few, merely served to confirm the premonitions of the many for whom the prospect of political liberalization had never held much promise in any case. Rather, most Chinese, especially those in the impoverished countryside, had staked their hopes on the Four Modernizations' pledge of a better life. When these aspirations were corroded away by the cynicism bred into the Chinese outlook by past political campaigns, a reaction well underway during my last few months of research, not a few Chinese came to see the Four Modernizations as little better than a political ploy by Deng to rally those disaffected by the Cultural Revolution behind him and his wing of the Party. One of my more politically sophisticated acquaintances put it the following way: "Who doesn't want China to be strong? Who doesn't want a better life? Who doesn't want an end to leftist campaigns? By appearing to support these goals, Vice Premier Deng gained support from nearly everyone, until they realized that the Four Modernizations campaign was just a way for him to consolidate his power." There must have been many Chinese who agreed with him because within two years of the movement's inception, rapidly waning public support, even among the cadre class, led the official press to complain with an air of injured innocence that some people, cadres as well as common folk, were reacting to the modernization program "as if it were just another political campaign."

In retrospect, Deng's triumphant return to power was invested by too many people with too many hopes. When these failed to materialize, he was saddled with a huge credibility problem. Whereas in 1977–78 many Chinese, buoyed by the end of the Cultural Revolution and the arrest of high-ranking leftists, were prepared to believe that Deng could solve China's many afflictions, they quickly discovered that in the absence of basic institutional reforms, changes in personalities counted for little.

The attitude of scoffing skepticism that Chinese soon came to adopt was not unduly cynical considering their past experience. The People's Republic has compiled quite a cookbook of failed formulas for instant modernization in its short thirty-year existence. In the early fifties there was the Soviet model with its emphasis on heavy industry. Then during the Great Leap there was the Maoist way with its exaltation of human will and muscle power. During the later years of the Cultural Revolution a variant of this, a concoction characterized by extreme egalitarianism, put in a brief, unproductive appearance. After so many false starts, the Chinese may perhaps be forgiven for casting a jaundiced eye at the newest addition to this string of unsuccessful recipes.

Even to me, the similarity of the Four Modernizations to past campaigns was unmistakable. From the Party's sanctification of the goal of modernization above all others and the setting of astronomical production objectives to the drumroll of propaganda urging all to sacrifice for its sake, it was a slice from the same millennarian pie. During the frantic early phase of the drive for economic expansion in 1978 and 1979, Beijing (1) rushed into multi-billion-dollar deals for turnkey steel and petrochemical plants, many of which it had to scuttle two years later as construction snags appeared and costs mounted alarmingly, (2) announced plans to mechanize 85 percent of agricultural work by 1985 just as the shift to family-centered farming undercut the use of tractors and other farm machinery, and (3) promised that incomes would rise by a factor of four by the year 2000, from less than $25 to $1,000 per capita,* only to quietly reduce this to $800 in 1981. This short boom-and-bust cycle, with its uncanny family resemblance to past follies, suggests a PRC leadership still compulsively spinning grandiose plans for the future to the neglect of matters nearer at hand.

Yet even if China is able to learn the lesson of its recent past and, freeing itself from what Vice Premier Yao Yilin called in 1981 the "age-old malady of seeking quick results," batten down for the long haul of gradual growth, it still must somehow find a way to deal with a host of difficulties—the accumulation of sufficient capital, the acquisition of advanced technology, the reform of the corrupt and complacent state bureaucracy, the plugging of the critical expertise gap—so complexly intertwined that the solution to one problem often inflames another. The People's Republic is predisposed, as a totalitarian state, to bull its way forward after the brute fashion of the Soviet Union, but it totally lacks the industrial brawn that is a prerequisite of this strategy. The 1930s Stalinist strategy of extracting the huge sums necessary for basic capital construction from the peasantry cannot be employed without driving enormous numbers of already impoverished rural dwellers below the subsistence level entirely. Neither is Beijing willing to go into extensive debt to Western banking institutions to finance its economic program for fear of bringing on a Polish-style economic fiasco. Lacking the foreign exchange to make the wholesale, across-the-board purchases of foreign technology that it initially envisioned, the PRC must rely heavily upon the slower process of schooling specialists abroad as a means of gradually developing an indigenous industry, while worrying that those sent to the altars of Western science may bring back as well idolatrous ideas about individual freedom and representative

---

* Even this revised goal will require an average economic growth rate of over 7 percent a year until the end of the century, but in 1981 the Chinese economy grew by only about 4 percent.

democracy—if they return at all. Handicapped by scarce capital and primitive technology, Beijing has come to appreciate the advantages of the kind of relatively inexpensive and technically unsophisticated light industry that has provided a steppingstone to modernization in Taiwan, Hong Kong, and Singapore, but lacks the managerial finesse and entrepreneurial drive needed to make this particular economic miracle happen.

Not that Deng and Co. haven't tried. Sprouts of capitalism that would have been quickly uprooted as "poisonous weeds" a few years ago are now being carefully transplanted into the socialist soil of China. Such Western economic principles as the pricing system, the profit motive, and material incentive have been adopted wholesale. What is missing in all of this hopeful pseudo-capitalism is unfortunately what is most essential: the vitality of the free market itself. High productivity and astute management are not the result of routinized applications of rote formula, as Deng's bureaucratic economists seem to think, but are adaptive consequences of the economic struggle for survival among competing economic entities. Until Beijing relaxes the dead grip of central planning and allows the invisible hand of the marketplace to hold sway, the Chinese economy will be efficient, responsive, and productive only to the limited extent that these characteristics can be imposed from above.

So too with Beijing's aspirations to emulate efficient, well-managed, and productive Western enterprises by granting more managerial autonomy to factories and their parent department, encouraging the study of Western management techniques, and appointing technical experts to assist generalist cadres. Most middle bureaucrats and managers remain more familiar with the Maoist canon than with modern business practices, and the PRC is too thinly endowed with specialized talent—especially after its dissipation in the relentless cycle of campaigns—to promote experts to positions of responsibility in more than a fraction of the billets where they are needed. Even where a specialist is elevated to the rank of assistant factory head, he is usually handicapped by a lack of real power, which remains in the hands of politically astute and well-connected cadres. A young worker related to me how his 59-year-old father, an electrical engineer and one of the tens of thousands of Western-educated specialists and capitalist managers rehabilitated after Deng's accession, had been appointed third assistant director of an electric generator factory in Foshan City. His father had been pleased with his new position until an incident occurred that made him aware of the hazards of having responsibility without authority. The factory director, a cadre with no formal engineering training, asked his opinion concerning the purchase of a large, second-hand lathe from the military, to which the engineer responded that the lathe should not be bought because it could not do the precision cutting their work called for. But the factory director, hoping to boost production, overruled his objections and approved the purchase anyway. As soon as the lathe was installed and put into operation, it was discovered that, as the engineer had foreseen, its cutting tolerances were not close enough for the factory's needs. "The factory director shifted the blame onto my father," the young worker recalled angrily to me. "He stood up at the factory meeting and denounced my father for allowing the purchase of technically inadequate machinery. He said that my father had wasted the state's money and damaged the Four Modernizations. My father didn't say anything. He just bowed his head. He was afraid because he is a rehabilitated reactionary. He told me that he only has a year or two until he retires and he doesn't want any trouble."

By far the most surprising capitalist inroad has been the limited legalization of the private enterprise sector. Foreclosed in the early and middle fifties as the state took monopolistic control over all economic activity, it sprang unexpectedly back to life in the late seventies with the sanction of self-employed street vendors and mom-and-pop shops. The Communist Party abandoned an even more sacred principle of socialism—that the state should be the sole employer—when it announced in November 1981 that every self-employed person would henceforth be allowed to hire as many as two helpers and five apprentices. However radical a departure from Mao's way the reestablishment of the private sector may seem to be, it is less a rejection of the founding father's orthodoxy than a temporary palliative for some of its more obvious deficiencies in the area of retail trade and service. Neither will the miniscule private sector create sufficient social drag to brake China out of its Communist orbit. Even if current predictions are fulfilled and it expands tenfold to several million workers producing several percent of the total GNP, private enterprise in the PRC will still be mere flotsam on the surface of a vast inert sea of socialized industry and commerce.

There remains more irony than promise in the selective use of cryptocapitalist methods to inject new life into a stunted socialist economy. As the no-nonsense repression of China's fledgling Democracy movement made painfully clear, the easy virtue of Deng's ideology is limited to liaisons with capitalist economic forms. Deng may be prepared to bed the theories of Adam Smith if it will increase the GNP and thereby strengthen state power, but under no circumstances will he embrace those of Thomas Jefferson. In political matters, he remains a strict Leninist, a firm believer in the need for Party dictatorship, in this respect not all that different from Mao himself.

Acute though its other difficulties are, the Chinese Communist Party's most pressing problems revolve around the people it rules: first, their sheer numbers, which keep labor costs so low that it is rarely cost-effective to mechanize; and second, their deepening doubts about the Party and its ability to modernize China, which undermine morale and hence hold production to low levels. While the population program appears to have strikingly reduced the birth rate in many areas, its indisputable long-term advantages appeared to me to be offset over the short run by the negative reactions of Chinese families forced to forgo or even abort desired offspring. Family planning is one more factor in a disaffection so profound and widespread among the population that Deng Xiaoping himself declared anxiously in early 1980 that the Party faced a full-blown "crisis of confidence." I myself often found people not merely cynical but downright dispirited, doubting not just the claimed superiority of their socialist system but even its bare-bones adequacy as an engine of economic change. I remember a conversation with a young agricultural technician about the relatively high standards of living that Chinese had achieved in Taiwan, Hong Kong, and Singapore. It ended with his bringing the moral back home by observing pessimistically, "We have been liberated for thirty years. If socialism is so superior, how come we are so backward and poor?"

Even more than the admittedly knotty problems of capital, technology, and managerial know-how, it is the existence of such

incapacitating doubt and disbelief that threatens to paralyze plans
for progress. If Mao's oft-repeated boast that 90 percent of the
population actively supported the ongoing revolution was, to
judge from the Chinese I spoke with, nothing more than wanton
hyperbole, it is nevertheless true that the Party repeatedly demonstrated during the PRC's first three decades of existence an ability
to mobilize the Chinese masses nothing short of awesome. While
the regime is still able to undertake drives with limited, clearly
defined goals such as birth control, the age of full-scale ideological
campaigns on the order of the Great Leap Forward may be over.
In reaction to an overbearing and ultimately intolerable politics,
most Chinese have become unbelievers, passive resisters who are
left unmoved by exhortatory slogans along the lines of the current
"Plunge into the hot struggle for production and give all to the
realization of the Four Modernizations." The ironical upshot of
this backlash is that China's only real resource—its people—has
rebounded to become perhaps its heaviest liability. With the exception of mid-ranking administrative cadres and apparatchiks,
who are absolutely committed to the current order because they
could be sure of surviving under no other, there is scarcely a
group in China today whose unstinting support the Party can
count on. Neither is there any segment of society unselfishly working for the Four Modernizations, however much it has benefited
from the various forms and policy changes of the last three years.
Cadres rehabilitated from labor camps were glad to be back, but
many simply go through the motions of work; workers were
cheered by the reinstitution of bonuses, but remain lethargic and
undisciplined; teachers were gratified at the return to the basics,
but their commitment to their calling, to say nothing of the over-
arching order, is still anemic; peasants were pleased to be promoted from collective farm hands to tenant farmers, but have
not translated these sentiments into allegiance to the state. "Do
you really think that China can modernize?" I was asked time
and time again by Chinese from all walks of life, usually in that
dead tone of voice that answers a question in the act of asking
it.

Even more unexpectedly, many officials in the lower grades
pessimistically portrayed China's future to me in terms almost
as bleak, and Communist Party members in private often gave
scant credit to their organization's ability to make good on even

part of its promise of an impending prosperity. Corroboration that my assessment of the cadre state of mind was, if anything, not negative enough came from no less authoritative a source than the *People's Daily*, which complained in a long article in early 1982 that "only a relatively small number among the hundreds of thousands of cadres and Party members . . . are really convinced that our country is now at a stage of great change and great development." Such misgivings on the part of those in positions of leadership do not augur well for China's development.

Besides intellectuals, of whose profound estrangement there can be no doubt, it was my impression that the most alienated segment of society was youth. Most representatives of the generation born after the revolution I had a chance to talk with at any length seemed uncommitted to any ideal, officially sponsored or not, and were certainly unconvinced that China will be able to modernize in this century. I remember my last conversation with Wenfang, the unemployed young woman from an establishment family whom I had gotten to know in Guangzhou, one day before my scheduled return to Hong Kong. She had completed her transformation into a Hong Kong tourist by somehow acquiring nylon stockings and pumps and, accompanied by a girlfriend in similar guise, had slipped past the gate guards of the Dongfang. But, perhaps because I was going on a journey that she could never make, Wenfang was not her usual vivacious self, and as the three of us walked slowly through the central garden of the hotel, an awkward silence descended.

"We are really so backward," Wenfang said finally, as much to herself as to me.

"Don't you think that things will get better?" I countered. "I mean, with the Four Modernizations—."

"The Four Modernizations," she cut me off in very un-Chinese fashion, "are nothing more than propaganda. You can't take them seriously. None of my friends pays any attention to them. Will things get better?" she repeated darkly. "I don't think so. Maybe in the next world. Or maybe in Hell."

The official explanation for this crippling lack of public confidence has varied. In the first years after their fall, the Gang of Four were remorselessly pilloried for all of China's many ills, including the yawning gulf between the leaders and the led. This simplistic scapegoating gradually gave way to a more complex and, on the surface, more credible account which centered on the damage done to public trust during the universally hated Cultural Revolution, belatedly acknowledged to have been not merely the handiwork of the Gang, but that of Mao himself. By 1982, with the Cultural Revolution receding in time and the Dengists struggling to push through bureaucratic reforms, the demoralizing effect of ineffective, corrupt, and privilege-seeking cadres was being mentioned as an additional factor.

Though a step in the direction of the truth, the present version still stops a long way short of clearing up the mystery of how the stock of government and Party has come to sink so low. Specific problems are cited piecemeal, without reference to the more fundamental systemic deficiencies that gave rise to them in the first place and are the ultimate cause of popular dissatisfaction. The back-door machinations and power-mongering of officialdom may be mentioned, but not the underlying problem, the all too evident emergence of a new ruling class of "leading cadres," an aristocracy which by hidden connections and out-and-out privileges enjoys a standard of living far higher than the people it ostensibly serves. Mao may be held to have made some "errors" in his later years, but without a hint that in many respects the system of totalitarian control that he built over his decades of power remains largely in place, containing Chinese aspirations for more freedom of thought and action. The Cultural Revolution may be decried, but the campaign approach that it exemplifies continues to be relied upon, despite the fact that it was above all incessant political movements that frittered away the capital of naive trust that the Communist regime was initially endowed with. How little the Party really understands the national mood was made starkly clear by the *People's Daily* article mentioned above, which called for reinforcement of the Maoist slogan "politics in command" and the strengthening of "ideological education." The solution to the current authority crisis, the Party newspaper concluded, was a major ideological campaign.

———◆———

Central to the Communist Party's recent efforts to make peace with its disgruntled populace and come to terms with its radical past is its critical reassessment of the late Chairman Mao. Mao had been "70 percent good, 30 percent bad," Deng Xiaoping was quoted as saying in November 1978, thereby opening a rancorous dispute in the upper ranks of the Party on their former leader's merits and demerits.

As the leadership conducted its largely secret debate over Mao's personal quotient of good and evil, ordinary Chinese were mulling over the fact that the infallible prophet-liberator of the continuing revolution, the paragon they had been taught in school to refer to as the "red sun of our hearts," had been officially pronounced capable of error. Deng's intention had been to dismantle the "cult of personality" that had been built up around Mao, distance himself and the Party from Mao's radical programs, and also, I suspect, avenge himself and other high-ranking cadres who had been demoted, purged, and persecuted during Mao's despotic last decade. While it was a simple matter to order Mao statues razed, Mao posters torn down, and the celebrated Little Red Book of Mao quotations withdrawn from the bookstores, all measures that were taken in 1979–81, Mao's close identification with the Party made it impossible to make a clean break with his past policies. Mao had been the Party's principal actor, primary symbol, and undisputed ideological authority for so long that for this organization to bring charges against him was, as one of my Chinese friends tartly put it, "like slapping one's own face."

Despite the Party's efforts to suppress public criticism of the former Chairman, the process of de-Maoization unavoidably undermined the image of the monolithic Communist Party and weakened its claims to political legitimacy—an effect similar to the effect of de-Stalinization in Khrushchev's Russia. But the problem was even more acute than this parallel suggests, for Mao had not merely been China's Stalin, he had been China's Lenin as well. The Gang of Four could be vilified as a cabal of power-hungry upstarts with a minimum of unpleasant historical side effects. Mao, however, had been in command from the creation. The founding father's failures would implicate not only the Communist Party but all that had been held inviolable—the achievements of the regime's thirty years, the superiority of the socialist system, and even the sacred revolutionary struggle itself. It was necessary to lay the leftist errors of the eleven-year Cultural Revolution and the three-year Great Leap Forward at Mao's feet and confirm that the painful period of recovery following the Great Leap Forward known as the "three difficult years" had indeed been, as scattered earlier reports had indicated, a time of terrible suffering for the Chinese people, but in such a way as to save face for the former leader and the Party he had led for so long.

Even before the Party reached a public verdict on what became known popularly in China as the "good Mao, bad Mao" problem, it was already trying to protect itself by placing its past beyond criticism.* I chanced to visit an acquaintance in Great Virtue Commune in mid-1980, shortly after internal Party directives had set out the coming reevaluation in draft form, and discovered counterfeit history in the making. His normally tidy desk was piled high with production reports from the Cultural Revolution, and he explained to me that the Party had ordered all references to radical Maoist policies and slogans of the time expunged. Perhaps because he had already spent two days painstakingly going over these old reports, cutting out a section here, pasting in a correction there, I found him fairly exercised about the whole business. "This is history," he said, hefting up a 2-inch-thick, folio-sized report with both hands. "How can you rewrite history? But that's what I have to do." He set the report back on his desk and went on agitatedly. "Everyone knows that the Cultural Revolution was wrong, that the Great Leap Forward was wrong. For half of our history since the liberation—fifteen years out of thirty—we have followed an incorrect line. This is a fact. The Party wants us to forget the past, so I have to rewrite all of these old reports. But how can we possibly forget? We should learn from these mistakes, not just pretend that they never happened."

Intended in part to restore the confidence of the vast numbers of people who had suffered under his policies, the official reevaluation of the decades of Mao's rule with its startling admission of

---

* Only in 1982 was the Central Committee finally able to reach consensus, passing a 27,000-word document that, though crediting Mao with the Communist victory, also held him responsible for a number of "practical mistakes" during his forty-one-year reign. The most devastating criticism of the man who in his later years had been canonized as a "great teacher, great leader, great commander, and great helmsman" concerned his dominant role in the Cultural Revolution, when the Party and the people, the report admitted, "suffered the severest setbacks and the heaviest losses." The product of compromise between those who had profited by it, the report was a hodge-podge of praise and calumny. Though politically necessary, this appeared to me to be the worst possible solution: criticism pointed enough to convince people of what they instinctively knew all along, that Mao had been the biggest radical of them all, but too blunted to cleanly exorcise his leftist policies once and for all.

a fifteen-year default of Party authority seemed to me to have just the opposite effect. To my cadre friend, the furtive way it was carried out was but one more indication that nothing had happened since Mao's death that could not be readily reversed, a sense that was shared by many I spoke with. I found that despite the fall of the Gang of Four, there was widespread worry that political radicals would again come to control the Party; that five years after the modernization program began, there was still little conviction that Beijing would be able to hold to its present course for any length of time; that in spite of what everyone agreed would be bitter opposition from all quarters, Mao's dreaded prophecy of more Cultural Revolutions to come would somehow be fulfilled. By the end of my stay in China, I was convinced that nothing short of decades of sustained economic growth would be sufficient to restore a basic level of confidence in the Communist Party and government, but by this time I had come to agree with the Chinese people themselves that, with the regime unable or unwilling to break out of the vicious vicissitudes of political campaigns, the necessary policy stability will not be forthcoming.

Like a mirage that first waivers and then winks out entirely upon closer approach, so did the shimmering image of the People's Republic as an egalitarian, just, unselfish, and liberated society vanish as my stay in China lengthened. But even as the grim and barren landscape of real life was coming into view all around, one Party claim still seemed to me to hold true, namely that the establishment of the "New China" had benefited the Chinese peasant. I did not know it at the time, but I was still a captive of the paramount myth of the Chinese revolution.

The promise of peasant salvation had been a critical factor in the civil war, on the home front winning over peasants in large numbers to fill the ranks of the Communist armies, overseas undermining support for the Nationalist Chinese by convincing well-meaning liberals that the Communists were merely agrarian reformers. After the Communist Party came to power, it launched a self-congratulatory campaign depicting the establishment of the PRC as marking a kind of Manichean divide between the forces of light and darkness, good and evil. While before the revolution peasants were told how much better off they would be after they were "liberated," they were now told how much worse off they had been before. These efforts, I was to find out, had not convinced the peasants so much as they had made them very cautious about voicing views at odds with the official line.

In the West, however, the myth had grown increasingly popular in the sixties and seventies, usually justified under the rubric of "accepting the Chinese revolution on its own terms." For those who believed that the lot of the peasants, who constitute over four-fifths of the Chinese population, had actually improved dramatically, much could be forgiven, even brushed aside as nonessential. Even after the violence of the land reform, the repression of the Hundred Flowers, the famine of the GLF, and the anarchy of the GPCR, the noted sinologist and Harvard University historian John K. Fairbank, the most prominent proponent of this relativist view, was able to write that "valued in the Chinese peasant's terms, the revolution has been a magnificent achievement, a victory not only for Mao Tse-tung, but for several hundreds of millions of the Chinese people."* It would be unfair to ask how many peasants Fairbank had spoken to in coming to this conclusion, because until my year in China literally no one had been allowed to interact freely with Chinese peasants (except the Hong Kong Chinese, and to protect their relatives, they weren't talking), much less take up residence in a rural community. Pearl S. Buck, for example, who as the daughter of American missionaries had grown up in a Chinese village, tried for years to gain permission to revisit rural China to no avail. But to judge from my experience, a few conversations with Chinese peasants and a look around would not necessarily have revealed the truth even to someone with her background. Well into my stay in the countryside, I would have agreed with Fairbank that the revolution, if not quite "magnificent," had been an achievement of sorts for the Chinese peasant.

A visit by an old village cadre named Lao Baixing on my second night in the village I lived in had early confirmed me in my prejudices, causing me to uncritically accept the premise that 1949 had meant a turning point in local peasant fortunes. Without prompting, he briefly set out his life history—how his father had passed away when he was an infant, how he had grown up under

* *China Perceived* (New York: Random House, 1974), p. xvii.

conditions of considerable hardship, and how, during the war of resistance against the Japanese (1938–45), he had seen his mother die of starvation. He told me that his own prospects had taken a turn for the better in 1951 when he had begun his long tenure as a local official by serving as an official of the peasant's association. Later that same year, already in his early thirties, he had finally taken a bride.

Then he began to talk about the changes that had occurred in the village over the last three decades, making a series of comparisons between past and present to highlight progress made. "We now have a lower middle school, whereas we had only a primary school before the revolution," he said. "The river dike in the northwestern part of the brigade, which often flooded over before because the two clans that owned the land would not cooperate in building it higher, has now been raised and joined with the main commune dike. There is a brigade health station now, while before there were only private doctors. Widows with children and old people without family are much better off than my mother and I were. They receive 5 to 10 *rmb* a month and are given free health care and education. The village used to be controlled by a landlord clique; now the Party cadres serve the people. Our rice rations come from the state, not like before when private rice merchants made a profit." All this and more he told me, making a convincing argument for postrevolutionary improvements in peasant life that formed nearly a perfect fit with my expectations. I dutifully recorded them in my notebook and considered the case closed.

Thereafter, I wasn't even asking the right questions. Sure that the good earth had been transformed by the revolution into something better, I spent my time working out patterns of change since that time. Not that I blindly accepted Beijing's claims that life had begun in 1949—I had learned better than to do that— but I still took almost as an article of faith that the peasantry was the great beneficiary of Communist rule. I persisted in this belief even as my research increasingly laid bare the dark underside of Chinese life. If the initial achievements of the Party vis-à-vis the peasantry had not been substantial enough to compensate for its shortcomings, my half-conscious conviction of the time went, then this would call the very revolution itself into question, something I was as yet unprepared to do.

So it was that the first time a peasant told me that things
had been better before the revolution, I put him down as a crank,
one of the malcontents who inhabit the corners and crevices of
every society. Yet it puzzled me that he had not been a landlord,
rich peasant, or other disenfranchised element of the old rural
elite, but a poor peasant, one of the great beneficiaries, suppos-
edly, of the revolution. Gradually, by sheer happenstance, I began
backing into odd bits of information that indicated that life in
the precommunist era had not been as hellish as it had been
made out to be. "We elderly used to wear cool summer clothes
of black satin, but now the state takes all of our silk" emerged
from an ancient peasant woman whose life history I was recording.
"After the establishment of the state sales store in the early 1950s,
there was nothing to buy" came out during a discussion of rural
marketing. "There are fewer thieves now because no one has
anything to steal," I heard in wry answer to a query about local
crime.

But it was not until an encounter with the old gravedigger
of neighboring Sandwharf Brigade that I was led to reexamine
my presuppositions in earnest. He was a veritable village pariah
who, like his father and grandfather before him, had originally
lived out away from Sandwharf near the community's main burial
grounds, not welcomed in the village proper except when a death
occurred and he was called in to prepare the body for burial.
He had only moved into the village proper at the harrowing end
of the Japanese occupation thirty-five years before when deaths
due to disease and famine were an everyday occurrence.

On this particular day, I had gone out to the burial grounds
with several related village families to observe a reburial ceremony, colorfully called in Cantonese "restoring the dragon" (*fu
long*). The grave of the grandmother of the several family heads
was to be opened, her bones gathered up and laid out on a large
sheet of red paper for worship, and then reinterred upright in a
large pottery urn called a "golden pagoda," the miniature crypt
that would be her final resting place. In it, she would sit cross-
legged in above-ground alignment with the beneficent geomantic
forces of the earth dragons, which would thus flow to her descendants.

The gravedigger, a wizened scarecrow of a man, had already
dug down to a depth of about 4 feet by the time we arrived,

and as I watched, his spade began to uncover the top of the casket. The wood had partially rotted away, but he was still able to pry up the lid in nearly one piece. Then, crouching and working his hands through the damp, moldy earth underneath, he began to come up with pieces of bone itself—a knobbed length of thigh-bone, a few odds and ends of vertebrae and such, and then a nearly intact skull. I asked him a few questions as he dug, but he took little notice, mostly just mumbling to himself. One of the deceased's grandsons told me in a quiet aside that the grave-digger was a "liquor-ghost," the local expression for wino. I gathered that he probably thought it the better part of prudence to fortify himself with a liter of rice liquor before going about his business of disturbing the dead.

"My, look what we have here," the gravedigger clucked loudly, and everyone turned to regard the long bronze-colored spike that he was clutching in the air. Maybe it was the liquor taking hold ("In wine there is truth," the Chinese also say), or maybe it was because of my unanswered questions about changing customs, or maybe it was just the pleasure of the marginal man at being, for once, the center of attention—for whatever reason, the gravedigger launched into a monologue. "Look at these beau-tiful casket spikes," he said, digging out a couple more as he spoke. "These spikes are real copper. This is an old grave. They don't use spikes like this anymore. Now they just use cheap iron nails that rust away in a year or two. And look at this wood. Forty years in the ground and still not rotted away, not like the cheap caskets that we use now. In the old days, people used to have more money. I would get a thick 'red envelope' for each funeral, enough sometimes to buy a month of rice. Now I'm lucky to get 5 *rmb.*"

While everyone, including myself, listened in stunned silence, he turned to me and said, "You want to know what has changed. I'll tell you. Since the revolution things have been real bad. We have to eat 'black rice' [rice of low quality]. We have to wear cheap, rationed cloth." Then with a curse he concluded, "Even the rice liquor is not as good as it used to be."

With that, the gravedigger, looking suddenly spent, fell silent. An embarrassed quiet descended over the burial grounds as the others present stood frozen awkwardly around the open grave. Finally the oldest grandson, who was also a production team cadre,

reached over and took the three copper spikes from the gravedigger (I found out that he later sold them to the state sales store
for 2 cents apiece) and then said as if to no one in particular,
"We all have to make a living with our ten fingers." With that,
the ring of onlookers dissolved, and the gravedigger squatted
back down in the grave to collect the rest of the bones. No one
mentioned his outburst again that day, either to confirm or contra-
dict it, but it had indelibly etched itself on my mind, and I resolved
to see how much of what he had said had been the truth.

Sifting truth from myth proved to be more difficult than I
had imagined. Of all the clichés of fiction that the Chinese Communist Party over the decades has worked to get accepted as
matters of fact, none has been more zealously hyped than the
tale of peasant salvation. The Party even enlisted the peasants
in this effort, teaching them that the proper attitude toward the
unreconstructed past was to "speak bitterness," a highly ritualized
form of storytelling about preliberation times in which all landlords are arrogant and rapacious, all merchants unctuous and
usurious, and all peasants humble and, above all, wretchedly exploited.

Direct questions on the merits of the revolution usually trig-
gered this "speak bitterness" reflex, eliciting a dismal recital of
past unenlightenment and present gratification much like I had
gotten from the old village cadre Lao Baixing. My handful of
trusted friends were more frank, but I could not be sure their
views were representative of the villagers as a whole. It was only
after I reflected back on the gravedigger's grievances that I saw
that I could bypass the barriers of fear and conditioning by addressing the peasants in terms of their own categories of personal
well-being, asking when they had eaten well and when they had
eaten poorly, when they had lived comfortably and when they
had done without, when had been the best of times and when
had been the worst.

In my final weeks in the village I went on to interview over
100 villagers, ordinary peasants and ex-tenant farmers as well
as brigade cadres and former landlords, to obtain a balanced por-
trayal of the past. I heard old peasant men and women, their
faces furrowed with the toil of years, recalling that they had eaten
better in the twenties and thirties than at any time since. Poor
peasants described to me how they had once belonged to landed

eating associations which each Chinese New Year threw a grand and gluttonous feast. I listened to sturdy middle-aged peasant women rave over how well stocked the shops had been after the Japanese left and how they had been able to get good prices for their produce. Even younger cadres told me that times had been good in the years from 1946 to 1949, when, despite the beat of distant war drums, the economy was thriving and there were "10,000" goods on sale in the marketplace. In short, I heard the villagers themselves give the lie to the Communist Party's claim of having saved the peasantry from a wretched, earthbound fate.

In the composite sketch of peasant life in living memory that I pieced together from these individual accounts, the twenties and thirties stood out as a time of unprecedented prosperity. Southwestern China was under the benign leadership of Sun Yat-sen, Chiang Kai-shek, and the Kuomintang, and the rural population of the region enjoyed a time of peace and plenty. It was this time of good food and feasting that the peasants, whose hearts are but a short remove from their stomachs, called their "golden age." The good life abruptly came to an end with the Japanese invasion, which, in the Pearl River Delta, led to mass starvation and emigration. After the defeat of the Japanese in 1945, civil war soon engulfed northern China, but the south still enjoyed several years of resurgent prosperity before the People's Liberation Army came. Thereafter, to the peasants' way of thinking, the quality of life gradually declined. Only in the last several years, they agreed, have conditions improved to approximately those of the period 1949–52, when the Communists had yet to implement their rural program of collectivization and market control. Though real, the advances in rural health care, education, welfare, and flood control mentioned by Lao Baixing (which would have occurred as well under a Kuomintang likewise committed to rural reconstruction) turned out to matter far less to the villagers than I had initially assumed. For peasants who had been forced to tighten their belts after they lost their family farms and the freedom of the market, they were scant compensation indeed.

So vast is China, so varied are her climate and geography, and so unevenly endowed are her agricultural regions that no simple historical schema can encompass the experience of her 800 million peasants. Perhaps in the North China plain and the

Chinese northwest, with their long winters and unpredictable summer rains, where prerevolutionary peasant conditions were to all accounts considerably worse than in the south (not least because they were for twenty-five years the crucible of an ongoing war), the "New China" has surpassed its lackluster southern showing. It may be that in the inhospitable mountain districts that border every region improvements have been more apparent, although on my car trip to the inland province of Guizhou I found a crushing hill-country poverty that eclipsed anything in Appalachia. But where conditions approximate those in the Pearl River Delta— the fertile deltas of northern Guangdong and Fujian provinces with their year-round growing seasons and lucrative cash crops, the vast river and lake country of the upper, middle, and lower Yangtze River with its bountiful rice harvests and rich lacustrine resources—peasant destinies have probably paralleled those of the commune I studied. For the 400 million peasants of the South China heartland, the liberation has probably proved to be an empty, undigestible myth.

Supporting evidence comes from the only other in-depth investigation of a rural community carried out in postrevolutionary China. In 1957, the well-known Chinese sociologist Fei Xiaotong did a restudy of the village of Kaixiangong that he had originally described in his 1936 book *Peasant Life in China.** The study was quickly suppressed, but not before he had reported that in this community, located in Jiangsu Province on some of the richest agricultural land in China, peasant incomes had scarcely increased in two decades. Earnings from rising grain yields had been almost entirely offset by a decline in income from family sideline enterprises.**

Further corroboration that the decades since the revolution have not ushered in an era of peasant prosperity comes from the regime itself, which recently acknowledged that it is only in the past several years that per capita grain consumption, that sensitive barometer of rural well-being, has reattained the levels

* Fei Xiaotong, *Peasant Life in China* (London: Routledge & Kegan Paul, 1936).
** Fei was to pay for his impudence in questioning the sacred myth of the peasant liberation. Retribution came quickly as he was attacked in the official press for attempting to discredit the achievements of the agricultural collectives and for casting aspersions on socialism. The month after his study appeared, he was publicly humiliated and forced to recant his "bourgeois intellectual" views on this and other matters before the National People's Congress.

of the years immediately following the revolution. What this otherwise extraordinarily candid admission failed to mention was that long years of collective farming under the "grain first" policy have reduced the variety of crops grown and included in the diet. Though peasants may once again be eating as much grain as they were thirty years ago, they are probably still not as well off nutritionally as they were before.

This retrogression also comes through in a widely circulated story about Deng Xiaoping, which says that when he was sent in disgrace back to his native Sichuan in 1975, he was so shocked at the poverty and deprivation that he encountered in the province once known for its natural bounty as "the heavenly country" (*tianfu zhi guo*) that he wept openly. Like my oldest peasant acquaintances, Deng was born shortly after the turn of the century and would well remember what conditions had been like in the 1920s. As a pragmatist, he would also have grasped the lesson that peasants will feed, clothe, and house themselves quite well, for the most part, if they are simply left alone. Deng's reforming zeal in loosening restrictions on peasant agricultural, sideline, and marketing activities may follow from his recognition that for the Chinese peasant, the liberation has meant not salvation, but stagnation.

———————◆———————

Late in May 1980, on one of my last evenings in the commune, I received an unexpected evening call from Lao Baixing, the cadre who had first lectured me on the revolution's supposed accomplishments. It was a memorable visit, neatly closing the circle on my inquiry into rural life even as it once again bore witness to the difficulty of penetrating the realities of the Chinese world.

Lao Baixing and I had become good friends over the course of my stay in the village. He stood out among the people I met in rural China as well informed, insightful, and articulate, and I had sought out his opinions on topics ranging from funeral arrangements to birth control. Welcoming what I took to be a parting visit, I opened a bottle of Shanxi wine, a burgundy with a dusky flavor that I kept for special occasions. The clerks in the state sales store had told me that this wine had aged in the bottle for at least ten years, because at 5 *rmb* a bottle it was priced out of reach of the villagers, so I had set it aside for times like these. Lao Baixing was silent as we finished the first glass.

"Do you remember my first visit?" he asked me as I refilled our glasses. I nodded, reading his remark as the beginning of a reminiscence. I could not have been more wrong. "To be honest," he went on slowly and steadily, "my mother and I did not have it that bad before the Japanese came. We lived with my father's older brother, and my mother raised silkworms with her sister-in-law. I was able to attend three years of primary school, about average for the time. It was only after the Japanese came that things got really bad. After they left, we had some good years from 1946 to 1949. It was money I saved as a tenant farmer of fish and sugarcane during this time that I used to get married." Layers of deception were tumbling away as he spoke.

"Times were *good.* People had *money.* You could buy *anything,*" he continued, putting a twist on the last word in each sentence like a spin on a billiard ball. "Goods have never been abundant since then. There are always shortages. Before, if you had money you could buy anything. Now a lot of things go through the back door, and only those with foreign currency [from remittances from relatives overseas] or officials can afford it. The people in power now have many more special privileges than before the liberation. They can purchase fish or high-quality rice that the masses can't even if they have the money."

"Another thing that they say about the old times is how the village heads oppressed the masses," he mused, sipping slowly on the wine. "You know, our village leaders then, the village gentry, were not bad men." He used the traditional term of respect for gentry, *shenshi,* rather than the word *dizhu,* or landlord, which has come to have a pejorative connotation. "Even if one or two were bad men, they had little power. The brigade cadres now have much more power to control people than the old village leaders. Now they can fine you, or struggle you, or assign you to a difficult task. Now you even have to have their permission on a travel permit to leave the county or spend the night outside the brigade. They decide everything for their own benefit, even though they say that it is for the people."

We chatted a while longer, but it was evident that he had said what he came to say and he soon got up to go. I walked him out to the main gate of my house, satisfied that I had succeeded in unlocking the involuted secrets of the Chinese countryside that the Communists had for so long kept shrouded under myth and model commune. But as it turned out, I had still not fully fathomed the abyss of Chinese complexity. "There is one more thing you should know," Lao Baixing said, hesitating momentarily by the gate. "That first night, when I came and talked to you about the liberation. I was instructed to come."

Index

DATE DUE

DEMCO 38-297